THE LIFE OF CHARLES, THIRD EARL STANHOPE, COMMENCED BY GHITA STANHOPE, REV. AND COMPLETED BY G.P. GOOCH

THE LIFE OF CHARLES, THIRD EARL STANHOPE, COMMENCED BY GHITA STANHOPE, REV. AND COMPLETED BY G.P. GOOCH

Stanhope, Ghita, 1881-1912 and gooch, G. P. (george Peabody), 1873-1968

www.General-Books.net

Publication Data:

Title: The Life of Charles, Third Earl Stanhope, Commenced by Ghita Stanhope, Rev. and Completed by G.p. Gooch
Author: Stanhope, Ghita, 1881-1912 and Gooch, G. P. (george Peabody), 1873-1968
Publisher: London : Longmans, Green
Publication date: 1914
Subjects: Stanhope, Charles Stanhope, Earl, 1753-1816
Great Britain – Politics and government 1760-1820
Great Britain Parliament – Reform

How We Made This Book for You
We made this book exclusively for you using patented Print on Demand technology.
First we scanned the original rare book using a robot which automatically flipped and photographed each page.
We automated the typing, proof reading and design of this book using Optical Character Recognition (OCR) software on the scanned copy. That let us keep your cost as low as possible.
If a book is very old, worn and the type is faded, this can result in typos or missing text. This is also why our books don't have illustrations; the OCR software can't distinguish between an illustration and a smudge.
We understand how annoying typos, missing text or illustrations or an index that doesn't work, can be. That's why we provide a free digital copy of most books exactly as they were originally published. Simply go to our website (www.general-books.net) to check availability. And we provide a free trial membership in our book club so you can get free copies of other editions or related books.
OCR is not a perfect solution but we feel it's more important to make books available for a low price than not at all. So we warn readers on our website and in the descriptions we provide to book sellers that our books don't have illustrations and may have typos or missing text. We also provide excerpts from each book to book sellers and on our website so you can preview the quality of the book before buying it.
If you would prefer that we manually type, proof read and design your book so that it's perfect, we are happy to do that. Simply contact us for the cost.

Limit of Liability/Disclaimer of Warranty:
The publisher and author make no representations or warranties with respect to the accuracy or completeness of the book. The advice and strategies in the book may not be suitable for your situation. You should consult with a professional where appropriate. The publisher is not liable for any damages resulting from the book.
Please keep in mind that the book was written long ago; the information is not current. Furthermore, there may be typos, missing text or illustration and explained above.

1

THE LIFE OF CHARLES, THIRD EARL STANHOPE, COMMENCED BY GHITA STANHOPE, REV. AND COMPLETED BY G.P. GOOCH

PREFACE

DISRAELI once spoke of Shelburne as one of the suppressed characters of English history. Shelburne's friend, Charles, third Earl Stanhope, is another. While Lady Hester has tempted not a few biographers, both in her own country and abroad, it was not till nearly a century after his death that the career of her distinguished father found a chronicler. He has been hitherto vaguely known as a man of eccentric habits and impossible opinionsâ ' the Quixote of the nation," as he is described in the ' Rolliad." The present biography, commenced by his great-great-granddaughter, at length reveals him as one of the outstanding personalities of his time, an inventive genius of the first order, and a fearless reformer who played a leading part in public life for forty years. The son-in-law of Chatham, the nephew by marriage of Grenville, the comrade and then the enemy of Pitt, the protege of Wilkes, the formidable antagonist of Fox during the Coalition and of Burke during the French Revolution, the valued supporter of Wilberforce, the friend of Franklin and Condorcet, Grattan and Price, the ally of Shelburne and Lauderdale in their opposition to the Great War and of Lord Holland in his championship of religious liberty, the butt of Gillray and the bogy of Horace Walpole, the hero of the youthful Coleridge and Landor, the oracle of the little band of Parliamentary Reformers who never lost courage or hope, the patron of Lancaster's schools, the friend of Fulton and Rennie and himself an inventor of the first rankâ few of his contemporaries touched the life of their age at so many points. When Ghita Stanhope's lamented death occurred in 1912, she had brought her narrative down to the outbreak of the French Revolution, which formed the turning-point in her ancestor's career. I was requested by her parents, the Hon. Henry and Mrs. Stanhope, to revise and continue the work which had been to her a labour of love, and a perusal of her manuscript left me in no doubt as to my reply. She had supplemented her studies in the family papers at Chevening by researches in the Record Office, the British Museum, and other archives, and had traced his footsteps through the maze of printed memoirs and correspondence, pamphlets and Parliamentary debates, broadsheets and caricatures. His education at Geneva, his plunge into English politics at the age of twenty-one, his share in the early movement for the reform of the franchise, his zealous and effective support of his brother-in-law during the first and happier years of his long ministry, his ardent championship of the principles of the French Revolution, his invention of the steamboatâ these and other topics are described by Miss Stanhope with the aid of new material. In preparing her manuscript for the press, I have divided it into chapters and made a few corrections and additions. Chapters I to V, the larger part of Chapter VI and the whole of Chapter X, except the last section, are from her pen. The latter embodies the results of prolonged research, and forms a valuable contribution to the history of naval construction and administration.

My own direct share in the book consists of Chapters VII to IX and XI to XIII, which describe the second half of Stanhope's crowded life and the unhappy relations with his family. My cordial thanks are due to Earl Stanhope for granting me unrestricted access to the rich collection of papers at Chevening and for permitting the reproduction of Gainsborough's portrait of his ancestor. I also desire to express my gratitude to Countess Stanhope for allowing me to discuss with her certain questions relating to the family history. I am indebted to the Dowager Countess of Ilchester for supplying me with copies of Stanhope's letters to Lord Holland, preserved at Holland House, and for permission to reproduce Opie's portrait, which was exhibited at the Royal Academy in 1803 an(1 was bequeathed by Stanhope to his friend and executor. If Miss Stanhope had been alive, she would have recorded her indebtedness to Sir E. Maunde Thompson and Dr. Holland Rose for assistance and encouragement. Other obligations are acknowledged in the notes and appendices.

G. P. GOOCH. March, 1914,

CHARLES, third Earl Stanhope, was born in London, on August 3, CHAP. 1753. His grandfather was the celebrated commander in the I. War of the Spanish Succession, and Prime Minister of George I. His grandmother was the daughter of Governor Pitt. His father, Philip, though little known in politics or society, was a conspicuous figure in the scientific world. 1 Even as a child the second Earl showed a pronounced taste for all scientific pursuits; but at first this predilection was sternly repressed. Left an orphan at the age of seven, his education had been confided to the care of his brilliant kinsman, Lord Chesterfield, who, considering classics and belles lettres to be the most essential part of a gentleman's education, forbade all mathematical studies to the boy who was one day to earn the verdict of Lalande that he was the finest English mathematician of his age. Yet he did not neglect the classics, for he could recite the whole of the ' Iliad' and the ' Odyssey ' in the original, and was master of several modern languages. Though he left no work by which his name could be remembered, he spent his life in study and research, and was on intimate terms with most of the learned men of the day. Through his instrumentality Torelli's edition of ' Archimedes' was published by the Clarendon Press, and he defrayed the expense of the posthumous edition of Robert Simson's worksâ a copy of which he sent to every learned society 1 See the opening pages of the article on the third Earl, in Public Characters of 1800-1.

CHAP, in Europe. He was a patron of scholars, and many works of L science were dedicated to him, among them the third volume of Priestley's ' Experiments on Air." As an old man, he had the privilege of introducing Benjamin Franklin to Lord Chatham.

Succeeding to the title at the age of seven, he took his seat in Parliament on coming of age in 1735. Though he did not take an active part in affairs, he was by no means without political convictions, and steadily opposed Walpole, under whom he had grown to manhood. ' All this week," wrote Horace Walpole, on April 8, 1742, at the crisis of his father's fate, ' the mob has been carrying about his effigies in procession. The chiefs of the Opposition have been so mean as to give these mobs money for bonfires," among them the Earl of Stanhope. 1 His most memorable public appearance was in 1743, when he raised the question of the Hanoverian troops. His speech was delivered ' with great tremblings and agitations '; but it was carefully prepared and vigorously phrased. He concluded by moving for an address to the King to terminate the employment of the ' Mercenaries who had been engaged in the previous year without consent of Parliament. His shyness, absorption in study, and long residence abroad rendered him an unfamiliar figure at Westminster. On one occasion in later life, when, after a long absence, he went down to the House of Lords in a plain dress, an attempt was made by the doorkeeper to bar his entrance with the words: ' Honest man, you have no business in this place!" 'I am sorry, indeed replied Stanhope quietly, ' if honest men have no business here 2 In 1758, he is recorded by Horace Walpole to have spoken well on Habeas Corpus. 3 On finally returning to England, in 1774, he opposed the American War and supported Wilkes in his conflict with the Government. When at length Lord Stanhope, in the words of Horace Walpole, ' lifted up his eyes from Euclid and directed them to matrimony 4 he chose Miss Grisel Hamilton, daughter of Charles, Lord Binning, and elder sister of Thomas, seventh Earl of Haddington. He chose wisely; for no one came into her society without observing the charm of her manners and the cultivation of her mind. Without sharing the recondite studies of her husband, she seems to have entirely sympathised in his pursuits and opinions. Her household was ordered with exact regularity and discipline. She carried on a large correspondence; and, though her spelling and punctuation did

1 Letters, ed. Toynbee, i. 208.

2 Stanhope's History of England, 1713-83, iii. 138-40.

3 Letters, iv, 140. 4 Ibid., ii. 77, not rise above the level of her time, her letters were unusually CHAP, discreet. Lady Mary Coke, eager for news from Paris and L the last Court scandal, expressed herself as ' much disappointed by Lady Stanhope's great discretion." ' This may be very prudent," remarks Lady Mary, ' but 'tis very disagreeable when one is curious."

There were only two children of the marriage: Philip, born in 1746, and Charles, born in 1753. Philip was sent to Eton, and his parents entertained the highest hopes of him; but he inherited from his mother's family the tendency to consumption, which had proved fatal to so many of the Hamiltons. He was removed to the purer air of Geneva, where he was under the care of the celebrated Dr. Tronchin. There he grew steadily worse, but bore his sufferings with the greatest gentleness and resignation. His mother sends bulletins of his health to Charles at Eton. 1 ' I wish you would write to your brother; it would please him very much. You don't know how much he loves you, and how often he talks of you and how happy he is to hear you are good." Charles wrote the desired letter; but when it reached Geneva, Philip was too ill to answer it himself. He sent a reply ' wrote by me," says Lady Stanhope, ' when I was sitting up at night with him."

' Geneva: June 26, 1763.

' My sweet Charly,â I received yours to-day. Nothing makes me so happy as hearing from you. Do not neglect your duty to God and keep out of bad company; never do anything that you would wish to hide from anybody, for you can lack nothing from God; never tell an untruth, but be honest and good in every respect, and never mind naughty boys laughing at you for being so. I am not well enough to write myself, but will when I can."

But the hoped-for day never came. On July 6, 1763, before Charles received this letter, Philip died and was buried at Geneva. He had just celebrated his seventeenth birthday.

' Our loss is very truly great," writes Lord Stanhope to Lord Le Despencer, 2 ' as we could not have been blessed with a child of sweeter or more amiable and affectionate disposition. It is however our duty to use our utmost endeavours to support it with resignation and to take all possible care to preserve his brother, who promises us all the consolation our melancholy situation can admit. This goes by a messenger that we send to 1 Lady Stanhope to Hon. C. Stanhope, April 6, 1763. Chevemng MSS.

2 Egerton MSS., 2131, fol. 78,

CHAP, cause an article to be inserted in the papers to contradict an absurd account of my poor son's illness and of the circumstances of our family given in yesterday's General Evening Post. The visit with which you and Lady Despencer flatter us will be most heartily welcome to us, as no one can be with greater sincerity and affection than I am, ' My dear Lord, ' Your most faithful, ' and most humble Servant, ' STANHOPE."

Chevening: Aug. 12, 1763.

The account to which Lord Stanhope refers appeared in Lloyd's Evening Post and the Public Advertiser, and demonstrates that the writer of society news was no less inaccurate and impertinent than his successor of the present day. There is a certain engaging simplicity about the communication which betrays its flunkey origin. ' The reputation of M. Tronchin x draws hither a multitude of foreigners. Lord Northampton, who has upwards of thirty persons in his retinue, has hired a furnished house for which he pays sixty guineas a month. Lord and Lady Stanhope have honoured us with their presence for near nine months: they have just lost their son, my Lord Mahon, whose disease, the spleen, baffled all M. Tronchin's skill, and by whose death an estate of Â 20,000 sterling per annum goes from the family. That young nobleman, in favour of whom his grandfather left this estate under condition that if he died before he was of age it should pass to another branch, had attained but to the age of seventeen years. My Lord and Lady Stanhope set out for London last Thursday."

Charles now became Viscount Mahon, and, as their only surviving child, was more than ever the object of his parents' solicitude. They resolved that his health should not be exposed to the English climate, or the care of his mind to the capricious attentions of the English schoolmaster. He was recalled from Eton (where he had been sent when nine years old), and the family decided on settling in Geneva. In surrendering him, his tutor writes to Lady Stanhope: ' He has an excellent understanding, though he does not seem to relish books. He has an excellent heart and disposition. Never have I known his equal 1 Theodore Tronchin (1709-81), one of the most celebrated doctors of the eighteenth century, and the earliest advocate of the hygienic treatment of invalids.

for so early a sense of honour." 1 He had struck the keynote CHAP, of the boy's character. In later years, Charles was frequently compared to Don Quixote, whom he resembled not only in appearance but still more in valour and high-mindedness. Lord Stanhope had been educated at Leyden and Geneva, and was absorbed in science and philosophy; but one wonders at the calm with which the excellent Grisel bore the transplantation. ' As long as Charles goes on well, I don't think of myself; and if his father has his books he is well everywhere, so I don't complain." She left many friends in England. ' I have been making a very melancholy visit to the country," writes Lady Hervey, 2 ' to my old and best friends, Lady Stanhope and her family. 'Tis a last farewell to those worthy people, with whom I have passed the greatest and much the most agreeable part of my life. She and her lord are going with their only remaining son to Geneva, where they think, and I can easily believe, he may be much better educated than first at one of our great schools and after at one of our universities. As the boy is but eleven years old and is to complete his studies abroad, 'tis very unlikely that I shall live to see their return. 'Tis a very heavy and unexpected blow upon me and affects my spirits very much." 3 The object of their expatriation was even more health than education. Lady Stanhope had a high opinion of Dr. Tronchin's abilities, and the greatest praise she can give to Chatham is 'You, my dear Lord, are my political Tronchin." 4 She thus describes the doctor's methods. ' Charles is very well, but we have put him under the management of Dr. Tronchin, who says he wants only to be strengthened, a moderate diet, a good deal of exercise and fencing as it opens the chest. He has also ordered him to read and write chiefly standing at a high desk. We follow these rules strictly. One other article is to keep him warm in his body, dry in his feet; a thin nightcap and a light hat or no hat at all." 5

Between the related families of Pitt and Stanhope an almost weekly correspondence was maintained, carried on chiefly by Grisel and Lady Chatham. Lady Stanhope's letters are all preserved, and constitute an interesting journal of their life abroad. The younger people also exchanged civilities. Thus Grisel writes: ' Charles has sent Miss Pitt some Geneva jewels, Pierres de Sante, which are found in the mountains of Savoy.

1 Rev. F. Dampier to Lady Stanhope, May 21, 1764.

"The ' bewitching Molly Lepel' of Lord Chesterfield's ballad.

3 June 3, 1764. Letters of Lady Hervey.

4 To Lord Chatham, October 30, 1769. 5 October 1764.

CHAP. There is a pair of ear-rings, a thing for her neck with a cross, â " that Jews may kiss and Infidels adore," and a thing for her cap. I hope she'll like them." x Charles, ' who is learning perspective sends two of his drawings to Lord Chatham. 2 To these attentions the young Pitts responded, as we learn from Lady Stanhope. ' I received your letter, my dear Lady Chatham, with the pretty drawing. The moment Charles saw it, he said, "Oh, that's Chevening Church, who did it? " and smiled when I told him. Mons. Liotard and Charles' drawing master happened by mere accident to be both here at the instant I received it. They observed several little touches that were remarkably well and shewed a great genius. They bid me let the person who did it know that they ought to continue practising, and imperceptibly they would soon come to perfection in drawing. I assure you I set high value on the first essay, and desire you will give Lady Hester a kiss from me." 3

The Genevese system of education was cheap and excellent, and the devotion to culture was deep and genuine. In England knowledge was forcibly implanted in the infant mind by severe and barbarous methods. The Genevan shopkeeper, and even the artisan, was familiar with the works of Locke, Montesquieu, and Newton. In an age when not a single free library existed in England, Geneva boasted a collection of nearly 40,000 volumes accessible to all the inhabitants. 4 The influence of Calvin had extended further than ecclesiastical or political reforms; for at his instigation a kind of tribunal had been established which attempted to regulate, even to the most minute detail, the private conduct of the individual. Nothing was too insignificant for its laws, which impressed on the Genevese character a more than Spartan austerity. The day began at six in winter and at four in summer; fires and windows that closed properly were considered a veritable luxury. The greatest frugality was enjoined. The old law of the Reformation, ' to have on the table at most two dishes, meat and vegetable (without pastry)," was still regularly observed, and simplicity of manners often went so far as to unite masters and servants at the same board. La bonne serge and le drap noir were the only dress authorised by the law, and lace and trimmings were rigorously proscribed. 5 The Genevese attributed much of their good fortune to the 1 Lady Stanhope to the Rt. Hon. W. Pitt, October 1764.

2 April 30, 1766. 3 October 2, 1769.

4 Coxe, Travels in Switzerland; and Dr. Moore, Letters from France and Switzerland.

5 Gaberel, Voltaire et les Genevois, p. 32.

maintenance of these laws. ' La prosperite de Geneve wrote CHAP. Senebier, ' fut long-terns le fruit heureux de ces sages loix; elles contribuerent puissamment a maintenir la purete de nos anciennes mceurs, qui ont fait notre lustre et qui ont si fort contribue a notre conservation." Writing in 1786, after a period of warfare, he adds: ' On peut meme preuver qu'une des causes de nos malheurs est la diminution de Finfluence de ce tribunal sur les individus 1 In 1764, the Genevese still adhered with almost passionate tenacity to a Spartan simplicity of morals and manners; and they dreaded the invasion of luxury only less than the incursion of a foreign prince. ' Rome was lost they said, ' when the Censors were no longer able to raise their voice against those whose vices unfitted them to belong to the Republic; Sparta fell with the credit of the guardians of public morals Painting, music, literature, and the drama naturally suffered under this iron hand, and the great men of Geneva have been chiefly scientists, philosophers, and mathematicians. Apart from other advantages, this austerity of manners added to its desirability, in the eyes of anxious parents, as a place of education. There were no objects of dissipation, theatres, or public places of amusement. Geneva was always included in the grand tour' of young gentlemen travelling abroad with their tutors. M. le Chevalier de Boufflers writes plaintively to his mother in 1772: ' C'est une grande et triste ville habitee par des gens qui ne manquent pas d'esprit et encore moins d'argent et qui se servent ni de Tun ni de Fautre He quaintly describes the seriousness of the Swiss character: ' Le peuple suisse et le peuple fran9ais ressemblent a deux jardiniers, dont Fun cultive des choux et Fautre des fleurs 2

Charles was infected with the spirit of the place not only in learning, politics, and science, but in dress. His mother sends to Kent for bats and balls that he may play cricket. ' I am consulted on all occasions she writes; ' but I never see or hear of buckles, etc.; on the contrary I call him the Quaker 3 â He would not wear powder, and to be without it was considered as eccentric as a lady of to-day in a crinoline. At last he yielded a little, and Lady Stanhope was hopeful. ' I think she writes, ' my boy sits more quietly to have his hair dressed 4 But this meekness did not last long, and the fashion occasioned one of his rare differences with his mother. ' He is a very good, 1 J. Senebier, Hist. litt. de Geneve, i. 192.

2 Lettres de M. de Bouffters pendant son voyage en Suisse, p. 23.

3 Lady Stanhope to Lady Chatham, June 7, 1768.

4 March 13, 1769.

CHAP, well-principled boy writes Lady Stanhope, ' but don't you find I- it difficult to make him distinguish firmness from obstinacy? Good sense and experience, I find, does more than many lectures on the subject. He was once a little devil, but he has not the least remains of that. I don't tell you he is not by nature warm-tempered, but he has so much sense to command it that if by any chance he is affronted, you would be surprised to see what command he has over himself. An uncommon sweetness of temper makes him do all he thinks will please." 1 But in matters of fashion he was resolute, and Lady Stanhope has to yield. ' The affair of powder is given up; he says it makes his head ache and then he can't think." 2 At the same time not only was powder de rigueur, but men wore their hair long and had it elaborately dressed. Fanny Burney gives an amusing account of one of the King's equerries who went early to bed so that his servant might put his hair in curl-papers in order to make a splendid appearance on the morrow.

Charles disdained all outward graces. ' New fashioned toupees observes his mother sadly, ' he certainly cannot wear for some time, as he has cut his off to save the trouble of dressing it. Some favourite lady may some time or other change all these matters; till then I despair of his being quite a la mode." 3 In cutting off his hair, he had only followed the example of the dearly loved Dr. Tronchin (known in his youth as ' Apollo ' Tronchin), who, when studying at Ley den under Boerhave, had been accused of spending too much time doing his hair, and replied by appearing at class next morning with a close-cropped head. Lady Stanhope finally summoned

Lady Chatham to her assistance. ' Charles is so afraid of being a petit-maure that he will I fear run into the other extreme. Some fathers think when the head is well furnished other things are less necessary, and therefore attend little to them; but as mothers sometimes see with other eyes, they think a few outward accomplishments also necessary. I shall be greatly obliged if you will sometimes say something on this subject, as all that comes from your house is greedily listened to. When I complain of any little singularity or negligence in dress, the answer is, Lord Chatham always wears a plain coat. You may see by this that what you say may do good. He is now in a society of young ladies and gentlemen, married and unmarried, which I hope will brush him up a little, and rub off his natural shyness, as he likes company and goes into it with pleasure 4 1 December n, 1766. 2 January i, 1773.

3 To Lady Chatham, February 17, 1772. 4 February 26, 1770.

Lady Stanhope's efforts were unremitting. ' I have set CHAP, my good friend Mme. Diodati (once Mile. Tronchin) to plague I. him she writes. ' I am little in hopes that he'll fall in love with her, as it can only be a platonic passion, and her stay won't be long enough to make it lasting. He has a great friendship for her brother whom you saw." 1 But though Charles was not in general susceptible to feminine charms, he at last succumbs: the object of his admiration being a lady of somewhat mature yearsâ a thing not uncommon at his age. ' The Duchess of Northumberland here for some days; she has done us the honour to dine here twice, and Charles is at last in love, deeply smit with her affability, free of pride and aims of a fine lady and so cheerful bearing with gout, and she no less with him." 2 ' On New Year's day he voluntarily made about a hundred and twenty visits to ladies as well as gentlemen. He did not indeed find all at home, but I was glad to find his readiness to do it." 3 However much his ' natural timidity' may have prevented Charles enjoying these amenities at the time, he entertained a lively recollection of some of them. Many years later, he wrote a facetious letter to his old tutor: ' Si j'etois a Geneve aujourd'hui je ferois au moins 150 a 200 visites pour baiser toutes les jolies dames de ma connaissance. Nous n'avons pas de ces bonnes coutumes dans ce paix-ci. J 4 Lady Stanhope consoled herself for the fact that her son would never be merely a young man d la mode. 'I am better pleased than had he spent the same time at a card table, the practice of most of our young folks who all grow milk-sops and can't bear anything." 5 She relates with indignation an anecdote of the foppery of the youthful Charles James Fox. ' Some months ago, the son of a certain black eye-browed gentleman took a trip abroad. When he landed he was met by an old schoolfellow, who asked about his movements. He answered " he was just taking a trip to buy a suit of clothes at Lyons for the Birthday." ' 6 Except in matters of dress, Lady Stanhope never interfered; for, as she truly observed, ' little meddling makes long friends." All his life he was devoted to his mother. When she was ill at Geneva, with Lord Stanhope absent in England, ' my little companion nursed me with the greatest care and tenderness, and I had no physician but him." 7

From his father Charles inherited a taste for science and 1 August 31, 1770. 2 May 3, 1772. 3 January 3, 1772.

4 Stanhope to Le Sage, January r, 1786. Chevening MSS.

5 To Lady Chatham, January 3, 1772.

6 March 18, 1771. 7 May 10, 1770.

io LIFE OF CHARLES, THIRD EARL STANHOPE

CHAP, habits of industry, which showed themselves at a very early L age. ' Charles writes his mother, ' is making a short-hand letter to his father, and he thinks he is improving Byrom's shorthand. He has just shewn me ten pot-hooks which he says means " they made a strenuous struggle for liberty." He is not pleased that I have no vast ambition to learn his manner of writing; he has been tormenting me lately with syllogisms." l Charles writes to his father: ' Dear Papa, I am ashamed of having stayed so long without writing, but I was inventing a way to hinder the variations of the pendulum by heat and cold, and I was very loath to write till I could send you more of it." 2 A neat-coloured drawing is appended. He learned Greek with Lord Stanhope and read Xenophon with pleasure. Later, he read Locke ' On the Human Understanding' and Blackstone's Commentaries.

Under the guidance of Georges Le Sage, one of the most learned men of his day, Mahon applied himself eagerly to mechanics, philosophy, and the higher branches of geometry. He cared little for the classics, belles-lettres, or that dallying with the fine arts which the eighteenth century euphemistically summed up as ' polite learning." At seventeen, he won the prize offered by the Swedish Academy for the best essay on the construction of the pendulum. This essay, written in French, is printed among the transactions of the Swedish Academy, and a great number of his drawings of clocks and pendulums were finely engraved by Geissler of Geneva. Charles is held up as a model to his kinsman, the young Lord Pitt, ' the powdered Beau." ' I trust," writes Chatham, 3 ' he will follow as well as he can Lord Mahon in the career of letters, arts and manly exercises, and I am sure I need not wish more for him." During 1769, Chevening was lent to Lord and Lady Chatham, who, according to the steward, saw ' a pretty deal of company, so we have of late lived wonderful merry." Chatham busied himself about the estate, and laid out a road through the park still known as Chatham's Ride.

Charles was not a mere bookworm. Besides his military exercises he rode well, and two years in succession was ' head of the manege." He played bowlsâ ' a game very different to that which goes by the same name in England 'â and cricket, and he seems to have acquired some skill in shooting. He grew quickly, and his mother describes him as ' a very awkward boy 1 Lady Stanhope to Lady Chatham, June 19, 1769, 2 Viscount Mahon to Earl Stanhope, June 3, 1770. a Unpublished correspondence of Lord Chatham.

at present." 1 He was very fond of skating. ' His father and CHAP. I sat an hour in the cold to see him. There was a party of L good skaters, and he in time may make one; at present he is like a father-long-legs, for, not being perfect in the exercise, arms go as well as legs for him to keep his equiliber, and he went faster than any of them." 2 ' He is now of the Society of Artists, which makes him happy. He has been at some balls, which is not what he likes most, but I believe he dances well." 3 ' The English here have lately set up a club which the people here call the Parliament. We are told that Charles has spoke with the true spirit of an Englishman, and at every meeting acquires a greater facility, not being at all daunted." 4

At this time Geneva was, in the French expression," une ville fort courue." It was filled with invalids, who came to consult the famous Tronchinâ ' les devotes du pere Tronchin," Voltaire called them. Many travellers, again, came in the hope of seeing Voltaire. He was the prey of the idle and the curious, and he sometimes took to his bed and declared himself ill in order to escape their unwelcome attentions. Neither Lord Stanhope nor his son, however, joined the pilgrims; for, though recognising his love of liberty and justice, the peer disapproved of the patriarch of Ferney. Other less conscientious English travellers did not suffer their religious scruples to interfere with their curiosity. With the object of seeing Voltaire Lady Mary Coke visited Switzerland in 1769, and came to see Lady Stanhope. ' Though I had other acquaintances at Geneva I passed every evening with her," she writes to Lady Greenwich. ' Lord and Lady Stanhope have been here several years. Their behaviour to me was more obliging than I can well express: I think I never met with so much attention and goodness. They lost their eldest son about four years ago: a loss that poor Lady Stanhope has not recovered, though she is excessively fond of the present Lord Mahon, who seems to promise everything they can wish. His painting would surprise you; he cuts out people in paper as well as others can draw them. He has invented, I was told, a mathematical instrument which I was assured is better for the purpose it was intended than any other of the kind; yet he is but seventeen years of age. They have fixed no time for returning to England."

Among other visitors were the Duke of Buccleuch with his tutor Dugald Stewart, Adam Smith, a friend and frequent correspondent of Lord Stanhope, Wilkes, and Lord and Lady Holland 1 To Lady Chatham, October 3, 1768. 2 January 14, 1770.

3 February 3, 1769. 4 January 22, 1774.

CHAP, accompanied by Master Charles James Fox. Of Wilkes Lady L Stanhope writes: ' He has been here some time. I do not know him but by sight. On the public walks we once exchanged a few words, as I was impatient to tell him of what country I was. He is the pattern of all that is right in the eyes of our young people here, as I am told, for I see few of them. He says he has had an offer of being sent by our Government Envoy to Berne or Ambassador to Constantinople, and that all that has been done in regard to him is unjust." 1 The Duke of Hamilton arrived under the charge of Dr. Moore, author of a popular novel, ' Zelucco." He was accompanied by his youthful son, Jack, afterwards known to the world as the hero of Corunna. Another acquaintance was the young Prince of Mecklenburg-Schwerin (twelve years old), who sent a toy snake to Charles ' every morning to mend, till it grew no longer than my finger. He has bespoke the employment of Snake-mender if he should come to be Sovereign. He is a fine lively boy. He comes to see us frequently, and his greatest pleasure is supping with us en famille." 2 The Prince never forgot his Genevese friends, and, on coming to England in 1782, he wrote to Lady Stanhope, expressing a hope that he may again see ' votre tres cher fils."

Shooting was a favourite pastime, and the best shot was crowned King of the Arquebusiers. The writer in ' Public Characters the ' Who's Who ' of 1800, attributes to Charles such skill as a shot that ' at a given distance he could hit a mark the size of a shilling any number of successive times." Lady Stanhope, however, gives a very different account. 3 ' At the yearly feast of the Arrow, Charles had a most polite invitation both by letter and by a deputation of some of the members. We went to see the procession return, and when we came to the door of the garden out of the town, Charles came out and says ' I am King and Bourgeois." As he had never shot in his life, we thought he was joking, till he showed us the gold medal and the arrow at his button, the marks of Royalty. All are vastly pleased with his whole conduct, and he is much beloved for his affability and being free of pride, which won't do in such a place as this and indeed does ill anywhere." Lady Stanhope is evidently proud of the way her eighteen-year old boy acquits himself, and it is pleasant to think of his popularity with the simple, kindly Genevans, who gave him the freedom of the city; but there was 1 Lady Stanhope to Lady Chatham, September 22, 1765.

- September 6, 1769.

3 Lady Stanhope to Lady Chatham, June 16, 1771.

another side to the picture. ' So far so well," she continues but CHAP, it will draw us into a horrid expense. No stranger has been King L since 1680, at which the feasts and expenses were so great and that also of the town, that the crown then worn was taken away, and the King called only Commandeur, tho' by the people still King. We shall do what is moderate; no extremes."

Lady Stanhope took great pains to make the fete a success. ' My spouse," she records, ' partook of all but the trouble, which we took off his hands upon condition he would pay all, to which he agreed." Yet the expense weighs on her prudent soul. There had been some chaff between her and Lady Chatham on the haughtiness of Chevening; ' but," she says, ' the bills I have to pay will humble me very soon." Of the fete itself she forwards a full account to Burton Pynsent, in the hope that' this long Act may amuse the young folks. I told you a little how things were. My two Messieurs have had " une lettre de Bourgeoisie " in a silver box, and nothing can be more honourable than the expressions of respect to both. The thanks in return have given great satisfaction. The dinner, instead of being within doors, by the number of the invited increasing, we were forced to have without, for which purpose a colonade in all the rules of architecture was erected at Pre l'fiveque. An amphitheatre was built for ladies invited by me, and we were to have a dinner in the great room where we formerly had our ball. Another table for some bourgeois volunteers, boys who had exercised in the last militia exercise, in short for nearer 600 than 500 persons in all. No feast was ever so well ordered."

On the fateful day there was a deluge of rain. ' We were forced to put off everything, thinking it could not last, and at night it cleared up. Next day the same thing. Boatmen and barometers consulted, and little hope given of better weather; as victuals would not keep any longer, it was resolved to bring all back to town. You can't form an idea of the hurry and distraction this occasioned. It was after eight in the morning before resolved upon and ten before I knew that I should have the house for my company. All to bring back in the rain above half a mile from the place to the town, tables to new make in another form, chairs all to bring. However as order does much, it went as well as could, and all were well served and at night I gave a ball. Had it ended here it had been something; but the exercise of dragoons, the prizes to be shot for by the archers, the procession, all that was not over. At last we had as fine a day as if it were made on purpose. Charles behaved " on ne peut pas mieux " is what I have heard from all, on every occasion did what was proper and prudent, and I find is much beloved." Even as he liked plain and simple clothes, I. Charles was also temperate in his tastes. He drank water, and he had only ' a bottle of sirrup and water to drink healths. We have had verses from all quarters, the best of all from the perriwig makers, complaining how all trades have gained on this occasion but theirs, and if pomatum and powder goes out of fashion they'll be ruined. Charles never wears powder." 1

Soon after the fete Charles was appointed Officier Major of the Dragoons. ' We returned thanks by saying that he should have thought it honour enough to be of that Corps, but that this " mettait le comble a leur politesse." He must now have some lace on his waistcoat, and you would have laughed to have heard his conversation with his tailor, to be sure to contrive that it did not scratch his hands. He is a very important man, he thinks, as Commandeur. He has had the Ordonnances des Arches copied into a little book which he carries in his pocket." 2 In September he was presented with a medal by the Corps, ' very elegant and very pretty, and he goes out in form at the head of his troop. Gen: Johnston from Minorca passed here some days and says our troop made a very good figure, and that Charles rides extremely well. 3 He says it will be a beginning for entering into the militia. I am glad he has no turn for the army; 'tis only good for younger brothers; and besides we wish him to be independentâ nor will he, I believe, ever be otherwise."

Charles was very anxious to amend the Ordonnances of the Dragoons and Archers and restore some of their lost privileges; but, as his mother observes, ' Republicans are not easily convinced," though they admitted the justice of his proposed improvements. A commission was appointed; but it was dilatory and inconclusive. Such methods did not recommend themselves to 1 Lady Stanhope to Lady Chatham, July 15, 1771. These festivities created a stupendous sensation at Geneva. A M. N. Cheneviere published a book, Relation des rejouissances faites it Geneve V occasion de tnylord Charles Stanhope, Vicomte de Mahon. Geissler engraved a print, and an enthusiast burst forth into a metrical Â pitre a un ami en description des superbes Fetes donnees par Milord Mahon a Geneve le 28 Juin et le 4 Juillet. Copies of these, with the addresses and the bills, were religiously preserved by Grisel. At the request of the Archers Charles was painted by Prud'hon, and a duplicate of the portrait is at Chevening. He is represented in the uniform of Commandeur, standing very stiffly, with a drawn sword in one hand, pointing with the other to a rock, against which repose the arms of Geneva. A large open book is magnificently inscribed ' Les Loix." On this stands a pole bearing the cap of liberty. Geneva is seen in the distance.

2 To Lady Chatham, August 12, 1771, 3 September 3, 1771.

Charles. Towards the end of his year as Commandeur, he was pressed to continue in office. ' He said nothing, but went to the I. Council. There he got up and told them he should at the usual time give up the medal. They were thunder-struck, but he persisted. After he went out, I am told that they said (near fifty of them), "Jamais nous avons eu un Commandant comme lui, il est terriblement ferine, diantre il est roide comme une barre de fer." Deputies were sent to him, and, after much entreaty, he promised to retain office one month longer. ' At the laying of the foundation stone of their new building he made a little speech, which gave satisfaction. They clapped hands and made the drums beat." 1 ' In May 1773 he had the pleasure of seeing his Ordonnances pass unanimously 2 A few days later he was suddenly called upon to command the dragoons at a review. ' He has no fears about it, but he wished to avoid it if he could. He has one ruleâ if he must do a thing he spares no pains but does it as well as he possible can." 3 Lady Stanhope 'sat on pins and needles," but all passed off successfully. ' Charles commanded them perfectly well, and was admired by even old officers who have served in different countries and who said they never saw any command better. There was an immense crowd, and many blessings he had. A young stranger student commanding their troops was a new sight. He is adored by them. I can't tell what he does, but he has the good fortune to gain the affection of all the corps of which he is member." 4

Such were the circumstances of Lord Mahon's education; well calculated, no doubt, to develop intelligence and individuality, but wanting those qualities which make public school life so important a factor in an Englishman's education. To these early surroundings are due many foreign characteristics which his English contemporaries were at a loss to comprehend: his scorn of luxury and display, his devotion to science and philosophy, his impatience of the insularity of his countrymen. Above all, his love of civil liberty is directly traceable to his Genevan training. Even in early youth he was interested in politics; for, though the entire town and canton numbered but 40,000 souls, Geneva was the scene of many political squabbles. One party was accused of a design of throwing all the power into the hands of a few families, and thus establishing a complete aristocracy. The other resisted every measure supposed to have that tendency, and was accused of seditious designs. These disputes were maintained with a bitterness which reminds us 1 June i, 1772. 2 May 10, 1773.

3 June 10, 1773, 4 June 24, 1773.

CHAP, in its implacability and pettiness of the feuds of the Montagues L and Capulets. Lady Stanhope forwarded voluminous accounts of Genevan politics to the Chathams. Lord Chatham admired the Genevan system of government, and at one time entertained an idea of visiting Switzerland to study it. It is not surprising that Charles should have followed in the democratic principles of his family. ' He is a great politician writes his mother, ' and I don't think a complaisant one. He'll not sell his conscience, or I am greatly mistaken." 1 Dr. Moore relates how, ' walking one afternoon with a young nobleman, who to a strong taste for natural philosophy unites a passionate zeal for civil liberty, we passed near a garden in which one of those circles which support the magistracy assembles. I proposed joining them. "No," says my Lord with indignation, "I will not go for a moment into such society. I consider these men as the enemies of their country, and that place a focus for consuming freedom." ' 2 Beside the Consistory of the Clergy, which had power over education and morals, the government of Geneva was vested in the Senate or Little Council, whose twenty-five members were appointed from the ruling families. The Council of Two Hundred had practically lost the right of legislation, and the people, though very enlightened and numbering the best mechanics in Europe, had no voice in the decisions of their rulers. The inhabitants of the Republic were of three kinds: (i) the governing classâ consisting of the councils, the clergy, their families and dependents;

(2) the shopkeepers, manufacturers, and master-mechanics; (3) the journeymen and mechanics, who, besides lacking political rights, could neither set up in business for themselves, nor fill the lowest office, nor exercise the liberal professions. These persons, who formed the most numerous class in the city, were called ' natives," though they were in fact the descendants of foreigners who had settled in the place. Both the bourgeois and the ' natives ' were endeavouring to secure political rights, and each was furiously jealous of the other. 3 The Council, hoping to instil more liberal principles into the younger aristocracy, chose some of them for its assembly. Lord Mahon sought and obtained election, and at once used all his conciliatory powers to put an end to the dissensions. He endeavoured to revive an interest in the civic population in the breasts of the young patricians, and assiduously frequented every class of society. 4 1 To Lady Chatham, February 26, 1770.

2 View of Society and Manners in France and Switzerland, ii. 164.

3 Parton, Life of Voltaire, ii. 445.

These efforts, though unavailing, gained for him the respect CHAP, and affection of the lower classes. I.

Despite the seductions of the famous Clairon, the Stanhopes set themselves steadily against the playhouse. Almost lost among the second Earl's sober scientific books are a few on the ' Evil and Danger of Stage Plays: shewing their Natural Tendency to destroy Religion and introduce a general Corruption of Manners." In this opinion Lord Mahon coincided. ' A play-house is lately erected in the neighbourhood writes Lady Stanhope, 1 ' whether by connivance to take up the minds of the discontented or by what accident I know not, but it is crowded daily. This at a time when trade is going to decay, everything dear, consequently much poverty among the lower sort. From other causes this winter I fear we shall see great distress, which at present is greater than ever I thought to see in this country. Our general hospital, once rich, is now, I may say, almost broke. In short all who think see this with sorrow. We do not go, not that good example always does good, but one's conscience is easy when one don't give a bad one. Charles in his little province does all he can to discourage it, joking at some and rewarding others; he has, he tells me, lately given additional prizes to be shot for by those who have not been at the play. I told him this was bribery. He says he don't give it upon condition they don't go, but as a reward to those who have not been. He has pleased many by this, and it is become the ton among them to be against the play, so that he has prevented many from going. There are several of his subjects can't afford it; they are most of them people from whom he won't learn the politeness of courtiers, but from whom he may see a good deal of public spirit. In the middle station of life I believe it is that one learns to know manhood." 2

That the English had never been so popular at Geneva was largely due to the esteem in which the Stanhopes were held. When they finally left the city ' their carriage could with difficulty move through the multitude who were assembled in the street. Numbers of the poorer sort, who had been relieved by their secret charity, unable longer to obey the injunctions of their benefactors, proclaimed their gratitude aloud. The young gentleman was obliged to come out again and again to his old friends and companions who pressed round the coach to bid him farewell, and expressed their sorrow for his departure and their wishes for his prosperity. The eyes of the parents 1 October 4, 1771, 2 October 4, 1771.

CHAP, overflowed with tears of happiness, and the whole family carried I- along with them the affections of the greater part and the esteem of all the citizens." 1 ' On Tuesday, February 22, we set out from sweet Geneva writes Lady Stanhope. 2 ' I had not time in my last to tell you of the marks of friendship and honour shewn us on leaving noire seconde patrie. In coming out of our court we found the dragoons on each side of the street. Charles joined them, and went to the gates where he got into the coach, and they got on horseback and escorted us to the frontierâ the archers drawn up in line out of the gates, and the streets from our door crowded to the outside of the town. The officers went in a coach and six horses adorned with ribbons to the first post, where each made me a compliment. And there we took our last farewell. If the blessings of these whom we saw from our door to the last farewell can avail we may be happy. It may seem vanity to mention not only the concern of our private friends but of all the town; but it would be ungrateful were we not sensible of the uncommon marks of distinction and friendly affection shewn us by all ranks. You may guess how much I was affected. I cannot think of it with (fry eyes." 3

They arrived in Paris at the end of February, and lodged at the H6tel de Lancastre, Rue St. Thomas. Lady Stanhope could not move from her sofa owing to an accident. She was visited by a few friends, who were ' very obliging but not like those of Genevaâ les amis de czur are not to be met with everywhere. My two Messieurs courrent le monde and dine often abroad." 4 Even the grave Lord Stanhope becomes mildly dissipated in this charming Paris. ' My lord is quite a gay young man writes his wife to Lord Chatham. T'other night a lady made him dance, after which he saluted them all; this diverted me very much when I heard of it 5 Charles had given way to gold lace and laced ruffles, but still rejected powder. ' II y a ici un Milord Stanhope wrote Madame du Deffand to Horace Walpole;' il arrive de Geneve, ou il a ete dix ans pour l'education de son fils qui a vingt-un ans. Ni le pere ni le fils n'ont pas vu une seule fois Voltaire; quel homme est-ce-que ce Milord? ' 6 Lord Stanhope was intimate with 1 John Moore, View of Society and Manners in France and Switzerland, p. 164.

2 Lady Stanhope to Lady Chatham, January 31,1774.

3 March 9, 1774. 4 April 14, 1774.

5 Lady Stanhope to Lord Chatham, April 14, 1774.

6 Lettres de Mme. du Dejfand a Horace Walpole, ed. Toynbee, ii. 591, and esteemed by most of the learned men of the capital, and the CHAP, prize awarded to Mahon for his essay on the pendulum (of which I. success he heard while at Paris) procured him notice. Con-dorcet formed a high opinion of his abilities, and Adam Ferguson, who passed through on his way to join a pupil, ' carried my youth to many of his acquaintance in the learned world." 1 ' I hope writes Lady Stanhope, ' that Charles will spend his time well; at least hitherto it has been different to that of the generality of his country-men whom he has not had time to frequent." One of these was the handsome young Thomas Coke, later known as Coke of Norfolk, deeply occupied in flirting with Princesses and ' making considerable havoc among the young beauties during his stay." Charles went on several excursions with Lady Mary Coke and his

aunt, Mrs. Hamilton. On May 10 Louis XV died unregretted, and Louis XVI and Marie Antoinette ascended the throne amidst popular rejoicing. ' All seem pleased with their new Sovereigns and I believe with reason." 2 Lady Mary, Mrs. Hamilton, and Mahon went to see the vault at St. Denis where the King's body was to be placed, and returning at eight o'clock met the funeral procession coming at a gallop. Lady Mary considered the mob ' very great and very indecent, as so far from shewing the least concern they hooped and halloed as if they had been at a horse race instead of a funeral procession." On another occasion they spent the day at Versailles, particularly admiring the apartments of the Princesses, ' all hanging with black, so clean, so finely furnished, so agreeably situated." Before many years had passed, the young nobleman was to rejoice at the collapse of the absolute monarchy, the material splendours of which he was now privileged to explore.

1 Lady Stanhope to Lady Chatham, April 14, 1774.

2 To Lady Chatham, May 30, 1774.

CHAP. IN July 1774 the travellers returned to England, and early in IJ- September Lord Mahon was presented at Court ' in coal-black hair and a white feather." Lord Stanhope would not suffer him to wear powder because wheat was so dear, and the wits said he had been tarred and feathered. 1 His taste in hair-dressing, or rather the want of it, was indeed the first thing to strike his compatriots. They were right in their supposition that the young noble was not like others of his class. A young man of Puritan habits and democratic principles could find few companions to share his ideas. ' I am sorry to say writes Lord Chesterfield, ' that the youth of the present day have neither learning nor politeness. Their manners are illiberal and their ignorance is notorious. They are sportsmen, they are jockeys, they know nor love nothing but dogs and horses, racing and hunting." They played deep and drank deeper. Royal Princes were dead drunk at the Court balls, and in Piccadilly respected Statesmen were found in the gutter. Fox lost his patrimony at the gaming-table. His contemporaries thought temperance more eccentric than any sensual indulgence. Pitt's correct mode of life was the subject of indecent jests, and it is easy to suppose that they regarded Mahon's teetotal views with contempt, his scientific interests as little better than necromancy, his pursuit of reforms from which no benefit could accrue to himself as sheer madness. Even his hygienic ways, imbibed from Tronchin, must have appeared cra2y, and it was considered worthy of remark that ' he slept with no nightcap and the window open," a taste unknown in that most stuffy age. 2 1 Walpole's Letters, ix. 42.

2 Meryon's Lady Hester Stanhope, ii. 15.

Mahon had no desire to spend his mornings fitting on a coat, CHAP his evenings at Goostree's, his days at Newmarket. Nor did he II. associate with ' our English Bumpkin Country Gentlemen, the most unlicked creatures in the world." 1 With some persons, to work is an imperious instinct: it is impossible for them to idle, and they grudge themselves the time for rest. Such a one was Mahon. Among the young ' Bucks and Bloods ' he had no companions; and it is significant that his great friend was his cousin, William Pitt. Charles was the senior by some six years; but the disparity of age was compensated by Pitt's precocious development of mind. They had many characteristics in common. Both ' could answer to the charge of looking slender and thin." 2 Both were of unimpeachable integrity, and both had perseverance and resolution. George IV is said to have remarked of Hoppner's portrait of Pitt: ' Yes, yes, there he is with his dâ d obstinate face!" 3 But Mahon was far more unbending than his friend. Once pledged to a cause he never forsook it, however prejudicial to himself; while Pitt held ' that a man who talks of his consistency merely because he holds the same opinion for ten or fifteen years, when the circumstances under which it was originally formed are totally changed, is a slave of the most idle vanity." 4 At the outset, their politics were identical; and they were two of the first politicians versed in the principles of the ' Wealth of Nations." But in temperament they were different. Mahon was impetuous where Pitt was cautious, and zealous where he was cold. Without the awe-inspiring haughtiness characteristic of all the Pitts, Mahon was possessed of manners which forbade impertinence or familiarity. Led by his scientific tastes to mix largely with mechanics, he preserved a dignity which could never be hidden by any democratic professions of dress or conversation.

When Lord Chesterfield wrote, ' Custom, that governs the world instead of reason, authorises a certain latitude in political matters not consistent with the strictest morality," he expressed very delicately the corruption of the age. The intrigues by which Thurlow contrived to remain in the Cabinet during all mutations of government are well known. The conduct of Richmond was not above reproach. Lord Carlisle changed sides thrice in the course of a single year. Shelburne earned for himself the nickname of ' Malagrida," the Portuguese Jesuit Lord Mansfield was ready to prostitute the cause of justice to 1 Letters of Lord Chesterfield.

- W. Pitt to Lady Chatham, January 3, 1780. Chatham Papers.

CHAP, save the King's brother from the penalty of the law, and Lord! L Kenyon did not hesitate to support a grossly unconstitutional measure to accommodate his party. Fox showed no scruples in allying himself with a man whom he had declared worthy of impeachment and the scaffold; and Dundas' happy faculty of putting himself at anyone's disposal was neatly hit off by the caricature in which he is represented asking ' Wha wants me? ' Of the ministers there was always oneâ often severalâ ready to intrigue against the rest of the Cabinet; and one Prime Minister declared' I will never again be at the head of a string of Janissaries who are always ready to strangle or dispatch me on the least signal." Walpole's cynical observation that every man had his price was no idle sarcasm in the eighteenth century. But Mahon was never to be bought. His integrity was unswerving, and his position outside the lines of party.

The year 1774 was of critical importance in the life of Charles Stanhope for more reasons than one. In September he proposed to Lady Hester Pitt (his second cousin) and was accepted, to the great pleasure of all parties. 1 ' As to the young gentleman," writes Mrs. Boscawen, ' he is a happy man and has made an excellent choice. The world has long made it for him." 2 The match aroused considerable interest. ' Lord Chatham's eldest daughter," wrote Walpole to Sir Horace Mann, ' is married to Lord Mahon, Lord Stanhope's son and a descendant of your old Baileys and Binnings. So I make you my compliments." 3 ' I wish I could find words," writes his happy mother to Lady Chatham, ' to express what I feel at this moment. I often wished that I had a daughter, and in her I think I shall have one as dear to me as if so by birth. My boy is so good that I hope he'll make your daughter as happy as I expect she will make him, or I shall be sadly disappointed in both. I do think that it will be the cleverest match that has been for a great while; the union of two good hearts and two good heads surely must turn out well. I can't tell you how I long to embrace our Girl." 4 Of Lady Hester Mr. Cholmondeley (familiarly alluded to as ' Chum ') writes: ' I have the pleasure of knowing her to be without compliment one of the most accomplished persons of the age and to have availed herself of every benefit which could possibly result from the most refined and prudent education." 5 The engagement gave equal 1 Lady Mary Coke, iv. 406.

2 Mrs. Boscawen to Lady Chatham, October i, 1774. Chatham Papers.

3 Letters, ix. 109. 4 Lady Stanhope to Lady Chatham.

5 Thomas Cholmondeley of Vale Royal to Lady Stanhope, October 8, 1774. Stanhope Papers.

pleasure to the Pitts. Lord Chatham thus describes Mahon to CHAP. Grenville. ' Though the outside is well, it is by looking within II-that invaluable treasures appear; a head to contrive, a heart to conceive, and a hand to execute whatever is good, lovely or of fair repute. He is as yet very new to our vile world, indeed quite a traveller in England. I grieve that he has no seat in Parliament, that wickedest and best school for superior natures." l

Just before this was written, Charles had made a valiant effort to enter the school in which Chatham had won incomparable distinction. Parliament had been dissolved, and at the General Election he and Lord Montmorris 2 contested the City of Westminster, their candidature being warmly supported by the Lord Mayor elect, John Wilkes. That the Stanhopes were not altogether pleased with his patronage is not surprising. To Lady Chatham Lady Stanhope admits: ' I own having Charles set out in the world in the suite of Mr. Wilkes hurts me very much." 3 It was, however, quite natural that he should thus attach himself. Fresh from Geneva, and deeply imbued with constitutional principles, he saw with dismay the power of the Court party, of which Wilkes was at once the victim and the formidable antagonist. Added to this was the amazing personal fascination of the man. Though squinting, toothless, and ill-featured, it was his boast that with ten minutes' start he could ingratiate himself quicker with any woman than could the handsomest man. Even Johnson and Gibbon, who thoroughly disliked him, were forced to admire his fine manners and his wit. When he presented a City petition to the King, even George, to whom he was peculiarly obnoxious, reluctantly confessed that he had never known so charming and well-bred a Lord Mayor. A final consideration was that Lord Chatham, Mahon's father-in-law to be, had been the fervent advocate of Wilkes in regard to the Middlesex Election of 1769.

The newspapers assert that all the outdoor servants and tradespeople of St. James's Palace were commanded to vote for the Court candidates, that the Chelsea outpensioners had the same instruction on pain of being instantly struck off the list, and that the Colonel of the first troop of Life Guards mustered his men and gave them peremptory orders to poll for Percy and Clinton. 4 Well might Bentham call King George' The Corruptor-General'; but at this time such incidents were too frequent 1 Chatham Correspondence, November 28, 1774.

2 Henry Redmond de Montmorency, second Viscount Montmorris.: Stanhope Papers.

CHAP, to excite much surprise. Mahon's colleague had no qualities II- to recommend him. The ' Rolliad ' repeatedly holds him up to ridicule, and he is described by one who knew him well as ' destitute of eloquence, invariably busy, yet never attaining his object; unsuccessful in every pursuit; but always on his feet to so great a degree as to convey the idea of ubiquity personified." Of the Tory candidates, Lord Percy 1 had represented Westminster since 1763. As his first wife was Bute's daughter, he had more than one reason to expect the support of the Court party. He was the eldest son of that Duke of Northumberland who, born Smithson, had raised himself to a higher sphere by marrying the heiress of the Percys. He applied to George II for the Garter, pleading that' he was the first Duke not to have it," to which the King retorted' that he was the first Smithson who had ever asked for it." Lord Percy was now absent in America ' cutting the throats of the Bostonians," 2 as the newspapers put it.

No doubt the Wilkes candidates made much of their opponent being engaged in an attempt to impose arbitrary and tyrannical measures on an independent people. His colleague, Lord Thomas Pelham Clinton, 3 is less conspicuous, and does not seem to have been blessed with the gift of oratory, for he is sarcastically referred to as ' that piece of still life, Lord Tommy Clinton." The Northumberland family had large properties in Westminster, and were commonly reputed to lay out about Â 40,000 a year with the inhabitants; whereas the Stanhopes had no house or possessions there, and, having recently returned from abroad, were regarded more or less as foreigners. For personal as well as political reasons the Duke of Northumberland would use his influence against any nominee of Wilkes, as, during the riots of 1769, the mob had forced him publicly to drink his health at Northumberland House. Undaunted by the forces ranged against him, Mahon plunged into the election with boyish impetuosity. His Address entreats the suffrages of ' the Worthy and Independent Electors of Westminster," 4 declaring that he ' will use his utmost efforts to obtain the expunging of that unconstitutional and most dangerous Resolution of the House 1 Hugh, Lord Percy, afterwards second Duke of Northumberland, born 1742, died 1817.

2 Middlesex Journal, October 6, 1774.

3 Lord Thomas Pelham Clinton, born 1752, married (1782) Lady Anna Maria Stanhope, daughter of second Earl Harrington; succeeded his father as second Duke of Newcastle, 1794.

of Commons, by which a person having a great minority of legal CHAP, votes was seated in that House as one of the representatives of lithe County of Middlesex; to obtain the repeal of the Septennial Act; to obtain also the repeal of the late Quebec Government Bill. I will contribute as much as in me lies he concludes, ' to re-establish that happy concord and mutual good-will which once subsisted, to the unspeakable advantage of this kingdom, between Great Britain and her colonies in America

In his usual unconstitutional and unkingly manner the Monarch busied himself with the Westminster election. On September 25 he writes to Lord North: ' I hear the Duke of Newcastle retracts from his agreement of joining Lord Thomas Clinton as a candidate for Westminster with Lord Percy, and this from no nobler an idea than the fear of some scurrilous abuse in the newspapers. Press him as a meritorious conduct towards me to nominate his son, and you may easily add that Lord Mahon cannot be a very formidable opposer as he will not open any houses. I understand the Duke's wise scheme is that Lord Percy should join Lord Mahon; but now after the advertisement the latter has published, I do not think him in the least preferable to Humphrey Coates 1 Our two lords were now elected to Wilkes's City clubs, and meetings were heldâ chiefly at the Standard Tavern, Leicester Fieldsâ to support their candidature. 2 On October 4 more than 5,000 inhabitants and electors assembled at Westminster Hall. 3 Wilkes, now Lord Mayor elect, was voted chairman and mounted on a table. The candidates were invited to support Acts for shortening the duration of Parliament; for a more equitable representation of the people; for excluding placemen and pensioners from the House of Commons; for an inquiry in what manner the enormous sums of money arising from the heavy taxes had been applied. Finally came a resolutionâ interesting as illustrative of the customs of the timeâ ' that they will insist that the gallery of the House of Commons shall always be opened and the proceedings of their representatives shall be made known to the people ' The electors announced their approbation by repeated shouts of applause Mr. Sawbridge nominated Lord Mahon. ' Nothing I can mention can ingratiate the noble Lord in your favour more than his public address to you. Bred 1 Correspondence of George III and Lord North, i. 203. Humphrey Coates was a wine-merchant of doubtful sobriety. He had conferred an obligation on Wilkes, who now refused to support him.

2 Morning Chronicle, October 14; Public Advertiser.

CHAP, up in constitutional principles he is not likely to depart from JI- them; I know he is endowed with many virtues; I believe he has a mind untainted with any vices. He has an independent fortune and, what is much superior, an independent soul."

Lord Montmorris then returned thanks in a grandiloquent speech. ' I am not," he said, ' a citizen of Westminster; but am I not a citizen of the world and as such better able to comprehend your interests? My country is here," he continued, pointing to the heavens. He compared himself to Pompey soliciting the votes of the Roman citizens, and declared that, like Pompey, he was ready to expire, if necessary, in defence of his constituents and country. Lord Mahon's speech breathes the spirit of liberty and independence, and contains none of the flights of his colleague. The reporter of these proceedings was struck by the ungainliness and lanky figure of Charles; for he observes, ' Lord Mahon certainly has not sacrificed much to the Graces!" 1 and describes his ' spasmodic speech ' and ' awkward boylike gesticulation." A still more hostile journalist describes him as ' a stuttering Geneva schoolboy, who can neither speak nor write his mother tongue." This was untrue. He had a forcible command of language, but his delivery was bad and his gestures frequently grotesque. Throughout his life he was so much in earnest as to be thoughtless of his appearance or the impression it produced on the minds of others. His written English is singularly easy and correct.

Personalities were the common weapons of political warfare. Lord Montmorris is spoken of as' an Irish adventurer engaged in a flagitious conspiracy against the real rights of the people." 2 The allusions to Lord Percy are less delicate, his appearance, his relations with his wife, his Smithson origin being discussed with unappetising candour. 3 The newspapers abound with squibs and lampoons, and the letters vie with the philippics of the Eatanswill Gazette. On Saturday night, October 8, all the houses were illuminated in consequence of Mr. Wilkes being chosen Lord Mayor," and a mob was abroad breaking the windows of those who refused to light up." Lord Montmorris and Lord Mahon happening to pass by Charing Cross in a coach, ' the populace, notwithstanding their earnest entreaties to the contrary, took the horses off, and drew them in triumph up St. Martin's Lane, Longacre, round Covent Garden, through the Strand to Northumberland House, and up the Haymarket with 1 Middlesex Journal. Public Advertiser, October 19.

the loudest acclamations of applause. In Piccadilly their CHAP. Lordships were obliged to get out to prevent the populace from II. drawing them to St. James'." 1

Preparations were now begun for the election, and the hustings were erected under the portico of St. Paul's, Co vent Garden. 2 Early on Tuesday, October n, ' a prodigious concourse of people assembled in Co vent Garden, the booths in the centre of the square and all the avenues leading to it being equally crowded. All the candidates being upon the hustings and some preliminaries being gone through, the Returning Officer insisted that each candidate should enter into a bond of Â 200, to answer for the expenses necessarily attending the taking of the poll. The Whig candidates came forward to the front of the hustings and harangued the Electors for near half an hour. This gave great offence to the friends of the other party. A scene of the most shameful indecency now ensued, a general cry of Come to poll, hissing, groaning, clapping and huzzaing, in order to prevent those noble Lords from being heard. Lord Mahon would not however be interrupted, but finished his speech. Just before one o'clock the poll was declared open and all went peaceably for a few minutes till a party of butchers with marrow-bones and cleavers made their appearance, bearing a blue silk flag with the motto Percy and Clinton friends to Liberty, which they displayed directly opposite to the hustings. The populace exasperated began to fling dirt at the flag, and the universal cry was Belt them, belt them; but they continued to wave their banner, till some persons on the hustings seized it and tore it to pieces 3

As the poll was to remain open several days, canvassing proceeded apace. The votes of the electors are entreated for ' Lord Percy, their late humane member." His mother, the Duchess of Northumberland, worked unceasingly. Writing to Sir Horace Mann Walpole says: ' Wilkes has met a heroine to stem the tide of his conquests; who, though not of Arc or a Pucelle, is a true Joan in spirit, style and manners. This is her Grace of Northumberland, who has carried the mob of Westminster from him, sitting daily in the midst of Covent Garden, and will elect her son and Lord T. Clinton against Wilkes' two candidates, Lord Montmorris and Lord Mahon." 4

Charles worked hard, his aunt writes to Lady Stanhope. ' I went to him this morning before eight. He was just going out, 1 Morning Chronicle, October 10, 1774.

2 Middlesex Journal, October 6.

3 Public A dvertiser and General Evening Post.

CHAP, made 1500 visits yesterday and very successful; he had 50 IL letters laying by him, and in such a hurry that he hardly took time to drink his milk. I was going with my nieces, and in turning into a street I saw him shaking hands with a very dirty blacksmith. He told us that he had that morning made 800 visits (not then 12 o'clock) and had hardly met with any refusal; some few said they would not vote against them. I did not see Lord Montmorris, but as their coaches were standing together, I imagine he was going up the other side of the street. Each has cards with both their names on them. Charles never gets time to dine, sometimes catches a drink of chocolate, and nobody can find him but in the street! ' 1 The papers bear further testimony to his indefatigable energy. A person signing himself ' John Grubb' declares that ' the most zealous friends to the laws against entertaining voters must be satisfied, for so far from giving a pot of porter during the whole poll you neither of you look as if you had eat or drank yourselves The contest caused Lady Stanhope some anxiety. ' I am in pain for his health she writes, ' knowing what a working head he has, and what an upright heart, which makes him scrupulous where there is no reason to be so. How rare for a parent to have to complain that their child is too honest In spite of his exertions, Charles finds time to pay flying visits to Lady Hester in Kent. ' Give my love to my dear Charley if you see him writes his mother to Lady Chatham. ' I suppose he stayed as long as he could at Hayes. There is a play called " Love in a Hollow Tree." If Lord Pitt was at home to assist, I would desire to have one wrote and call it " Love and an Election "!" 2

In days when the din of the multitude often prevented the candidates from being heard, a powerful voice was a valuable possession. Many are the references to Charles' stentorian lungs. The ' Rolliad' described him as ' Mahon outroaring torrents in their course A lady, meeting him soon after his election, found it difficult to believe' that it was he that harangued the people so as to be heard quite across Co vent Garden for she thinks him ' remarkably silent 3 At the close of the poll each day the candidates came forward and addressed the crowd. Mahon was always well received. Writing to Lady Chatham, Lady Stanhope says: ' Colgate came here last night, having been in town Tuesday and in the midst of the crowd. He said he heard 1 Stanhope Papers. 2 Ibid.

s Hon. Mrs. Boscawen to Mrs. Delany, November 15, 1774. Delany Correspondence, v. 63.

nothing but praises of Charles on all hands, so much spirit in so CHAP young a man pleased them; perhaps some of them were friends H-of our girl." 1 In spite of his exertions, however, every day more votes were recorded for the Tory candidates. The Court party was exultant. ' The Westminster election continues very prosperous," writes the King; ' the poll could not be more favourable than this day; I have heard it pretty privately reported that Lord Mahon and Montmorris polled yesterday many very bad votes." 2 On October 26 the poll was closed and the numbers stood as follows:â

Lord Percy. 4994

Lord Thomas Clinton. 4744

Lord Montmorris.,. 2551

Lord Mahon. 2342

Wilkes and Sir Watkin Lewes were on the hustings, and there was a great concourse of people. ' The High Bailiff of Westminster who officiates as Returning Officer, and Colonel Phillipsâ representative of E. Percyâ publicly returned thanks (on the close of the poll) to Lord Viscount Mahon, for having been able, by the daily patriotic and constitutional speeches his lordship made to the people in a most manly and thundering voice, to prevent all riots whatever during the course of the election most especially at the close of the poll, which day has always produced a most shocking scene of insults, of riotings and confusion in all the former contested elections for Westminster. It was impossible for the mob to conduct themselves with greater decency and tranquillity than they did that day, and the friends of Lord Mahon and liberty will certainly rejoice to see that even his lordship's opponents have been obliged to bear a public testimony to the great candour and public spirit which has appeared throughout the whole of his lordship's conduct from the very beginning of this arduous contest." 3 A few days later Mahon addressed his Committee at the Standard Tavern, thanking them for their support and saying he heard they meditated petitioning Parliament for a new election; but he did not think proper to take any part in a petition, and if the present election were to be voided he would not again present himself as candidate. 4

It is probable that Westminster desired Charles to stand 1 Stanhope Papers.

George III to Lord North, October 14 and October 18.

CHAP, again at the election of 1777, for in that year Mrs. Boscawen 11 â writes: ' Lady Weymouth tells me we are to have no riots at Westminster about the election, which is a very good hearing. Lord Mahon, whom the Opposition would have been glad of, I suppose, says he spent too much last time, and Lord Montmorris is not to be found. I think that nobody will oppose Lord Petersham." 1 Of what these expenses were we can form a very accurate estimate; for a folio volume exists at the British Museum containing every bill contracted by the Tory candidates during this election. It is an entertaining collection, from the agents' ' disbursements for dinners to electors at 36 a head," and the bill ' from your Humbel Searvent Henry Flanaganâ eleven pounds and three shillings' for suppers and ' lickkers' at ' saveral times," to the letter from the proprietor of the Rose Tavern, ' although my bill is not very large I will venture to say no one man got so many votes as myself." The account of this last worthy publican for ' provisions and wine ' expended by the electors of Westminster reaches the modest figure of thirty pounds, the principal item being ' strong beer." 2

Preparations were now begun for the marriage of Mahon and Lady Hester; but Charles could not be induced to forego his ordinary occupations to attend to the important question of dress. His mother writes to Lady Chatham: ' Pray tell my son that I hope he'll recollect that his stocks have been this twelve month in rags and that there is no time to be lost in determining what he is to have, that they may be ordered." 3 The more momentous subject of Lady Hester's trousseau required more consideration; but Lady Mary Coke hears that ' Lady Chatham has chose her daughter's clothes very ill." 4 In the grandiloquent language so dear to him Lord Chatham requests his brother-in-law to be trustee to the young couple. ' The myrtle wreaths are duly twined, and the parchment bands in great forwardness, which are to unite our dear Hester to Lord Mahon. Every circumstance promises happiness, and to add pleasure to pleasure, parents and child hope you will allow us to mix your name in this very pleasing business, as a trustee to the settlements. Your colleagues 1 Hon. Mrs. Boscawen to Mrs, Delany, December 13, 1776, Delany Correspondence, v. 286.

2 Pel ham Papers, Add. MSS. 33123, ff. no, 149, c.

3 Undated; in 1774.

will be Lord Temple, Mr. Thos: Pitt, Mr. Cholmondeley. All CHAP, is ample as I wish." 1 The wedding took place at Hayes on H-December 19; and the rector, the Rev. Francis Fawke, 2 was moved to celebrate the auspicious event in verse:â ' When gentle hearts in faithful union join And mix the Hero with the Patriot's line, With every charm uniting every grace And all the virtues of the Temple race, The happy omen we with joy admit And bless the match of Stanhope and of Pitt

In a letter from Lady Stanhope, quoted by Lady Mary Coke, 3 we have an example of the terrible honeymoon en famille of the eighteenth century. ' As soon as the ceremony was over," she says, 'we all came here (Chevening). As Lady Stanhope has some of her relations in the house with her, the company has been pretty numerous. In consequence the marriage has been celebrated in the old style: the new one you know does not admit of a third person. Lady Stanhope expresses herself much pleased with her new daughter-in-law, and says they shall be in town very soon. They have taken Lord Cork's house in Queen Anne Street." She had three daughters: Hester, born 1776; Griselda, born 1778; and Lucy, born 1780. We next hear of the young couple at the Drawing-room of St. James, when ' the new married lady of Lord Mahon was presented by Lady Chatham to her Majesty, after which Lord Temple 4 gave them a grand entertainment at his house in Pall Mall." 5 On January 12, 1775, Mahon was admitted to the Royal Society, to which he had been elected in 1773 before leaving Geneva. Four days later he made a flying visit to Derby. 6 A vacancy had just occurred there, and Charles thought of offering himself; but a candidate was already chosen. Before the end of the year he made another attempt. In November one of the members for Bath died suddenly. Lord Temple and his brother, with that ambition for their family which was the particular characteristic of the Grenvilles, instantly wrote to Lady Chatham suggesting that ' Lord Mahon should proceed thither without delay in order to take a view of the carte du pais before it is occupied by another." 7 But nothing came of it, and Mahon had 1 Earl of Chatham to the Hon. James Grenville, November 28, 1774.

2 The friend of Dr. Johnson and translator of A nacreon.

: t Letters, iv. 449. 4 Uncle to Lady Mahon.

5 January 4. Middlesex Journal.

6 London Evening Post, January 18, 1775.

7 Hon. James Grenville to Lady Chatham, November 14, 1775. Pitt Papers, Record Office.

CHAP, to wait till he was elected for the Borough of Wycombe by the 11 â influence of Lord Shelburne.

Charles now published a slim pamphlet, ' Considerations on means of preventing fraudulent practices on the Gold Coin," written in 1773 at Geneva. The object of this treatise was to recommend certain methods of coining which would render an imitation difficult, except by very skilful workmen; and he suggests that no one would find it worth while to expose himself to the severe punishment inflicted on false coiners. The pamphlet contains several noteworthy suggestions, and ' actually proposed that method, since adopted with great advantage for copper pieces, of raising the edge to protect the impression." 1 ' I have got another noble author, Lord Mahon wrote Horace Walpole. ' He writes on the gold coin; if he can make gold as well as coin, he will be of great use to his father-in-law Garrick, and a very good prop to his administration." 2

In May, 1775, Charles, accompanied by his father, paid a visit to Lord Shelburneâ probably at his retreat at Streathamâ and there met Price, Priestley, and other interesting guests. 3 For some time after this we hear little of Lord and Lady Mahon, who continued to reside in the country. Charles occupied himself chiefly with his inventions, and discovered a method of securing buildings against fire. It depended on the now well-known principle that when there is no current of air there can be no fire. During the experimental stages the park at Chevening must have been the scene of many strange conflagrations. The invention at last proved so successful that he gave a grand display in September 1777, which carried conviction to the minds of all beholders. He shall tell his own story. ' I caused a wooden building to be constructed about 26 feet long by 15 feet wide. The first experiment was to fill the lower room full of shavings and faggots mixed with combustibles and to set them on fire. The heat was so intense that the glass of the windows was melted like so much common sealing-wax and ran down in drops; yet the flooring-boards of that very room were not burnt through, nor was one of the side timbers, flooring-joints or ceiling-joists damaged in the smallest degree." Sir John Pringle, President of the Royal Society, Wilkes, and other celebrities expressed their confidence by sitting in the upper room ' enjoying the luxury of ice-creams while the most intense fire was raging in the room immediately below them. 4 ' I then 1 Playfair, British Families of Antiquity, i. 427.

z Letters, ix. 209. 3 Rutt's Life of Priestley, i. 256, note.

caused a kind of wooden building, of full 50 feet in length and CHAP, of three stories high in the middle, to be erected quite close II. to one end of the secured wooden house. I filled and covered this building with above noo large kiln faggots and several loads of dry shavings, and set this pile on fire. The height of the flames was no less than 87 feet perpendicular from the ground, and the grass upon a bank 150 feet from the fire was all scorched; yet the secured wooden building quite contiguous to this vast heap of fire was not at all damaged, except some parts of the outer coat of plaster work." He also showed that it was impossible to burn a wooden staircase secured according to his method. ' Had our dear friend been born sooner," remarked Lord Chatham, ' Nero and the second Charles could never have amused themselves by reducing to ashes the two noblest cities of the world." 2 The method was to prove of practical utility to his own family. About 1797 a fire broke out at Chevening and raged furiously till it reached the part of the house Charles had made fire-proof, where its progress was at once arrested. 8 Mahon contrived some other inventions, which he believed to be of considerable importance in the art of building. His method of burning lime in a kiln, like a wind furnace, produced such intense heat as to vitrify it. Lime thus burned was found to make mortar more durable and harder than that in common use. Another invention of his early years was a method of covering roofs with a composition made of tar, chalk, and fine sand. By using this composition instead of slates and tiles, the roof could be made almost flat, thus allowing the attics to be built like the lower rooms. 4 In 1777 our inventor completed two calculating ' arithmetical machines," as they were called. The first, ' by means of dial-plates and small indices, moveable with a steel pin, performed with undeviating accuracy' complicated sums of addition and subtraction. The second solved problems in multiplication and division, ' without possibility of mistake," by the simple revolution of a small winch. It was half the size of a common table writing-desk, and ' what appears very singular and surprising to every spectator of this machine is that in working division, if the operator be inattentive to his business and thereby attempts to turn the handle a single revolution more than he ought, he is instantly admonished of his error by the springing up of a small ivory ball." 5 One of the machines is at Chevening, while two passed into the hands 1 Philosophical Transactions for 1778, p. 884; and Annual Register, 1779.

2 Chatham Correspondence, iv. 440.

3 Public Characters, 1800-1. 4 Ibid., pp. 95-6. 5 Ibid.

CHAP, of Babbage, and were given by his son to the Victoria and Albert IJ-Museum. They bear the dates 1775 and 1777, and are marvels of mechanical ingenuity.

When Benjamin Franklin came to England in hopes of obtaining a satisfactory settlement of American affairs, he was introduced by Lord Stanhope to Lord Chatham. 1 His scientific attainments aroused Mahon's lively interest; and when some years later a discussion in the Royal Society arose as to the relative merits of Franklin's pointed lightning-conductors and those with ' knobbed ends Charles warmly espoused the cause of his friend. He engaged Wilson, the objector, in such an animated dispute, and so completely disproved his theories by a number of successful experiments, that the latter ' went to the end of the room as if to avoid seeing them, and afterwards said he had not changed his opinions." In short a very pretty quarrel took place. Lord Mahon, vehement, logical, always able to prove his point, was pronounced in the right, and Franklin's scientific reputation vindicated; while Wilson was discredited and treated with contumely. 2 In Lord Mahon's ' Principles of Electricity," published a year later, many pages are devoted to proving the superiority of pointed lightning-conductors. The King took part in the dispute, not on scientific but on political grounds. It is said that he sent for the President and begged the Royal Society to rescind the resolution condemning Wilson's conductors and approving Franklin's; but Sir John Pringle, with all respect, declined. ' Sire," he said, ' I cannot reverse the laws and operations of nature." 3 A friend of Franklin wrote this epigram:â ' While you, great George, for knowledge hunt, And sharp conductors change for blunt,

The Nation's out of joint. Franklin a wiser course pursues, And all your thunder useless views

By keeping to the point."

At the end of 1777 and the beginning of 1778, Charles was engaged upon his ' Principles of Electricity," and carried out many experiments to illustrate his theories. ' I am to meet my sister," writes Pitt," as soon as she can find a leisure moment. Her great business is that of secretary to Lord Mahon, whose " Electricity " is nearly ready for the press and will rank him, I 1 Memoirs of Benjamin Franklin, i. 433. 2 Ibid., ii. 77.

3 Weld's Royal Society, ii. 101. See also Peter Pindar, who says that this dispute was the immediate cause of Sir J. Pringle's resignation.

suppose, with Dr. Franklin." 1 In this treatise he proves by an CHAP, elaborate mathematical demonstration, illustrated by a great H. variety of experiments, that the density of an electrical atmosphere super-induced upon any body must be inversely as the square of the distance from the charged body. He also took great pains to prove and explain the existence of what he describes as the returning stroke in electricity, by which fatal effects may be produced even at a vast distance from the place where the lightning falls. This new theory he considered as completely exemplified and established by the death of James Lander and two horses, killed in Scotland by the effects of a thunderstorm which was evidently at a considerable distance from the spot where the fatal accident happened. An account of this occurrence was drawn up, and, together with some ' Remarks' by Mahon, was published in the ' Philosophical Transactions ' for the year 1787. Priestley, who had already written his works on electricity, thought very highly of Mahon's treatise, which was translated into French in 1781 and into German in 1798. It was largely owing to this book that he was elected a member of the Philosophical Society at Philadelphia.

Lord Mahon figures in the dramatic scene which closed Lord Chatham's illustrious career. On April 7, 1778, the Duke of Richmond 2 was to move an address that all British troops be withdrawn from America, which was virtually an acknowledgment of her independence. Against the advice of his physician, Chatham rose from his bed and came to the House of Lords in order to protest against this course, and publicly disavow sympathy with the Rockingham Whigs. ' The scene was very affecting wrote Horace Walpole; ' his two sons and son-in-law, Lord Mahon, were round him." 3 ' As he tottered to his seat, he bowed courteously to the peers who had paid him the involuntary respect of rising to receive him. His dress was of rich black velvet, his legs were swathed in flannel. He looked like a dying man; yet never was seen a figure of more dignity. He appeared like a being of a superior species. His face was pale and emaciated; so emaciated that beneath his large wig, his aquiline nose and penetrating eye were nearly all of his features that were discernible." 4 In a faltering voice and in broken sentences, he 1 William Pitt to Lady Chatham, February n, 1779. Stanhope's Life of Pitt, i. 28.

2 Brother of the Lady Sarah Lennox admired by George III, and builder of Goodwood.

3 Letters, x. 218.

4 Seward's Anecdotes of Distinguished Persons, ii. 383.

CHAP, protested against ' giving up the dependency of America on the II. sovereignty of Great Britain and cried: ' If no other Lord is of opinion with me, I will singly protest against the measure! ' The Duke of Richmond having replied, Chatham again rose to address the House. He was seen to press his hand to his heart and stagger back, and would have fallen had not the Duke of Cumberland and Lord Temple caught him in their arms. The House was immediately adjourned. He lingered some weeks, and expired on May n, 1778, in his seventieth year. So high ran party rancour that his public funeral, which took place at Westminster Abbey on June 9, was attended by none of the Court party; while the Opposition was chiefly represented by that section of the Whigs which had claimed him as leader. Burke and Dunning were the pall-bearers. In the absence of his elder brother abroad, William Pitt was principal mourner, accompanied by Lord Mahon. 2 1 Parl. History, xix. 1023-6.

2 Though Copley's picture of ' Lord Chatham's seizure ' is best known, Shirwin gives a better representation of the scene and more faithful portraits of the principal actors. Particularly good is the likeness of Lord Mahon, who supports the recumbent statesman in his arms. Chatham and Mahon were much attached to each other and

corresponded on politics. See Chatham Correspondence, iv. 402-3, and 497-506. Mahon signs himself ' Your most dutiful and affectionate son."

THE failures and humiliations of the American War, following CHAP, on the persecution of Wilkes, stimulated popular discontent, III. and from 1778 the demand for reform grew rapidly. Wyvill created a new and powerful instrument of agitation in the county associations. The great Whig families began to flirt with the idea of reform; but, being in many cases owners of boroughs themselves, paid little more than lip-service to it. Their real desires lay rather in the direction of reducing the power of the King by abolishing the places and pensions which he employed to influence Parliament. These two currents flowed for a time side by side; but they were rather rivals than allies, and when Burke's measure of economical reform was carried, Parliamentary Reform was shelved. After their disappointment with the Whigs, the Reformers turned to Pitt, who entered on his career as a convinced advocate of their cause. But Pitt likewise proved a broken reed. This experience of the two great parties left an abiding bitterness in the soul of Charles Stanhope, and determined him to trust neither to Whigs nor Tories but to his own right arm.

Since the Middlesex Election, it was becoming the custom to bring the opinion of public meetings to bear on Parliament. In December, 1779, a great gathering was held at York, which, unlike those of 1769, was composed of influential and respectable persons. The Reverend Christopher Wyvill took the chair, and it was resolved to appoint a committee of their number to prepare a plan of association. Many counties welcomed the example of Yorkshire, and held large meetings. The cause was espoused by all the great Whig leaders, and the younger members of the party were equally zealousâ Mahon and Pitt among the number. Writing from Cambridge, Pitt says: ' The counties

CHAP, in this part of the world are beginning to awaken, and most of IJ L them will, I hope, adopt the Yorkshire measures. I do not yet hear anything to the honour of the west, which I am sorry for." 1 Kent was soon in the field; and early in January Mahon was elected chairman of its committee. 2 At the close of his life he wrote to his old friend, Major Cartwright: ' Though a younger man than yourself, I am your senior in reform. You first published on that subject in 1776, I in 1774." 3 No such pamphlet or publication has been found; but his categorical statement, which can hardly be gainsaid, shows how early he had begun to champion the cause. He frequently consulted Wyvill on questions of organisation and propaganda; while Fox, Burke, Dunning, Sir George Savile, Shelburne, the Dukes of Rutland and Richmond were among his other correspondents. Their letters are among his papers, with a vellum-bound volume, ' Proceedings of the Committee of the County of Kent." On October 19, 1780, we read that ' the Hon. William Pitt was added to the Committee." Each county committee deputed two or three of its members to meet in London to confer on the objects of the agitation. As one of the deputies for Kent, Mahon sedulously attended the meetings held throughout March. 4

Besides advocating reform in his own county of Kent, he interested himself in the Buckinghamshire Association. He was candidate for Chipping Wycombe, a close borough under the influence of Lord Shelburne, to whom he wrote regarding

Parliamentary Reform. Shelburne replied as follows:â ' High Wycombe: April 7, 1780.

' My dear Lord,â I am very sorry that the Buckinghamshire Committee has been appointed to meet in London, as they cannot be assisted by the country members without manifest inconvenience. I cannot with any propriety ask the gentlemen in this part to go out of the country. As to the business which it meets upon, I can only repeat to your Lordship that I cannot discover in the plan of the Yorkshire Association a single exceptionable principle. General union is acknowledged to be essential to our success. To this end there must be a reasonable lead somewhere. Where can it remain so safely or so honourably as with the Meeting of the County of York, who have uniformly proceeded hitherto with a view to measures and not to men, 1 Pitt to Lady Chatham, January 12, 1780. Chatham Papers, Record Office.

2 Wyvill Papers, Hi. 180, c. 3 Cartwright's Life, i. 82, note. 4 Wyvill Papers, i. 116, 129, 426, 429.

and regarding whom there does not exist the smallest well- CHAP, founded suspicion of the interference of party? Next as to the Hi-points which are made subjects of Association. It is acknowledged that the approaching election has a very great influence on the divisions now taking place in the House of Commons in favour of reform and redress of grievances. The county members have very generally voted on the public side, except a few who are likely to lose their seats by not doing so. What then is so natural or so reasonable as to follow where these principles lead, and desire that Parliaments shall be shortened, and an effectual addition or substitution of county members made to the present House of Commons? My principle does not go to influence the political opinion of any man. But I think it is a duty to declare my own, and your Lordship will do me a great deal of honour by communicating these as my sentiments to the Committee either individually or collectively, if those of absent persons shall be alluded to.

' I have the honour to be, with the greatest attachment, ' SHELBURNE." 1

The more far-seeing Reformers were now beginning to feel that even to obtain Economical Reform would only be to lop one head off corruption: the monster itself would not be destroyed. They commenced a further agitation for Parliamentary Reform and Parliaments of shorter duration. At this time the people had but little voice in the government of the country. Of the two great political parties of the day, Cartwright truly observed that the Tories believed in the divine right of Kings and the Whigs in the divine right of noblemen and gentry. The divine right of the people was left to be upheld by that small band of Radical pioneers who composed the early political societies. To set forth the need for Parliamentary Reform, Major Cart-wright, with the assistance of Dr. John Jebb and Capel Lofft, founded the ' Society for Promoting Constitutional Information." 2 Among its members were Home Tooke, Pitt, Fox, Sheridan, the Duke of Richmond, Wyvill, and Mahon.

Parliamentary Reform, however, soon divided the Reformers. All the Whigs favoured Economical Reform; but on the subject of Parliamentary Reform their opinions were at variance. While Shelburne, Fox, and their adherents were ready to give it their support, it was opposed by Rockingham and his followers, 1 Stanhope Papers.

2 Wyvill Papers, ii. 463; Bland Surges Papers, p. 178; Daly, Radical Pioneers, p. 114; Jephson, The Platform, i. 190.

CHAP, including Portland and Burke. At a meeting of the Bucking-Hi- hamshire Association, held on May 27, at Aylesbury, Lord Temple having declared himself antagonistic to Parliamentary Reform, Mahon rose as its champion. He moved the adoption of the York programme, which demanded a fairer representation of the people by adding to the House of Commons at least a hundred members, and asked for Parliaments of shorter duration. ' Triennial Parliaments," he declared, ' are the unalienable right of the subject and were illegally wrested from the people by the Septennial Act." x The value of his support was quickly recognised. ' The transaction of the business wrote Wyvill, many years later, ' necessarily required frequent communication between the deputies. Lord Mahon and Mr. Wyvill soon found they were agreed in their hatred to a corrupt system of administration, in their zealous attachment to liberty on the genuine principles of the constitution, and in their firm conviction that, without a radical reform of abuses in the frame of Parliament itself, the official regulation proposed by Burke, as the grand panacea for all our national complaints, would be found no better than transient anodynes, whose slight and insignificant effect would soon be overpowered by the deeply vitiated habit of our representative body. This general similarity in their principles and views produced an intimacy between the noble Viscount and the writer, which gradually became confidential. It was at Lord Mahon's house that he was first made known to Mr. Pitt; but whether the introduction was proposed by Lord Mahon or desired by Mr. Pitt he does not distinctly recollect. At this interview the sentiments of Mr. Pitt on the dangerous situation of the country at the time, on the corrupt state of Parliament, and the necessity for reformation at the request and interposition of the people, were similar to those of Lord Mahon and the other members of the General Deputation." 2

At this moment occurred an unfortunate episode, which seriously injured Reformers in the estimation of Parliament. In 1778 Sir George Savile had carried a Bill to relieve Roman Catholics from some of the unjust penalties inflicted upon them by the law. But the spirit of bigotry was not dead. There sprang into existence the society known as the Protestant Association, which elected as president Lord George Gordon, a fanatical youth of questionable sanity, who represented Ludgershall in Parliament. He was a tiresome speaker and one rarely listened to until he became noted for his vehement 1 London Courant, May 29, 1780. 2 Wyvill Papers.

'No Popery' harangues. On June 2, 1780, many thousands CHAP, assembled in St. George's Fields, and marched in four divisions III. to the Houses of Parliament. They filled the lobbies while Lord George presented to the Commons a voluminous petition against Savile's Bill. The House voted to adjourn its consideration until the sixth. A scene of alarm and excitement ensued. Lord George, running backwards and forwards to a window, informed the mob what was taking place, and held up certain politicians to execration. ' The House of Lords," wrote Horace Walpole in his sprightly way, ' was sunk from the temple of dignity to an asylum of lamentable objects. There were Lords Hillsborough, Stormont, and Townshend without their bags and with their hair dishevelled about their ears, and Lord Willoughby without his periwig, and Lord Mansfield, whose glasses had been broken, quivering on the woolsack like an aspen.

Lord Ashburnham had been torn out of his chariot, the Bishop of Lincoln had been ill-treated, the Duke of Northumberland had lost his watch in the holy hurly-burly, and Mr. Mackenzie his snuff-box and spectacles. Alarm came that the mob had thrown down Lord Boston and were trampling him to deathâ which they almost did. They had diswigged Lord Bathurst on his answering them stoutly, and told him he was the pope and an old woman." 1

Without the rabble thundered on the doors of both Houses, while within the members were considering if they must open the doors and fight their way out, sword in hand. ' Some of their Lordships with their hair about their shoulders, others smutted with dirt, most of them as pale as the Ghost in Hamlet, crowded together all speaking at the same moment and none listening to the other." 2 While others were shaking in their shoes, each palpitating peer uncertain who would be the next victim, Lord Mahon seems to have been the only person who acted with any decision or initiative. Fear was unknown to him. From the balcony of a neighbouring coffee-house 3 he addressed the disorderly rabble. He was well-fitted for such an effort. His voice was stentorian, his language energetic, his gestures forcible The Westminster Election of 1774 had made him known to many of the crowd. His eloquence was remarkably effective in quelling the tumult, and we are told by Walpole that ' Lord Mahon chiefly contributed by his harangues to conjure down the tempest." 4 Before the arrival of the Guards ' he had prevailed on so many of the people to disperse' that the Lords were able to depart in quiet.

The same night these ' pious ragamuffins' destroyed some 1 Walpole's Letters. 2 Parl. History, xxi. 669, note.

3 Walpole's Letters, xi. 189. 4 Ibid., xi. 192 and 195.

CHAP. Catholic chapels, and the riot became more and more formidable. " â On the sixth they burnt Newgate and opened other prisons, besides destroying and pillaging the houses of Lord Mansfield', Sir George Savile, and others. The mob, recruited by some 2,000 criminals, was out for plunder, and on the seventh, besides destroying King's Bench and New Bridewell, threatened the Bank. Finally 20,000 troops were collected and the rioters subdued. Insignificant and abortive in itself, the tumult did infinite damage to the cause of Reform. The Gordon Riots, it was said, originated in an agitation, an association, and a petition. These were the methods used by the Reformers, and would they not culminate in a similar result? In truth the largest share of the blame was due to dilatory ministers and an inadequate police, who suffered the riots to assume the proportions of an insurrection. The Government took the hint, and exerted itself to form a police sufficient to control mobs without the interposition of the military. At a county meeting held at the Star Inn, Maidstone, 1 on July 3, Mahon moved and carried ' that it be strongly recommended to all Noblemen, Gentlemen, Yeomen Freeholders, and Householders in the County of Kent, and to the sons of such persons, to provide themselves with a good musket and bayonet for the purpose of strengthening the Civil Power, and maintaining the peace of the said county; so that good order may without the aid or interposition of the military be effectually preserved within the same."

During these early years Pitt and his brother-in-law were on terms of the closest intimacy. In London he was constantly at Harley Street, and in the country he often rode over from Hayes to Chevening to see his little nieces, to whom he was tenderly attached. They were an uproarious party, and Pitt frequently alludes to their high spirits. ' His eyes told him they were in health says Lady Stanhope, ' and his ears told him they were in spirits." Hester was the tomboy, ' the Jockey Girl Griselda ' the little Book-devourer and Lucy ' the Beauty." Hester was always her uncle's favourite. When Griselda was born, he writes: ' I am told my little niece is a perfect beauty, though I own I am hardly persuaded of it, and have extremely offended the nurse by not preferring her to Hester." z Mahon was tenderly attached to his wife, and was alarmed by any signs of illness. ' Poor Charles writes Lady Stanhope on one occasion, ' is in the utmost distress." 3 While Lord and Lady Mahon were 1 Wyvill Papers, i. 254.

2 W. Pitt to Lady Chatham, October 14, 1778. Chatham Papers.

in London the two little girls were often left to the care of their CHAP. grandmother, who doted on them and reported so often on their IJ L doings that she felt compelled to apologise. Her husband, indeed, said that she never saw a child without coveting it. 1 ' Hester is quite wild she writes; ' I am forced to send assistance from here to keep her within bounds. Her Herculean nurse is now absent." 2 ' My namesake is so merry, she not only laughs all day but also all night, to the no small disturbance of those who during the latter would choose to sleep." 3 ' I am grown quite a fool about Hester. What a wonderful and amiable child it is. I have hopes her sister will be such another. Hester saidâ the next must be a boy, for two girls are enough for anybody. If like her a dozen would be welcome to me, so I am quite calm and feel no impatience on that score, though no doubt a boy would be welcome to us all." 4

Lady Stanhope was doomed to disappointment. In February 1780 Lady Mahon gave birth to a girl in London, and from this time her health steadily declined. She died at Chevening, in July, at the age of twenty-five, leaving behind her the memory of a singularly beautiful character. ' She was," writes Lord Hadding-ton, her husband's cousin, ' a woman rarely to be met withâ wise, temperate, and prudent, by nature cheerful, without levity, a warm friend, and free from all the petty vices that attend little minds." 5 Her death caused Pitt keen sorrow, for she was his favourite sister, and it plunged her husband into despair. ' Poor Charles," writes his mother, ' has passed a melancholy day. I keep him amused as much as I can, and nothing but hindering him to think is of service. Alas! when he doesâ but I will not dwell on a subject that must be heart-breaking to us all. The sweet children are perfectly well, and thrive amazingly in the good air. I see them less than I should do, as I see poor Charles grow thoughtful when they are present, though he takes great notice of them, more I think than he used to do. Time alone can do good to us all." 6

At the General Election in the autumn of 1780 Mahon was one of the two members returned unopposed for Chipping 1 Lady Stanhope to Lady Chatham, December 20, 1789.

2 Ibid., 1777. 3 Ibid,, December 20, 1778.

4 Ibid., January 20, 1780.

5 Life of Lady Hester Stanhope, by the Duchess of Cleveland.

6 Lady Stanhope to Lady Chatham, August 6, 1780.

CHAP. Wycombe; and few legislators of that time entered on their III duties with more disinterested zeal. Throughout October we find him in correspondence with Wyvill respecting a proposal that in the coming session Sir George Savile should ' take a lead in moving the great question for ameliorating the parliamentary representation by the addition of one hundred Knights." 1 Sir George hesitated to introduce this proposition so soonâ ' unless a rational and feasible plan can first be prepared and will be supported by the bulk of the minority in Parliament." 2 Mahon was all impatience; but Sir George Savile was too prudent a politician to yield to this youthful impetuosity.

On October 23 Charles wrote Wyvill the following characteristic letter:â ' My dear Sir,â I send you herewith the unanimous resolutions of our Kentish Committee, which I trust will meet with your approbation, and with that of your respectable Committee of the County of York, to whom I beg you will have the goodness to present those resolves. Our Committee wish to prevent, as much as possible, unnecessary procrastination; and are at the same time truly anxious to shew in the most decided and public manner their high respect for the great and meritorious County of York, and their strong desire of co-operating with the valuable Sir George Savile, one of their representatives in Parliament, in the promoting of the important and necessary object of equalising and purifying the representation by adding to the House of Commons at least one hundred County Members. I have the honour to be, with the highest esteem and sincerest respect, 'My dear Sir, ' Your most faithful and 'affectionate humble servant, ' MAHON, Chairman.

' P. S.â I send you inclosed a copy of my letter to Lord Rocking-ham. I have wrote many letters to a like effect to other persons. We shall certainly be very strong in this new Parliament. For God's sake, my decir Sir, let us be well aware of even seeming to concede any fur, he, either in respect of matter, manner, or time. We shall lose all by procrastination, for, to use the late Earl of Chatham's expression on this subject, "We have taken possession of strong ground, let who will decline to follow us."

1 Wyvill Papers, iii. 263-276, September 29 to October 2.- Wyvill to Mahon, September 29, 1780.

Nothing but firmness can procure us the united support of CHAP, opposition." x IIJ-

When Parliament met on October 31 Charles lost no time in making his political debut, for on the same day he took part in the debate on the choice of a Speaker. Knowing that the re-election of the late Speaker, Sir Fletcher Norton, would be disagreeable to the King, Lord George Germaine moved to elect Mr. Cornwall. Charles opposed the motion, and 'made an energetic eulogium on the virtues of Sir Fletcher Norton'; 2 but the election of Cornwall was carried by a large majority. He had no qualifications for the post, unless a capacity for strong drink can be thus described. This weakness is satirised in the ' Rolliad," in a passage which compares Lord Mahon preying on the Speaker's patience to the vulture devouring the liver of Prometheus:â ' There Cornwall sits, and, oh unhappy fate! Must sit for ever through the long debate; Like sad PROMETHEUS, fastened to his rock, In vain he looks for pity to the clock; In vain the effects of strengthening porter tries, And nods to BELLAMY for fresh supplies; While, vulture-like, the dire MAHON appears, And, far more savage, rends his suffering ears."

Feeling that it could afford to be generous, the House passed a vote of thanks to Sir Fletcher Norton for his services. The motion was strenuously supported by Lord Mahon, 3 who contended that ' the House had at all times an indisputable right to control the King's civil list as freely and as fully as any other part of the expenditure of the public revenue."

A week or two later the young member received joyful intelligence. ' Being just returned from the House of Commons he writes +o Lord Shelburne, ' I am happy to be able to inform your Lordship that Sir James Lowther has told the Duke of Rutland he intends bringing in William Pitt for one of his vacant seats; at the same time I must beg your Lordship not to speak publicly of it yet. I confess I am vastly glad of the event, as I have the highest idea of the honour and integrity of William, and have no doubt he will do himself great credit in the public service." 4 The prophecy met with a speedy fulfilment. On February 26, 1781, Pitt spoke on Burke's Bill for Economical Reform, and his talents at once commanded the admiration they 1 Mahon to Wyvill. Wyvill Papers, iii. 275.

' 2 Part. History, xxi. 803. 3 Ibid., xxi. 882.

4 Chevemng MSS.

CHAP, were ever afterwards to excite. Charles was present on this III. historic occasion. ' This moment I have received a letter from Charles wrote Lady Stanhope to Lady Chatham," saying William Pitt spoke like an angel, and pleased everybody vastly. I admire your son, and may say as he did at four years old: In all my reading I never met with such a character!" No wonder Lady Chatham rejoiced at the success of her son, who bore his triumph very modestly. ' The account you have had he wrote to his mother, ' would be in all respects better than any I can give if it had not come from too partial a friend. All I can say is that I was able to execute in some measure what I intended, and that I have at least every reason to be happy beyond measure in the reception I met with 2

In March Mahon married Louisa, only child of the Hon. Henry Grenville, who had filled in succession the posts of Governor of Barbados and Ambassador at Constantinople. He was a younger brother of Lady Chatham, so that the second Lady Mahon stood in relation of cousin-german to her predecessor. There is no evidence of a love match, and, allowing for the stilted language of the age, Lord Mahon's account of her is not very enthusiastic. In announcing his marriage to Lord Shelburne he says: ' The solitary state in which I have been left by the very trying misfortune I experienced last year has made me resolve on settling again. There is a person with whom I have been acquainted from a child, and of whom I have had since that time infinite reasons to have a favourable opinion 3 Her granddaughter, the Duchess of Cleveland, remembered her as a ' worthy well-meaning woman, but stiff and frigid with a chilling, conventional manner 4 She was devoted to society, and can have had few tastes in common with her husband. ' She got up at ten o'clock, went out and then returned to be dressed, if in London, by the hairdresser; and there are only two in London, both of them Frenchmen, who could dress her. Then she went out to dinner, and from dinner to the Opera, and from the Opera to parties, seldom returning until just before daylight 5 Such is the unflattering picture, drawn many years later, by Lady Hester, whose evidence, however, is not of a very trustworthy character.

1 To Lady Chatham. Chevening MSS.
2 W. Pitt to Lady Chatham, February 27, 1781. Chatham Papers, Record Office.
3 February i, 1781. Chevening MSS.
4 Life of Lady Hester Stanhope, by the Duchess of Cleveland.

The honeymoon must have been brief, for we find Mahon again CHAP, in his place at the meeting of deputies on March 24. 1 The Hi-meetings were now transferred to St. Alban's Tavern, the Corporation of London having ' thought fit to retract their courtesy to the deputies, and to abolish their Committees of Association." On April 3 he laid before the House a petition from the Goldsmiths to be put on an equal footing with the manufacturers of other countries by fixing the standard of gold. He spoke again on the subject when the Report of the Committee was presented; but questions of this kind aroused only a languid interest. In May he took part in the protracted debate which followed Sir George Savile's motion for a committee to consider the petition of the Delegated Counties; 2 and he was one of the tellers when Sawbridge, with admirable persistency, rose to make his annual motion for shortening the duration of Parliaments. 3 A few days after the prorogation he wrote the following letter to his friend Wyvill:â ' Chevening: July 24, 1781.

' My dear Sir,â Your letters which I have just received give me the greatest pleasure, inasmuch as I am truly happy to find that the principle of the Motion was not disapproved of by your Committee, but only the expediency of resolving it, till it was known whether or no it would be attended with success. I have only one thing to recommend, and that I take the liberty to recommend very particularly,â to express in your letters that the compensation should be perfectly optional; and that it is meant that those proprietors of Boroughs, who do not desire to part with them for any compensation completely, should retain their present rights. Would it not be proper to write (amongst others) to the Duke of Rutland, the Duke of Richmond, Mr. Thomas Pitt, and Sir James Lowther? I have seen Mr. David Hartley, and have also conversed with Mr. William Pitt on the subject of our idea of an optional compensation, who both approve it extremely. I have also seen Lord Rockingham, who does not yet seem to meet us. He is still of opinion that the country at large does not care for these kind of objects. ' Believe me, my dear Sir, ' With the highest respect, ' Your most faithful and affectionate ' MAHON 1 Wyvill Papers, i. 384-94. 2 Parl. History, xxii. 199, 3 Ibid., xxii. 257,

CHAP. Throughout 1781 North's ministry had been repeatedly III. threatened with defeat. With India in revolt and Ireland on the brink of rebellion, involved in wars with America, Spain, France, and Holland, it had survived more adversities than any other government. Supported by the King it withstood the unremitting attacks of the Opposition, and bore unashamed the exposure of those corrupt practices which had so long maintained it in office. Its death-blow came from America with the surrender of Yorktown. Parliament met two days later, and the Opposition redoubled its efforts. On February 22, 1782, General Conway moved ' that the war on the continent of North America might no longer be pursued for the impracticable purpose of reducing the inhabitants of that country to obedience." Fox, Pitt, and Barre supported the motion, and Mahon cited some opinions of Lord Chatham in regard to the war, which North promptly denied; but after an acrimonious debate Conway's motion was defeated by the' melancholy majority ' of 194 to igs. 1 The Prime Minister had long wished to resign; but, yielding to the ' peremptory entreaties ' of the King, he had identified himself with a policy which his better judgment could not approve. The end came when Coke of Norfolk moved for the recognition of American Independence. All night long the House sat. At 8.30 in the morning the House divided, and amid breathless silence the result was announcedâ 177 noes against 178 ayes! Coke, at the instigation of Fox, at once moved that the address to the King should be taken up by the whole House, and he was chosen to present it. 2 North announced his resignation to the Commons, and the Whigs took office under Lord Rockingham.

The state of Ireland was the first of many difficulties to engage the attention of the new Government. The Irish Parliament was pressing for legislative independence. On the same evening that the new ministers took their seats, Eden, whom the loss of place had suddenly converted into an Irish patriot, moved the repeal of the sixth of George I, which asserted the right of England to make laws for the sister kingdom. Fox and Mahon rebuked him for the intemperate haste with which he pressed such a measure upon new ministers, and Conway, by threatening a vote of censure, obliged him to withdraw his motion. Like Fox, Mahon was a supporter of Home Rule. Lord Charlemont wrote to a friend: ' I send you enclosed a speech of Charles Fox which I know will give you pleasure. Lord Mahon at the end of the debate spoke to this effect: " Mr. Speaker, I attended in my place to-day to have an opportunity of asserting the CHAP. independence of the legislature of Ireland in case anyone should Hi-have presumed to controvert it; but, as I have the happiness to find that it is allowed on all hands, I shall content myself with thus having declared my opinion." These I am told were his words." 1 Mahon was, as usual, averse from half measures, considering that Poynings' Law and the sixth of George I should be repealed in toto or not at all, and he expressed these sentiments in a letter to Grattan. When the Irish Commons met on April 16," every heart panting with expectation ' to hear Grattan bring forward his declaration of legislative independence, the great orator concluded his magnificent speech with a reference to the opinion of Lord Mahonâ ' an Englishman who understands good sense and constitution 2 Grattan's reply deserves attention for its explicit statement of his views on the questions then agitating Ireland.

' My Lord,â I had the honour of receiving your Lordship's letter, which I should have answered instantly, but I was prevented by illness. I entirely enter into the spirit of your Lordship's objection to a partial repeal of the 6th Geo. I. Undoubtedly it would have been inadequate either to the purpose of jurisdiction or of legislation. I took the liberty of stating in the Commons yesterday your just and liberal sentiments with respect to Ireland, and stated your just distinction and motive which was universally well received and admitted. We have unanimously passed an address to His Majesty, setting forth the causes of our discontents and jealousies. I am sure your Lordship will think there is no one head of that Address that Ireland ought to depart from, and which Great Britain ought not in justice and wisdom and may not with magnanimity surrender. After the legislative claim is surrendered, the remainder, very material to the rights and feelings of the Irish, is nothing to England. The determining our prospects in her House of Lords or Court of King's Bench is very dilatory, expensive, and shameful to us, but of no use to you if you renounce the supremacy of legislature.

You lose nothing which is real by a final settlement, and you will gain the confidence of Ireland. Your Lordship will find this kingdom has defined her grievances, and is not progressive in her discontents. Your Lordship will be pleased, moreover, to consider that it was impossible to contemplate 1 Twelfth Report of Historical MSS. Commission. Charlemont MSS., p. 380.

2 Debates of Irish Commons, ii. 337.

CHAP, the British Constitution and not to loathe the defects of our own. III. If we have the spirit of liberty, you ought to blame yourselves and the contagion of those great qualities which have distinguished Great Britain. I shall conclude my letter, which I fear has tired your Lordship, with the observation that, if it had come to a question between liberty and the King of England, those who admitted her supremacy would have fought for the latter, and those who denied it would have died for the former. ' I have the honour to be, with great respect, ' H. GRATTAN." 1

On May 3 Wilkes introduced for the sixth time his motion to rescind the resolution relating to his expulsion, 'as being subversive of the rights of the whole body of electors." It was opposed by Fox and Dundas, but supported by Mahon and carried by 115 to 47; and by order of the House all orders or declarations respecting the Middlesex Election were expunged. 2 During its brief career the Rockingham Ministry did much to purify Parliament. It passed Bills disfranchising revenue officers and disqualifying contractors from sitting in Parliament, and accepted Burke's Economical Bill of 1781; but there were limits to its reforming zeal. In May Pitt moved for an inquiry into the state of Parliamentary representation. The proposal was seconded by Sawbridge and supported by Savile, Fox, and Sheridan; but it was ' the people outside Parliament who wanted it reformed, not those inside," and the motion was defeated by 161 to 141â the largest minority till 1831. Immediately after its rejection a meeting was convened at the Thatched House Tavern of Members of Parliament and deputies ' favourable to Parliamentary Reform." Lord Mayor Wilkes presided, and Pitt, Cartwright, Jebb, Mahon, and the Duke of Richmond were among those who assembled to discuss what steps should be taken. It was agreed that a petition should be signed and laid before the House next session. In view of Pitt's harsh opposition to Reform a few years later, it is interesting to note that the minutes of this meeting are in his handwriting.

No better success attended the efforts of Mahon, who, on the 23rd, introduced a Bill for preventing expense and bribery at elections. At this time the poll was held only in one place, and in country districts it was a costly affair for the candidate to convey thither all the electors. To remedy this he proposed that the sheriff should be empowered to adjourn the poll from one 1 Mr. Grattan to Lord Mahon, Dublin, April 18, 1781.

place to another in the county, to suit as far as possible the CHAP, convenience of freeholders. We have now achieved the same III.

result by the multiplication of voting stations. Pitt favoured the Bill, but Fox, Sheridan, and Powys were violently opposed to it. In committee Mahon consented to give up several points in order to make it more palatable to the House, and he struck out the words forbidding candidates to hire horses and carriages for the conveyance of voters to the poll. The clause still provided that money for the purpose should not be paid to the elector under the penalty of disfranchisement, and of incapacity to the candidate of sitting in Parliament. This clause was warmly supported by Pitt; but, when we consider the state of the franchise in those days, it is not astonishing that most of the country gentlemen should have regarded it as too severe, and it was rejected by a majority of twenty-six. Mahon, having lost the incapacitating clause, which contained ' the very pith and marrow of my Bill declined to proceed further with it in a mutilated condition.

Meanwhile the dissensions in the Whig Cabinet were becoming ' scandalously apparent." Thurlow was suspected of caballing with the King against his colleagues; the two Secretaries of State, Fox and Shelburne, were at daggers drawn; and when Rocking-ham died somewhat suddenly on July i, Fox resigned rather than serve under Shelburne, who was appointed First Minister. In Shelburne the King hoped to find a man, like North, who would be a tool in his hands; but, with or without reason, he was treated with distrust by many of the Whig party. Though steadily liberal in politics and one of the ablest debaters in the House of Lords, he had a reputation for insincerity. Even his colleagues declared ' it was impossible to separate his intentions from his verbiage and professions x and Burke denounced him as a Catiline and a Borgia. In seceding from the Cabinet Fox carried with him his ally, Lord John Cavendish, the Chancellor of the Exchequer. The vacant post was at once offered to Pitt, who thus attained one of the highest offices in the Government at the age of twenty-three.

Parliament had been prorogued till December 5, and on the I2th Mahon took part in a debate on the value of Gibraltar, which arose out of Conway's motion for a vote of thanks to General Elliot. Three days later he supported Thomas Pitt, who rose to move the order of the day after Fox's motion for ' such articles of the provisional treaty as relate to the recognition 1 Buckingham's Court and Cabinets of George III, i. 76.

CHAP, of the independence of America." In his speech Mahon ' anim-III. adverted smartly on Mr. Fox." 1 During the Christmas holidays we find Pitt summoning his brother-in-law to London, probably to concert with him a measure on Parliamentary Reform.

' Downing Street: Dec. 28,1782.

My dear Lord,â I am in great hopes you will be able to come directly to town. This is just the time in which we must fix on something; and I think in a day or two we could go through all the necessary discussions before any practical steps are taken., xr â.,, ' Yours most affectionately, 'W. PITT." 2

We owe a vivid picture of Charles Stanhope during his early years in Parliament to his fellow-member, Wraxall, who, though he knew him but slightly, was deeply impressed by his personality. ' Lord Mahon was then one of the representatives for Wycombe. His ardent, zealous, and impetuous mind, tinged with deep shades of republicanism and eccentricity which extended even to his dress and manners, was equally marked by a bold originality of character, very enlightened views of the public welfare, inflexible pertinacity and a steady uprightness of intention. His eccentricities of dress, character, and deportment, however great they might be, were nevertheless allied to extraordinary powers of elocution as well as energies of mind. If he had flourished a century and a half earlier, he would unquestionably have rivalled Ludlow or Algernon Sydney in their attachment to a commonwealth. His person was tall and thin, his countenance expressive of ardour and impetuosity, as were all his movements. Over his whole figure, and even his dress, an air of puritanism reminded the beholder of the sectaries under Cromwell rather than a young man of quality in an age of refinement and elegance. He possessed stentorian lungs and a powerful voice, always accompanied with violent gesticulation." Yet, while insisting on his oddities, Wraxall pronounces him ' a man who at every period of his life, whether as a commoner or a peer, displayed the same ardent, fearless, indefatigable and independent character." 3 These qualities, added to his great abilities, had already made him one of the leading figures in the Whig party.

1 Parl. Hist., xxiii. 305.
2 Stanhope's Life of Pitt, i. 71.

PARLIAMENT reassembled on January 22, 1783; and it seemed CHAP, impossible that Shelburne's Ministry could last. The number of IV. his followers in the House of Commons amounted only to 140, those of North to 130, and those of Fox to 90. The Prime Minister wished to attack North's party, but Pitt emphatically declined to be associated with him in such an attempt. With his Cabinet already tottering Shelburne could not risk the defection of his Chancellor, and opened negotiations with Fox. But Fox was already in treaty with Lord North, and three days later they cemented that unnatural alliance known as the Coalition. Shelburne resigned, and for nearly eight weeks the nation remained without a Government, while the King vainly endeavoured to secure a Ministry which would be less obnoxious than the Coalition. He entreated Pitt, though a youth of twenty-four, to take office; he besought the veteran Lord Gower; he made a despairing effort to detach North from Fox, and declared that he would abdicate rather than submit. After exhausting all his powers of persuasion and intrigue, King George was compelled to take the Coalition on their own terms. They chose for their titulary chief the Duke of Portland, a docile peer of conspicuous mediocrity, well suited to his position of figure-head. Fox and North were made Secretaries of State, and Lord John Cavendish resumed his post at the Exchequer. When the King was forced to receive his Ministers at Court, an old gentleman present predicted the speedy fall of the Coalition. For when Fox kissed hands, he observed the Monarch turn back his ears and eyes, ' just like the horse at Astley's when the tailor he had determined to throw was getting on him." 1 The King treated him, however, 1 Memorials of Fox t ii. 29.

CHAP, with less dislike than North, whose conduct inspired him with IV- disgust. Yet, as the Duke of Buckingham justly observed, 1 the disgrace of the junction certainly lay more heavily on the Whigs than on Lord North; for Fox had spent his whole life in assailing the person and policy of Lord North, whose principles were utterly opposed to his own." x

The length of the inter-ministerium had greatly delayed public business, and soon after the new Ministers had taken their seats Lord John Cavendish introduced his Budget. He issued a new loan, the terms of which, though not very advantageous to the country, were, he declared, as good as could be procured, owing to the hurry in which they had to be concluded and the folly of the late Minister. Within a week it bore a premium of 8 per cent. ' Lord Mahon," relates Wraxall who was present, ' attacked the terms of the loan with his usual impetuosity of voice and manner." 2

There were two great objects that a Chancellor of the Exchequer should never lose sight of, the one, the diminution of the national debt, the other, increasing the revenue by taking off some of the taxes. The latter might appear paradoxical, but nothing could be more clear than that many of the articles of the Customs had been greatly depressed by the imposition of taxes beyond what they could bear. Moreover, high duties never failed to encourage smuggling. A friend of his, lately on the Continent, had fallen in with a wealthy Englishman in France, who, having been driven from England for smuggling, had amassed a very large fortune by pursuing his old practice. This man had claimed Lord North as his best friend, for, by imposing such heavy duties on the articles usually smuggled to England, he had made the smuggling trade so beneficial that a man could scarcely fail to make his fortune by it in a very short time. Lord John Cavendish made no attempt to meet the attack, prudently retiring behind the Speaker's chair, whence, records Wraxall, ' he peeped out during the debate." Fox proceeded to ridicule the arguments of Mahon. He had heard a similiar doctrine from Lord Shelburne in another place. This brought Pitt, who was sitting next to Mahon, to his feet. He upheld Mahon's assertions, and returned Fox's satire with an irony more bitter and infinitely more dignified, and ' between them the discussion was maintained with equal acrimony and ingenuity for a long time." 8 Finally North bantered Mahon and Pitt with good-humoured pleasantries on ' the beautiful theories they had built 1 Court and Cabinets of George III, i. 230.

2 Memoirs, iii. 95; and Pavl. Hist., xxiii. 936.

up with such magnificent eloquence and attempted to vindicate CHAP, his financial administration.! v-

On June 6, in the debate on the second reading of Mahon's Bill to prevent Expense at Elections, 1 its author explained that, as a measure had been passed to prevent bribery, he now proposed to curtail the expenses obligatory on candidates. Among other items he would like to suppress the giving of cockadesâ a practice which entailed an enormous outlay, for many haberdashers charged for a hundred times more ribbon than they had in their shops. The measure was ridiculed by Fox. ' The noble lord he said, ' had formerly brought in a Bill, some of the clauses of which were agreed to by the House and others rejected; upon which the noble lord had got rid of that Bill and brought in two new ones, putting the clauses the House had approved into one Bill, and the clauses which it disapproved into another. The former of these had passed, and the latter was the measure then under consideration Several members bore testimony to the heavy expense of cockades: one maliciously remarking that perhaps Mr. Fox had not experienced it, as he understood that' some friend of the right honourable Secretary had defrayed his expenses for him." Pitt supported the Bill, but Fox's motion, ' that it be read a second time this day three months," was carried.

Though Burke's Act had cleared away some sinecure offices, a great many remained. Some of them were so important that in 1812, according to Romilly, the salary of the Tellers of the Exchequer amounted to about Â 26,000. Lord John Cavendish made an attempt to abolish a few of these appointments, but he continued others not less indefensible. Pitt having stigmatised this plan as ' barefaced and unreasonable," Mahon let loose a torrent of indignation. The noble lord had not only proposed that the present possessors of those scandalous places in the Exchequer, and those who had a reversion of them, should have the salary continued, but desired to keep up those exorbitant places for the future, and to give them those extravagant emoluments for professedly doing nothing. A more scandalous profusion of public money, a more profligate attempt to maintain the unconstitutional influence of the Crown, was scarcely to be met with in our history. Mr. Fox said it was no measure of the undue influence of the Crown, because persons who had places for life were not under influence. Would the right honourable gentleman dare to say that the expectation of those places was 1 Parl. Hist. xxiii. 993.

CHAP, no means of influence? There was a time when he regretted

IV- the recent change of administration, but now he sincerely rejoiced at that event; for it had given the right honourable Secretary and his colleagues a complete opportunity of proving what they were. 1

On July 16 Parliament was prorogued, and in September Pitt went abroad for a holiday. On his return he wrote to Mahon a letter which reveals their close personal and political relations.

' Berkeley Square: November 3, 1783.

' My dear Lord,â I was in hopes to have seen you and those with you at Chevening, all of whom I wished extremely to see before this time, but I have had so much to do ever since I have been in town that I have found it impossible. The meeting is now so near that time is every day more precious, and there is abundance of objects that require examination. I trust you will be in town in a very few days, for there are several things in which I am quite at a loss without you. If anything detains you, pray let me know and I will endeavour to meet you at Hayes, but I rather trust to seeing you here. Adieu.

' Ever most affectionately yours, 'W. PITT. ' 2

On the reassembling of Parliament in November, Fox introduced his Bill for the better government of India, the debates on which are rendered memorable by the eloquence of Burke. On this eventful occasion Mahon was one of the Tellers. The Bill was detested in the country, and, in presenting a petition against it from his constituency, he denounced it as infamous. The right honourable gentleman, whose child this monstrous and, he hoped, abortive production was, had in a former debate spoken of himself as a general, under whom the less danger was to be dreaded, seeing that were the right honourable Secretary inclined to encroach on those sacred rights of the constitution in defence of which he had spent a great many years, the various officers who still acted with him would certainly desert their posts; but he forgot that the left wing was commanded by the noble lord (North). From this ominous junction doubts of the consequences had certainly prevailed; and, in his opinion, this obnoxious Bill was one of the first fruits of such a corrupt tree. 3 The Bill passed the Commons by a large majority, but in the Lords it was 1 Parl, Hist., xxiii. 1067-9. 2 Stanhope, Life of Pitt, i. 107.

violently attacked by Thurlow. ' If this Bill should pass," he CHAP, said, ' the King will take the diadem from his own head and IV-place it on the head of Mr. Fox." But George III was equal to the emergency. Through the medium of Lord Temple he circulated a written message, saying that' whoever voted for the India Bill was not only not his friend, but would be considered by him as an enemy." The

Lords thereupon threw out the Bill by ninety-three to seventy-six. On the same day a friend of Burke rose in his place, and, having alluded to the rumours that the King was caballing against his ministers, proposed a resolution that' it is now necessary to declare that to report any opinion or pretended opinion of His Majesty upon any Bill or any proceeding depending on either House of Parliament, with a view to influence the votes of the Members, is a high crime and misdemeanour, derogatory to the honour of the Crown, a breach of the fundamental privileges of Parliament, and subversive of the constitution of this country Pitt rose, and, stigmatising the resolution as ' unnecessary, frivolous, and ill-timed," moved the order of the day. He was seconded by Mahon; but North and Fox both urged the propriety of considering the Resolution, and, when the House divided, a majority of seventy-three was recorded in its favour. 1

As soon as the division in the Lords became known, the King hoped his Ministers would resign; but they were resolved to let him bear the full odium of the transaction, and suffered themselves to be dismissed. The following day Pitt was nominated Prime Minister. Shouts of laughter greeted the announcement that he had been appointed. He was but twenty-four, and without any Cabinet colleague in the House of Commons to assist him against such formidable opponents as Fox and North, Burke and Sheridan. Mahon declined the offer of a place in the Ministry; but he assisted the new Cabinet with advice. ' At Pitt's," writes Wilberforce, ' we had a long discussion; and I remember well the great penetration shewed by Lord Mahon. " What am I to do," said Pitt, " if they stop the supplies? " " They will not stop them," said Mahon, "it is the very thing they will not venture to do." ' 2 The next day Parliament was adjourned, to reassemble on January 12. Two days later Pitt introduced his rival India Bill, which was rejected by a majority of eight. But Fox's majority slowly dwindled, and the populace recognised in the young Minister the spirit of his 1 Parl Hist., xxiv. 202. 2 Wilberforce's Life y i. 48-9.

CHAP, father; while his disinterested rejection of a sinecure, which his IV. narrow means would have made most welcome, aroused the enthusiasm of the country.

Fox had sacrificed his avowed principles for the sake of office, and he was beginning to pay the penalty. Nearly three thousand of his own constituents presented to the King an address condemning the India Bill, and commending his Majesty for dismissing the Coalition. In a large meeting at Westminster Hall, Mahon moved that' the common cause of this country was involved in the support of the present administration." The Whig leader made an abortive attempt to retaliate by calling a rival meeting, but ' the hisses, catcalls, and other discordant tokens of disapprobation obstructed every effort made by him to captivate the multitude with his eloquence." At length ' he thought prudent to quit the chair and retire several paces backwards to the Court of Common Pleas." His retreat, however, was cut off, for ' here he was confronted by Lord Mahon, who waved his hat, the Hall resounding with acclamations. The situation of Mr. Fox becoming evidently more perilous, the curtain which separates the Court of Common Pleas from the Hall was dropped, on which a general cry of " Who's behind the curtain? " now prevailed." 1 Mahon then stepped forward, and was immediately lifted on the shoulders of the electors and borne to the other side of the Hall, amidst the acclamations of the meeting. In this position he made a speech, declaring himself an enemy to the Receipt Tax, the Coalition, and Fox's India Bill. '

I detest," he cried, ' that system of corruption by which taxes have been multiplied and the price of provisions enhanced. I wish for a Reform of Parliament and a House of Commons which shall speak the real sense of the people. These great purposes will be answered if the present Ministers are supported against the Coalition." He then moved the adoption of an Address agreed on at a former meeting, and the show of hands was at the lowest computation nine to one in favour of his resolution. After this Fox, finding it impossible to be heard, left the Hall amidst the groans and hisses of the people.

A few days later, in debate, North mentioned this tumultuous meeting as in no way indicative of the people's true feeling for his colleague. The noise and riot, he declared, owed their origin to two noble lords who were there present, not to the unpopularity of Fox. On his own behalf the Member for Westminster advanced several specious explanations of the people's dislike. Mahon 1 See the pamphlet, A Full and Authentic Account of the Proceedings in Westminster Hall.

retaliated ' with great severity and ability records Wraxall. 1 CHAP. The right honourable gentleman, he began, had made the most IV-unqualified assertion he had ever made in that House. The words were these: ' I am sure that, as to Westminster, I never had more of the real warm zeal and hearts of the people than in the present moment." The right honourable gentleman, when he thought proper to make this declaration, had undoubtedly forgotten that in this same speech he had said, but a few minutes before, that ' he got great unpopularity by the warm and decided support he had given to the tax upon receipts; that he had also been rendered unpopular by the ideas which the public had taken up relative to his India Bill, which it was impossible for the people to understand." He had also owned ' that his coalition with the noble lord in the blue ribbon had produced to him great unpopularity, great odium, and great obloquy." ' Does popularity, then, consist in unpopularity? Does he take groans for applause and hisses for approbation? There was a time when the right honourable gentleman did in a very great degree possess the confidence of the people. There was a time when what fell from him in popular assemblies fell with that weight and was attended to with that silence and respect as if an oracle had been speaking. Why? Because the public at that time believed him to be their friend; because they credulously thought he was fighting their battles. But now men's eyes are opened; he is no longer seen in the light of a tribune of the people. Did the right honourable gentleman in Westminster Hall last Saturday receive the same kind of applause as three years before? The voice of the people was, it is true, heard on that day; but in what words? In the short but expressive words of " No Coalition! " "No India Bill!" " No Grand Mogul!" " No Turncoat!" "No Traitor! " " No Dictator! " " No Catiline! " ' This slashing speech was the greatest Parliamentary success that the young member had yet achieved.

Following the example of Westminster, Yorkshire, the most important of the counties, presented an address condemning the Coalition. The leading Tories of Buckinghamshire also resolved to present an address expressing their abhorrence of the measures of the late Government. Accordingly a meeting was held at Aylesbury," the most numerous and respectable that has been remembered in the county of Bucks."

After the adoption of the address had been proposed, Burke rose to express his disapprobation, but was prevented from speaking by ' repeated 1 Memoirs, iii. 298.

hisses and groans ' from the crowd. Lord Mahon came forward and persuaded them ' to hear Mr. Burke fairly." ' He was upon the whole well heard says the Morning Herald, ' allowing for the warmth and earnestness with which the freeholders espoused the address." 1 Mahon then replied, and the address was adopted. Fox at first ridiculed these proceedings. They did not, he said, express the real sense of the people. The painful conviction of their truth was only to be forced upon him at the General Election, when the members of the Coalition were smitten hip and thigh.

Pitt's popularity was hourly increasing. The Corporation of London presented to him the freedom of the City, and he went in procession to dine at the Grocers' Hall. On the return journey at night a crowd of artisans dragged up St. James's Street the coach in which sat Pitt himself, Lord Chatham, and Mahon. Opposite Brooks's, the stronghold of his political opponents, the carriage was suddenly attacked by men armed with bludgeons and broken chair-poles, among whom it was asserted were seen several members of the club. Some of the rioters made their way to the carriage, forced open the door, and aimed blows at the Prime Minister, which were with some difficulty warded off by his brother's arm. At length Pitt and his companions made their way into White's Club. The servants were much bruised and the carriage nearly demolished. 2 In referring to this occurrence the authors of ' Political Eclogues," ashamed to name Pitt, transfer their raillery to Lord Mahon:â â Ah! why Mahon's disastrous fate record? Alas! how fear can change the fiercest Lord. See the sad sequel of the Grocers' treat; Behold him dashing up St. James Street, Pelted and scared by Brooks' hellish sprites, And vainly fluttering round the door of White's. 1

On March 25 the King put an end to the session, and dissolved Parliament. It was at this moment that Horace Walpole wrote angrily of Mahon as ' a savage, a republican, a royalist." 3 Of all the contests that of Westminster attracted most attention. It is, indeed, the most famous of electoral battles. The Prince of Wales identified himself with the cause of Fox, while the Duchess of Devonshire and other lovely ladies canvassed for him with a zeal which exposed them to the coarse taunts of their opponents. The lady champions of the Government 1 Morning Herald, March 23, 1784. 2 Stanhope, Life of Pitt, i. 152. 3 Letters, xiii. 143.

candidates were not as attractive as those of Fox, and were unkindly handled by the wits. - 'What troops too of females 'mongst CHARLES' opposers, Old tabbies and gossips, scolds, gigglers, and prosers! And hags after hags join the barbarous din, More hateful than serpents, more ugly than sin

Admiral Hood's great naval services made him the prime favourite, and it was for him and Sir Cecil Wray that the Court exerted all its influence. Mahon, the candidate of 1774, was also indefatigable in their interest. Every day he might be found upon the hustings, and proved himself, in the words of Wraxall, ' a most formidable and pertinacious adversary." x In the ' History of the Westminster Election," 2 this zealous canvasser is sketched by a Foxite rhymer:â ' Lord Mahon, Lord Mahon, Though you came very soon, And acted much like an old stager; If Pitt had been there. He'd have seen in despair The defeat of his doughty Drum-major,

Lord Mahon, The defeat of his doughty Drum-major."

When the poll closed after forty days Fox had a majority of 236, the numbers being:â

Lord Hood. 6,694

Fox 6,234

Sir Cecil Wray 5,998

There was a great procession to Devonshire House, and the streets were illuminated. Festivals were held at Carlton House, and the Prince of Wales appeared at a dinner given by Mrs. Crewe in the buff-and-blue uniform of the Whigs, and gave the toast, ' True Blue and Mrs. Crewe!" to which she wittily replied," True Blue and all of you!"

Fox was not at the end of his troubles, for Wray complained of irregularities, and presented a petition to the High Bailiff demanding a scrutiny. That dignitary, who was strongly opposed to Fox, consented to grant it. The new Parliament met the next day, and the Whig leader would have been excluded pending the scrutiny had he not been enabled to take his seat for the close borough of Kirkwall. It was a piece of good fortune that he could plead his own cause in the House of Commons; and the 1 Memoirs, iii. 297. 2 Ibid., 453,

CHAP, incident was productive of some of his most admirable speeches. IV- Before the debate on the address was begun a Whig called attention to the case, and moved that the High Bailiff ought to have made an immediate return. The motion was no censure of the High Bailiff, but invited a decision upon the right of a returning-officer to delay a return for any period. Mahon, in a closely reasoned speech, upheld his conduct. It was the first division in the new Parliament and showed the strength of the Government, for the motion was defeated by 283 to 136. The question was debated at wearisome length. ' It is the dullest business," writes a suffering member, 'that ever came before the House. There never was a case of so much bustle and absurdities that has given and will continue to give such general plague and disgust to the infinite regret here of every one except Lord Mahon." 1 At last the House, by a large majority, affirmed the legal character of the scrutiny. Incidentally the episode was beneficial, as it was the cause of more than one amendment in the election laws.

In June Alderman Sawbridge brought forward a motion to amend the representation; but Pitt, Wilberforce, and others, attempted to dissuade him on account of the pressure of other business. ' In my opinion," said Pitt, ' it is greatly out of season at this juncture. But I have the measure much at heart, and I pledge myself in the strongest language to bring it forward the very first opportunity next session." The Alderman persisted, and, after a long debate, the motion was rejected by 199 to 125, Pitt himself being one of the majority. Mahon, on the other hand, voted with Sawbridge. Throughout life he acted on the principle of seizing every opportunity to support the measures of which he approved.

It was during this session that Pitt effected several important fiscal reforms. The tax on tea in particular gave rise to numerous frauds. While thirteen million pounds were consumed every year in England, only five and a half were sold by the East India Company, the illicit trade thus being more than double the legal. These frauds Pitt determined to check by reducing the tax from 119 to 12 J per cent. Though this would diminish smuggling and the reduction would soon be compensated by increased consumption, a loss of revenue must at first occur. To meet this deficit he imposed a tax on the windows of all houses above a certain size.

Historians have given Pitt credit for the reduction of the tax CHAP, on tea; but its initiation was due to Mahon, as the Prime Minister IV-candidly acknowledged. 'The noble lord he said, 'has a peculiar right to speak on the subject, having originally suggested the reduction of duties as beneficial to the revenue." During these debates a ludicrous incident occurred. Mahon commonly spoke from the row behind the Treasury Bench; and' so strongly records Wraxall, an eyewitness, ' did he always enforce his arguments by his gestures as to become sometimes a troublesome neighbour. Just as he was commending his friend and relation, the First Minister, for his endeavours to knock smuggling on the head at one blow, he actually dealt Mr. Pitt, who sat below him, a smart stroke on the head. This manual application of his metaphor convulsed the House with laughter, and not a little surprised the Chancellor of the Exchequer; but it seemed neither to disconcert nor to arrest the impetuosity of his eloquence x This scene suggested to the authors of the ' Rolliad' the following bitter lines:â 'This Quixote of the nation Beats his own windmills in gesticulation; To strike, not please, his utmost force he bends, And all his sense is at his fingers' ends."

On June 30 Pitt introduced his Budget which proposed taxes on hats, ribbons, coals, horses (except those employed industrially), linens, calicoes, bricks, and tiles. To this last there was some objection. Mahon inveighed against it, and denounced the argument of George Rose in its favour as ' the most weak, ridiculous, and absurd that could possibly be advanced This onslaught deeply annoyed Pitt, who was ready to discuss any amendment to his Budget, but naturally resented an attack on his Secretary of the Treasury. He retorted in a strain of irony; and this, writes his biographer, the fifth Lord Stanhope, ' appears to have been the first estrangement between these so lately most cordial friends 2 Notwithstanding this passage of arms, Mahon defended Pitt's financial schemes as a whole against the criticisms of Fox. ' The right honourable gentleman's speech was a heap of contradictions, and he had betrayed a degree of ignorance that proved him to be perfectly unfit to speak about finance. A dull man would have been silent upon the subject, and an ignorant man would have hearkened to instruction; but the ability of the right honourable gentleman on other subjects 1 Memoirs, iii. 402. 2 Stanhope, Life of Pitt, i. 175.

CHAP, had made him presumptuous in this, and his mind had so little IV. information and so many prepossessions that he probably never would be undeceived." 1 He proceeded to castigate the maladministration of North and the Coalition. ' Why," he asks, ' did they make no effort to fund the navy loan, leaving to present ministers the disagreeable necessity of laying heavy taxes on the country in order to discharge debts contracted by the improvidence of their predecessors? ' 2

In fulfilment of his promise Pitt introduced a measure for Parliamentary Reform during the session of 1785. In an eloquent speech he proposed to disfranchise thirty-six decayed boroughs, each returning two members, and to assign the seats to the largest counties and cities. A million was to be set apart to compensate the borough proprietors. He also proposed that copyholders should obtain the franchise in the counties. The measure had been concerted with the Yorkshire Reformers, but met with but little favour at the time. During the latter stages of the American War, when the people were at the mercy of a corrupt majority and labouring under heavy taxation, Reform stirred every heart; but now the country was regaining its prosperity under a Minister who enjoyed its confidence, and had grown more indifferent. Despite the support of a section of the Whigs the Bill was defeated by 248 to 174. From this moment Pitt abandoned the cause, and before long he began to oppose it. Though it is customary to date his separation from Mahon from the French Revolution, the shelving of Reform caused a certain coolness. Pitt's desertion of a scheme to which he was so solemnly pledged must have been repugnant to one of such unwavering convictions as his brother-in-law. Like Cartwright he believed that though moderation in practice might be commendable, moderation in principle meant being unprincipled. A few days after this defeat a meeting of ' those in favour of a Reform in the Representation ' was held at the Thatched House Tavern. A resolution declaring that Pitt's proposed Bill' would form a substantial improvement of the Constitution' was negatived by 63 to 39, Fox, Jebb, and Sawbridge voting against it, Mahon, Wyvill, and Home Tooke with the minority. 3

Early in January 1786 the spiritually minded Wilberforce notes in his diary: ' To Mahon's; he earnestly busy about useful things, but all of this life." 4 When Parliament met, the two friends were found co-operating. Mahon's motion for leave to bring in ' a Bill for the better securing the rights of voters at 1 Parl Hist., xxiv. 1284. 2 Ibid., 1286.

county elections ' was seconded by Wilberforce. ' Lord Mahon," CHAP. writes Pulteney," made a flaming speech against the Chancellor for IV. throwing out an Election Bill of his last year, and the Opposition heard him with greater shouts than they give their own people. He called the Chancellor an enemy to the House of Commons and to the people, and Divide et impera, he insinuated, was the only maxim with some folks. Whether this was a mere flourish of personal resentment, or whether he alludes to other divisions, I shall not pretend to guess; but he was heard with great attention by both sides." 1 A report was forwarded by the orator to his friend and comrade, Wyvill.

'London: February 14, 1786.

' Dear Sir,â I was well pleased with the reception I met with. Some persons may imagine that a different line of conduct would have been more likely to be attended with success. If I had not tried that last year, and had not reason to think that I was right (as to the success of the measure itself) in not tamely acquiescing in the manner in which the measure was lost, I should have been less ostensibly firm about it. I conceive some Reform to be the most necessary of all objects; and as long as there are hopes of success, I will not abandon the business. I have been informed by a Yorkshire gentleman of great credit that the gentlemen in that part of the country are displeased at nothing having been done last year, and at the rejection of my County-Election Bill. If this be so, I wish extremely you would relate it directly to Mr. Wilberforce in a letter to be shewn if necessary. And if you are, as I am, quite clear of opinion that the Bill for appointing different places of poll cannot be founded on any principle that will not be liable to endless difficulty and objection, except it be on the principle of making the Returning Officer and the Deputy Sheriffs ministerial instead of judicial Officers, I wish particularly that you would urge that circumstance. If a Polling Bill for Yorkshire be founded on that plan, it will fail when attempted to be executed in the county at any election. The measure will then be disgraced (even should it pass Parliament), as it would strengthen the objections to the plan beyond measure. The consequence of this would be that the object would be more completely damned than if nothing were to be attempted at all at present. If you agree with me in the outline of the above, I wish you to warn your two worthy representatives against consenting to take a bad plan in preference to a good one.

1 Rutland MSS., i. 282.

CHAP. Let them press for the best. It will not even be more easy to IV- attain a bad one. For it is not this Bill, or that Bill, but every Bill of Reform that is detested by men of certain principles. ' Dear Sir, ' Ever affectionately yours, 'MAHON." 1

Though Pitt seemed all powerful in the country, he was often thwarted by the reactionary members of his own Cabinet. In the present instance their dissatisfaction was openly expressed. ' The whole of this," wrote Thomas Orde to the Duke of Rutland, on July i, ' is caused by so ridiculous a matter as Lord Stanhope's Election Bill, which Mr. Pitt has strongly supported, and now carries through the House of Lords in spite of the remonstrances of the Chancellor and Lord Sydney, who had last year thrown it out." 2 A fortnight later the same gladiators again succeeded in dispatching the measure.

MAHON was now to exchange the scene of these strenuous con- CHAP, flicts for the more sedate discussions of the Upper House. On V. March 7,1786, the second Lord Stanhope died at Chevening. ' His life was an illustrious example of public virtue and private integrity, and his death is sincerely regretted by his friends," writes the Morning Herald. 1 'The late Earl Stanhope says another journalist," was a man of extensive reading. His genius was elevated, his knowledge various and profound, and his views general and extended. The noble successor to his Lordship's title and dignity is known to have long possessed his virtues." 2 Except in their love of natural science, however, there was little resemblance between father and son. While the second Earl was a gentle and scholarly recluse, happy in his family and his books, the third was born for action, and already, at the age of thirty-three, stood out conspicuously among the public men of his time.

Pitt now introduced the scheme he had promised in the previous session for the reduction of the National Debt. During the recess he had consulted with Dr. Price, whose ' Treatise on Reversionary Annuities ' and ' Appeal to the Public on the Subject of the National Debt' had gained him a high position as a financial expert. Though he made no public acknowledgment of its origin, he adopted one of three plans prepared by the eminent Nonconformist minister. He proposed to devote a million annually to establish a Sinking Fund, and to make it inalienable except by another Act of Parliament, its management to be placed in the hands of six Commissioners. The plan of annually setting aside a fixed sum for the payment of the National 1 March 9 r Public Advertiser, March 10.

CHAP. Debt had been suggested by the first Lord Stanhope in 1716, V. and occasionally employed by Ministers since the days of Walpole. Pitt maintained that the Sinking Fund should be carried on in times of war as in times of peace, in times of deficit as well as in times of surplus, deeming it wiser to borrow at simple interest in order that the Sinking Fund might develop at compound interest. The measure was received with extravagant applause; but Stanhope assailed it in the House of Lords, and published a pamphlet condemning it and describing a plan of his own. 1 ' Of the principle of the Bill he writes, ' I approve as much as I disapprove the Bill itself. A plan which neither pays off much debt in times of peace nor insures its being redeemed in times of war is a plan to delude the public. And the present Minister, who does not mean to delude the public, does evidently delude himself. He thinks, no doubt, that his plan for redeeming the National Debt is to save the nation; and if it be well managed it unquestionably may save it. But if it be c-onducted in the way proposed by the Bill now before the House of Commons we shall neither profit by peace nor be prepared for war." In the spirit of prophecy he goes on to foretell what actually took place. ' Wars may come and those new wars may accumulate such a load of debt upon the nation, that even when another peace shall come, the people may not be able to bear the enormous weight of additional taxes, which it might be necessary to lay in order to provide another Sinking Fund. Mr. Pitt's plan therefore may bring ruin upon this country." How nearly this prediction was fulfilled is proved by the statistics of the National Debt. At the end of the American War it was about 250 millions; at the end of the French War it exceeded 800 millions. Throughout the long struggle Pitt's Sinking Fund was maintained inviolate. The nation annually borrowed vast sums at high interest, and applied a part of them to pay off a debt which bore a low interest. This incredibly stupid arrangement of creating new stock at a loss to the Treasury in order to buy up old stock has been estimated to have cost the Government little less than twenty-five millions. 2

Curiously enough the chief weakness of Pitt's plan, its continuance in times of deficit, never seems to have struck Stanhope, who takes for granted the supposition of an annual surplus. But in his pamphlet he states other objections to the Bill. Firstly, the power given to the Commissioners might induce them to gamble in the public funds. Secondly, if the Sinking Fund 1 Observations on Mr. Pitt's Plan for the Reduction of the National Debt.

were alienable in time of unrest, a Minister might involve the CHAP, country in war in order to seize upon a large surplus without V. being obliged to have recourse to extra taxation. Thirdly, the repeated application of sums of money to any particular stock below par would raise the value of such stock in the market, and this would put the nation to the most enormous expense to redeem the capital. The chief feature of his alternative scheme was the conversion of three-per-cent. stock into one that should bear four per cent.â in other words, that the holders of three-per-cents, should for Â 400 of that stock receive in lieu Â 300 of stock bearing four per cent. To incline the stock-holder to this voluntary conversion, he was to have the right of priority of redemption on his agreeing to be paid off at a fixed price.

' Lord Stanhope wrote Storer to Eden, afterwards Lord Auckland, ' has just published a pamphlet, in which he states Mr. Pitt's plan for the payment of the National Debt is destructive to the country. It is said that Mr. Pitt took a great deal of pains to dissuade him from publishing it, but that his lordship was resolved. Consequently, for once, Mr. Pitt's eloquence was wasted." 1 Stanhope never allowed private considerations to turn him aside from what he conceived to be his public duty, and he introduced his plan to the House of Lords in a speech of singular ability. He read letters approving it from ' some of the first monied men in the country and some of the most knowing men in the City '; and moved ' that it is highly important to the public creditors, as well as necessary for the welfare of this country, that a lasting provision be made for the maintenance of the public credit, and that a plan for the reduction of the National Debt be made absolutely permanent; and, in order effectually to insure the permanency of such a plan, that it is essential that the public faith be fully pledged to individuals, by an express compact being entered into between the State and the creditors, so that the breach of such a compact should be equivalent to an act of bankruptcy." 2 However meritorious the scheme it was the manifest duty of his party to oppose it. The Home Secretary, Lord Sydney, the Tommy Townshend whom Pitt had raised to a peerage, declared that he ' did not feel it requisite to investigate the plan which the noble lord had stated to the House. Conscious of the extreme difficulty of persuading one so inflexible as the noble lord to withdraw his motion, he should move the previous question." Lord Camelford, who also owed his peerage to his kinsman Pitt, spoke more favourably

CHAP, of the proposal. ' I know well the integrity of the noble earl's V. intentions and his ardour in carrying into effect any measure he thinks is for the good of his country, and I am fully persuaded every word he uttered has come from his heart; but I disapprove the time of proposing such a resolution." The Opposition peers, on the other hand, were free to approve the merits of the plan. ' I never recollect a first speech in this assembly said Lord Stormont, ' which came with more weight or made a more evident impression on your lordships than that of the noble earl." ' Lord Stanhope's scheme," declared Lord Loughborough, ' has afforded me great pleasure and information. Its facts are strongly urged, its calculations demonstrably just, its reasoning clear and convincing." In spite of this formidable opposition Pitt's Bill passed and served to augment his popularity, and he appears to have regarded it as the chief monument of his fame. 1

The sharp disagreement on the Sinking Fund did not prevent Pitt warmly supporting his brother-in-law's County-Election Bill. ' I find from Lord Stanhope," wrote the Prime Minister to Sir Lloyd Kenyon, Master of the Rolls, on April n, ' that he has communicated to you his Bill for a register of freeholders in the different counties. If you should think it unexceptionable and should have no objection to take a part in introducing it into the House, your authority would give it great weight. I consider diminishing the expense and trouble of election as a very important public object, if it can be obtained." 2 The Bill was in charge of Wilberforce, and passed the House of Commons without much difficulty. ' I know," wrote Stanhope to Wyvill, ' that some of those who supported us had their doubts, that some few had more than doubts, that others were languid and far from eager, owing to the general supineness one day complained of by Lord John Cavendish with respect to all except party questions." 3 On the third reading Stanhope stated its principles to be nine in number:â i. No man could hereafter vote for any property which had not been registered for at least six months. This would prevent any man's coming on a sudden on the day of election, and stating himself to possess a freehold never heard of before.

1 These pages were submitted by Miss Stanhope to the late Sir Edward Hamilton, who wrote to her on May 23, 1908: ' I see nothing in your remarks on the Sinking Fund to which exception can be taken. The essential point to get hold of is that the plan was founded on a fallacy which Pitt did not see. It was a great feather in Lord Stanhope's cap to have taken exception and just exception to the plan of the man who was the greatest financier of his age or of any age."

2. No man, having purchased a freehold estate with a view to CHAP. vote, could vote unless he had been for twelve months enrolled on v-the register, as the holder of the freehold he came to vote for.

3. A man coming to the possession of a registered freehold estate by devise, descent, marriage, or promotion to a benefice in the Church, could, upon registering, vote directly.

4. No man could lose his vote by another's neglect.

5. The necessity of enrolment on the register occurred but once in a man's life. Freeholders living at a distance might enrol by attestation instead of travelling to the parish.

6. There was to be a register in each parish, and for each parish near those who were acquainted with the estate.

7. The poll-books were to be divided into parishes and to correspond with the registers.

8. A false oath should not be taken.

9. Returning-officers should no longer be judicial, but official and ministerial.

The criticisms on the measure were characteristic. Lord Sandwich ' saw no reason whatsoever to induce him to depart from the old system and adopt this new-fangled proposition. Great care, much pains and long expense he added," have brought our election laws to their present state of perfection." With as much reason it was opposed by the Bishop of Bangor, ' because it unhinged the whole code of laws our ancestors had formed." Every improvement then suggested by Stanhope was to be incorporated in the Statute-book; but his Bill was defeated ' by a coalition of the King's friends and the Whig aristocracy." 1 It was the first of many defeats and disappointments in the Upper House.

On February 13, 1788, began the memorable trial of Warren Hastings, which lasted till his acquittal in 1795. Interested in all questions of justice, Stanhope watched the proceedings with unremitting attention. 'From beginning to end," remarks the editor of the ' Speeches," ' he never failed in his attendance, nor suffered himself to be absent for an hour. He took notes of the evidence, and always shewed candour and impartiality in dealing with the difficult questions frequently arising during the course of the trial." 2 The session is further memorable for the first steps in Parliament towards the abolition of the slave 1 Wyvill Papers, iv. 114.

CHAP, trade. In May, 1787, an association had been formed of which v- Granville Sharpe was chairman. Of the twelve members who formed the Committee ten belonged to the Society of Friends, Among its most ardent supporters was Wilberforce, who in the same year vainly endeavoured to procure the insertion of some provisions against the slave trade in the treaty then being negociated in Paris by Eden. He next resolved to agitate the question in Parliament; but on his health failing, it was left to Pitt to give notice of a motion. A Committee of the Privy Council was appointed to take evidence of the African trade. Early in the year, Wilberforce had applied to Stanhope for help.

' For many reasons, I am clear, and Pitt is of the same opinion, that 'tis extremely desirable that petitions for the abolition of the trade in flesh and blood should flow in from every quarter of the kingdom: they are going forward in many places. I know how friendly you must be to my motion and I trust you will lay a load of parchment on the shoulders of the members of the county of Kent.

' Yours ever affectionately, ' W. WILBERFORCE." x

Wilberforce was not mistaken. With his customary zeal he at once joined the movement. But vested interests were powerful, and the threatened interference drew indignant protests from the merchants of London, Lancashire, and Bristol. Men of high position, and even clergymen, were not ashamed to defend the evil thing. Meanwhile Sir William Dolben, having inspected a slave-ship, was so shocked that he introduced a Bill to mitigate the horrors of the Middle Passage. It was supported by Pitt and Fox, and passed the Commons with some difficulty. On June 18 it reached the Lords. In moving its immediate commitment, Stanhope observed that the evidence they had heard proved to them that seven negroes, on the average, out of every hundred died in the three months' passage to the West Indies. The ordinary mortality of negroes in that time would not be ordinarily one per cent., but, ' allowing for the dangers of the seas, it might be two; so that it might be literally said that from the present mode of carrying on the trade, five persons out of every hundred were actually murdered." 2 He rejected Lord Heathfield's comparison of soldiers in a tent to Africans on board ship. ' The Africans," he said, ' are packed between 1 To Lord Stanhope, January 25, 1788. Stanhope Papers.

decks on platforms like books on shelves, and are thought to CHAP (be perfectly at their ease if they have just room enough to v-turn. Is that the case with soldiers in a tent? The air breathed between decks is rendered putrid by the closeness of the space and their own respiration; whereas a tent is continuously replenished with fresh air He then, records the ' Parliamentary History introduced some remarks on the nature of air as breathed by mankind. By being confined to a small space, by breathing the air over and over again, the vital part became tainted, as in the Black Hole of Calcutta, and thence came the danger of death. If it were possible to confine the air in which their lordships lived for a certain length of time, they would all drop down dead.

The Opposition was led by Lord Chancellor Thurlow, whose relations with Pitt were by no means cordial, and who found means to instil his hostility to the Bill into the mind of the King. When the measure, now fully amended, came up for third reading he played for delay, which would in that period of the session have prevented its passing. He suggested amendments which, if accepted, would have carried the Bill again to the Lower House. Stanhope at once pointed out that the King was to prorogue Parliament the next day, and therefore they must adopt it as it stood or reject it altogether. There was no alternative and no time to be lost. The House adopted his advice and negatived the Chancellor's amendments. ' And thus says Clarkson, ' at length passed through the Upper House, as through an ordeal of fire, the first Bill that ever put fetters upon that barbarous and destructive monster the Slave Trade. The next day the King gave his assent 1

Writing to Eden at Madrid Lord Sheffield thus referred to the debate: ' The Chancellor made an inimitable attack on Lord Stanhope, who had been running repeatedly to Pitt, who stood under the throne, and taking hints from him. Having dropped some domineering expression he said that their lordships felt the disadvantage of being turned over from the Minister to his deputy, which put him in mind of a passage in a pamphlet on the slave trade. The author stated that where the planter superintended the treatment of his negroes all went well; but when they were turned over to the deputy slave-driver the case was directly the reverse. He pursued the idea incomparably, perhaps not very decently for a member of the Cabinet. It is said all of that Board except Pitt and the Duke of Richmond are 1 Clarkson, History of the Abolition of the Slave Trade, i. 316; European Magazine, xiv. 53.

CHAP, averse to the Slave Bills, and also that the King does not approve v- of the business." x In the face of such obstacles success was a veritable triumph. To Wilberforce in his retreat at Kendal Stanhope reported the progress of the campaign, and received a grateful reply: ' I thank you, my dear Lord, for the proof of your kindly remembrance that was conveyed to me in your letter from the House of Lords. 1 sincerely congratulate you on your triumph, and it is the more gratifying to me because I confess it was unexpected. I know your Lordship's spirit and perseverance, and genius in suggesting expedients and solving difficulties, and I know your address in canvassing, whether the solicitation be to attend or to sweep away. To all this your success must be attributed." 2

The centenary of 1688 was celebrated all over the country with great rejoicings. ' Not a lady was to be seen without streaming orange-coloured ribbons, or gentlemen without rosettes of the same in their button-holes." 3 Coke of Norfolk gave a magnificent fete at Holkham. 4 The political societies commemorated the occasion by banquets. The Whig Club met at the Crown and Anchor Tavern, with the Duke of Portland in the chair; and Sheridan proposed the erection of a monument at Runnymede. On November 5 the Constitutional Club had a dinner of some 1,200 persons at Willis's Rooms, and sang a spirited ballad.

' Britons! revere, with hearts elate,
The glorious Revolution, That firmly fixed in Church and State Your heaven born Constitution.
In Fifteen Hundred Eighty Eight,
The Armada was defeated, In Sixteen Hundred Eighty Eight,
Our Freedom was completed.
In Seventeen Hundred Eighty Eight,
PITT'S wise administration Peace, Plenty, Splendour, Wealth, and Weight Diffused throughout the Nation." 5 1 Auckland's Correspondence, ii. 221.
2 Wilberforce to Stanhope, July 9, 1788. Stanhope Papers.
3 Life of Mrs. Schimmelpennick, i. 67, 4 Stirling, Coke of Norfolk, i. 352.

The Society for Commemorating the Revolution in Great CHAP. Britain had existed ever since 1688, its members being chiefly V. Dissenters who met annually on November 4, the date of King William's birthday. On this occasion ' a numerous and respectable ' company of about four hundred gentlemen dined at the London Tavern. Earl Stanhope, ' one of the most ardent and enthusiastic defenders of civil liberty who has appeared in our time," took the chair. The proceedings began at noon with a service at the Nonconformist Meeting-house in Old Jewry. ' The congregation then adjourned to the London Tavern, the chairman being preceded in walking up the room by one of the stewards bearing the original colours which King William displayed on his march from Torbay. Lord Carmarthen, Lord Hood, and other persons of distinction followed; and the company sat down to dinner. About an hour after dinner Lord Stanhope introduced the resolutions of the Committee, the principal of which was that a perpetual anniversary of thanksgiving to Almighty God for the blessings of the Revolution should be instituted, and that December 16, the day on which the Bill of Rights passed, would be the proper occasion for its celebration. It was then resolved to request Henry Beaufoy to move in the House of Commons for leave to bring in a Bill for this purpose."

Having chosen stewards and a Committee, the members next assented to ' Three Fundamental Principles." (i) That all civil and political authority is derived from the people. (2) That the abuse of power justifies resistance. (3) That the Right of Private Judgment, Liberty of Conscience, Trial by Jury, the Freedom of the Press, and the Freedom of Election are ever to be held sacred and inviolable. ' An excellent oration was then delivered by the Rev. Dr. Towers; the Character of King William was read by the Rev. Dr. Rees; and the day was crowned with songs of conviviality suited to the occasion." No less than forty-one toasts were drunk. In the evening the Monument was illuminated, and a transparent painting, emblematic of the glorious event, displayed in front of the tavern, containing the inscription ' A TYRANT DEPOSED AND LIBERTY RESTORED, 1688." 1 In accordance with the resolution of the Society, Beaufoy introduced a Bill to set apart a day of annual thanksgiving. It passed the Commons; but when Stanhope introduced it to the House of Lords it so roused the ire of Warren, 1 European Magazine, xxiv. 280-3; and An Abstract of the History and Proceedings of the Revolution Society in London. Printed by Order of the Committee, 1789.

CHAP. Bishop of Bangor, that, contrary to the usual form, he opposed V. it on first reading. ' The Revolution," he said, ' was taken notice of in a very particular manner in the service of our Church Further commemoration he thought unnecessary, and he was supported by the Chancellor. Lord Hopetoun was the only peer who rose to speak in favour of the Bill, which was thrown out.

While the celebrations were in progress the King became insane. The profligate character of the Prince of Wales and his notorious association with the Opposition made Ministers hesitate to confer the Regency upon him; while Fox, Sheridan, and his other friends contended that he had a right ' to assume the administration on his own behalf." The Ministers replied that Parliament alone had power to nominate a Regent, and their view was shared by Stanhope, who adduced the example of the Convention Parliament as a proof of the competency of the two Houses to supply the deficiency in the executive Government. To call this right in question, he declared, was to sap the foundation on which the claim of the House of Hanover to the throne rested; for if they had no right to give the crown to the Prince of Orange they had also no right to make the Act of Settlement by which the Hanover family obtained the throne. The bitter warfare was brought to an abrupt conclusion when, towards the end of February 1789, the King recovered his reason. In the House of Lords the address was moved and seconded with only a single comment. ' This came," says Wraxall, ' when Lord Stanhope, a man who at every period of his life displayed the same ardent, eccentric, fearless, independent character, stood forward to state his doubts on the principle as well as the propriety of the intended address to the throne." ' A Bill," he observed, ' is actually in progress, which contains a clause specifying the precise manner in which the King is to resume the reins of government on his recovery. The Queen and her Council are empowered to judge and decide when this act may take place. Now, the two Houses having in the first instance ascertained, by the testimony of the physicians, the royal incapacity, and having next specified the channel through which the nation may be satisfied of the Sovereign's complete restoration, is the present measure strictly parliamentary? I give full confidence to the fact of recovery, but it is essential we should act in consonance with order." The Chancellor, who probably was not prepared for such an objection from such a quarter, made nevertheless an ingenious, if not a convincing reply. ' No declaration of the two Houses would," he said, ' deprive the King of the right to govern, nor could any clause interrupt his re-assum- CHAP, ing the power on the total cessation of his disorder." Alluding V. to the Regency Bill with a sort of repugnance as a measure which he wished to be buried in oblivion, he denied that either the Bill itself or the clause inserted in it was founded on the testimony of the physicians. ' Parliament he asserted, ' had better proof of his Majesty's illness, namely, his having neither met the two Houses in person, nor issued a commission to execute the duty." Stanhope repeated his assertions, adding, nevertheless, ' I am a friend to Ministers, and do not mean any insinuation prejudicial to them. My intention is only to put them on their guard." ' I was of opinion at the time," says Wraxall, ' and I remain so, that, as a matter of parliamentary order, Lord Stanhope was right in his position." 1

During the months of the Regency crisis Stanhope's time was largely devoted to championing the cause of religious liberty. The English Catholics at this time did not exceed 60, 000. 2 Ruled by Vicars-apostolic since the reign of James II, their real leaders were the nobility and country gentry, on whose contributions the machinery of the Church in England depended. After the final defeat of Jacobite hopes in 1745 a friendlier feeling towards Catholics became general, and the Act of 1778 mitigated the penal laws and removed one or two disabilities. The Gordon riots showed that the embers of fanaticism were still smouldering; but Catholics were encouraged by their success in 1778, and in 1782 a Committee of prominent laymen, representing the old county families, was formed to promote their interests. Its leading figure was Lord Petre, a great Essex landowner, who had entertained George III and who was to display his patriotism during the Great War by equipping a corps of 250 men. But the real brain of the Committee was the Secretary, Charles Butler, a learned and devout lawyer of untiring zeal and great practical ability. Appointed for five years the Committee took no overt step during their first term; but, on their reappointment in 1787, they determined on an active campaign. Early in 1788 1 Memoirs, v. 335; Pavl. Hist., xxvii. 1301.

2 The admirable work of Bernard Ward, The Dawn of the Catholic Revival in England, supplies a good deal of information which was not before Miss Stanhope, and which has been added on revision.

CHAP, they addressed a Memorial to Pitt, who, after taking time for v- consideration, received a deputation and expressed his friendliness towards their aims. In response to his suggestion that authentic evidence of Catholic opinion in regard to the dispensing power should be procured, the Committee consulted the theologians of the Sorbonne, Louvain, Douai, Alcala, Valladolid, and Salamanca. The replies were unanimous in declaring that the Pope possessed no civil jurisdiction in England, that no officer of the Church could absolve an English citizen from his allegiance, and that there was no justification for breaking faith with heretics. These replies, surrendering the Ultramontanist claims which had shocked and angered England in the reign of Elizabeth, accurately expressed the convictions of the Catholic subjects of George III, who knew their loyalty and were eager to show it.

At this point Stanhope comes on the scene. Whether his assistance was invited or offered is not clear from the following account by Charles Butler of an incident which looms large in the history of English Catholicism. ' At this time a general attempt was made to modify the statutes of uniformity. One express object of Lord Stanhope's Bill was to give relief to the non-conformists of the established Church by liberating persons of every description from the penalties of nonconformity. But as there was a prejudice against the Catholics, his lordship thought it would be advisable solemnly to disclaim some of the tenets falsely imputed to them. For this reason, with long consideration and after perusing the works of some of the best Catholic writers, and conferring with the ministers of other churches and some of the leading men of all other parties, but without the slightest communication with any Roman Catholics, his Lordship framed the Protestation, transmitted it to Lord Petre, and recommended that it should be generally signed. Lord Petre instantly forwarded it to the Secretary of the Committee with directions to send copies of it immediately to the four Vicars-apostolic." The Committee made ' some alterations and forwarded it as instructed. The Protestation repudiated the right to murder or depose excommunicated Princes, or to absolve subjects from their allegiance. ' We acknowledge no responsibility in the Pope, and no ecclesiastical power has any jurisdiction in this realm." Licence to break faith with heretics was also repudiated. ' We do make this declaration," it concludes, ' without any evasion or reservation. And we appeal to the j ustice and candour of our fellow-citizens whether we, who thus solemnly disclaim and from our hearts abhor the above abominable and unchristian principles, ought to be put on a level with any other men who CHAP, may hold and profess those principles." x V.

The following correspondence from the Chevening archives suggests the zeal with which Stanhope threw himself into his task:â ' Buckenham House, Norfolk: November 8, 1788.

' My lord,â In consequence of the conversation with your Lordship some time ago on the subject of an Oath proposed to form part of a Bill for election matters, I communicated the purport of it to my particular friends. We have without hesitation determined that the said Oath contains nothing that a conscientious Catholic may not swear with entire safety, and no more than every good subject should swear to if required. Permit me to assure your Lordship how sensible I am of your kind attention to our cause.

1 Your Lordship's most obliged and obedient ' humble servant, ' PETRE."

' Chevening: November 14, 1788.

' My Lord,â I have received your Lordship's letter of the 8th instant and I am very happy that your Lordship's friends make no objection to the substance of the new oath. My first principle is, that every man has a natural and inalienable right to liberty of conscience, and that no man should be persecuted for his private opinions in matters of religion. But every person is at all times liable to be called upon to give due security to the State, whenever the State shall deem it expedient. Upon this principle I propose the new oath instead of the oaths now existing. My second principle is that if in any country the members of any religious sect are unjustly accused with being dangerous members of the community, frcm the public conceiving erroneous opinions of their faith, they are bound in prudence (before they make application to obtain more toleration) to undeceive and inform the public in order to remove the ground of suspicion and every pretence of persecution, and to enable the friends of toleration to stand forth in support of religious freedom, without being supposed by the public to hazard the political interests of the State. It was principally (if not altogether) for want of this necessary caution on the part of the Roman Catholics that the disturbances in the year 1780 were 1 Butler, Historical Memoirs of the Catholics, iv. 1-55. This celebrated document is reprinted in Appendix IV of this volume.

CHAP, occasioned. Upon this principle I took the liberty of hinting v- to your Lordship, in the conversation we had in town, that the British Roman Catholics as a body ought in my opinion, in the most formal and solemn manner, to give to the world, not an account of what they do believe, but an explicit disavowal of what they do not believe. I mean to speak, of course, of the principles which have been publicly imputed to them (I am ready to believe) perfectly unjustly. I am particularly engaged at the present moment; but, if I can find time before, or soon after, Christmas, I will endeavour, by stating upon paper, the particular principles which ought to be disclaimed. As a true friend of toleration I am desirous of promoting it. But none but a rash Protestant would wish to shock public opinion, which ought not to be shocked but efficaciously enlightened.

' STANHOPE."

On December 3 he forwarded the promised declaration or Protestation, advising that it should be signed by all the Roman Catholics in Great Britain, delivered to the two Secretaries of State and published in the London Gazette. In acknowledging it Lord Petre wrote as follows:â ' Buckenham House: December 5, 1788.

' My Lord,â I this morning received your Lordship's letter accompanied by the most obliging marks of your liberality towards the British Roman Catholics. For them and myself I cannot sufficiently return your Lordship our most sincere thanks for the trouble you have taken in drawing up the declaration. I am in daily expectation of some papers 1 which will tend to authenticate and strengthen the principles we avow in opposition to those abominable doctrines we are so unjustly accused of, which I will take the liberty of transmitting to your Lordship.

' I am, my Lord, ' Your Lordship's most obedient, humble servant, ' PETRE

The Protestation was signed by the great body of the English Catholics, including the four Vicars-apostolic and the majority of the clergy, and was laid before Parliament with their petition for relief. Stanhope's services were again gratefully acknowledged by the leading Catholic laymen.

The origin and authorship of the celebrated Protestation were at a later period hotly contested. Bishop Milner, who led the attack on ' Cisalpinism," declared his conviction that CHAP. Stanhope merely patronised it; that he composed it, he could v-no more believe than that he wrote the ' Summa of Aquinas." 1 Charles Butler, however, added a note in the third edition of his ' Historical Memoirs stating that Stanhope's authorship was most explicitly declared both by himself and by the Committee, and was never contradicted at the time. 'The contrary has since been asserted, but without the slightest proof." This categorical statement is decisive; but, as Butler himself mentioned, the Protestant Peer had consulted both men and books. The idea of a Protestation was not new, for Throckmorton, one of the most active members of the Catholic Committee, had urged it in I786. 2 The following important letter from a Catholic priest, written from London on December 17, 1788, summarises a lost letter of Stanhope and confirms the accuracy of Butler. ' In the Committee this morning Lord Petre read two letters from a nobleman of the first connection, with whom he had no acquaintance till the present opportunity offered of serving the Catholics. His Lordship says that he had been brought up in violent prejudices against us, but reading and reflection have convinced him of his early errors, and he thinks he cannot better atone for the mistakes of his youth than by exerting his endeavours to relieve an oppressed and calumniated part of his fellow-subjects. Two principles he lays down. First that toleration ought to be extended to all conscientious Christians of every denomination. Secondly that where a body of men is suspected, though unjustly, of maintaining erroneous and dangerous doctrines, the members of that body ought in prudence to take every opportunity of removing suspicions. For this purpose he drew up the declaration which you have seen, and in which he believes he has mentioned all the prejudices that Protestants entertain against Catholics as members of the political community. This Declaration is his own deed entirely, and the original is accompanied with notes and extracts, particularly from O'Leary's writings. I must observe that the words of the Declaration are almost entirely taken from O'Leary. However, as Mr. Walmesley (one of the Vicars-apostolic) had expressed objections, some changes have been admitted in hopes of obtaining his approbation. The Noble Lord will to-morrow morning see the corrections. He wishes we may be prepared for any favourable opportunity that may offer, more especially because he thinks that sufficient care had not been taken, when the last 1 Supplementary Memoirs, 50-2.

- Ward, The Dawn of the Catholic Revival, i. chap. vii.

CHAP, indulgence was granted, to prepare the minds of prejudiced v- Protestants. He hopes therefore we will not be backward in exertions to enlighten efficaciously the prejudiced part of the kingdom."

If further evidence of Stanhope's authorship be demanded, it may be found in a declaration drawn up and signed by Charles Butler to meet the scruples of a London priest. ' I do hereby most solemnly declare that Earl Stanhope himself told me, and that Lord Petre and Mr. Wilkes both repeatedly informed me that he told them, that it is not intended, either by the whole context of the Declaration or by any article contained in it, that Catholics should deny the spiritual authority of the Church or its Pastor." In like manner Milner was persuaded to sign by the words of a fellow priest, ' We all know the Instrument is inaccurate, but what would you have from Protestants and laymen who do not enter into our religious difficulties? ' Stanhope cannot be blamed for the fact that his well-meant efforts to prepare public opinion for Catholic relief should have led to a bitter feud. Consulted and trusted by the leading laymen he believed himself to be dealing with men competent to speak for their whole communion. If the Protestation, in its categorical denial of Papal infallibility, offended the susceptibilities of a minority, it was the fault of those who assumed responsibility for the document, not of its Protestant author. Moreover, there can be no doubt that its vigorous assertion of loyalty and its uncompromising repudiation of the extreme claims of the Counter-Reformation largely contributed to the passing of the great Catholic Relief Bill of 1791.

In addition to his work for the Catholics Stanhope introduced a comprehensive Toleration Bill. Though this measure was unsuccessful at the time, it is highly important in the history of religious liberty. He proposed to repeal a number of ancient and, for the most part, obsolete laws; and to give every one, except Papists, full liberty to teach and exercise their religion, and by speaking, writing, printing, and publishing to investigate religious subjects. 1 His erudite speech, introducing it, occupies more than thirteen columns of the ' Parliamentary History," and gives an extremely curious account of the persecuting laws that still remained on the Statute-book. Those which he most 1 Parl. Hist., xxviii. 113. An anonymous Letter to Earl Stanhope on the Subject of the Test, a copy of which is in the British Museum, recommends him to persevere in his studies, and sarcastically congratulates him on the various ' exertions of your arms and body by which so much grace is added to your Lordship's oratory."

desired to repeal made attendance at Divine service compulsory. CHAP. By Elizabeth's Act of Uniformity every person who, without V. reasonable and lawful cause, did not attend church, both on Sundays and holy days, might be fined one shilling on each occasion. By a second law of Elizabeth the fine was raised to Â 20 a month. By a third any person who obstinately refused to go to church was to be committed to gaol till he conformed; but if after three years he persisted in his refusal, he was to be banished from the Realm, his property was to be confiscated, and he was liable to death if he returned. Under James I it was provided that two-thirds of the lands of the offender might be taken; that every householder was liable to a fine of Â 10 a month for every servant, visitor, or visitor's servant, who abstained from church; and that informations, suits or actions, against those who did not attend church might be laid in any county and at the pleasure of any informer. The Toleration Act had indeed relieved Protestant Dissenters who believed in the Trinity from these penalties by authorising their places of worship; but it left those who, from conscientious reasons or from taste, abstained from attending any form of public worship liable to the ancient penalties.

There were several other statutes which it was desirable to repeal. The laws of Elizabeth rendering it compulsory to eat fish on fast-days had expired; but to eat meat on fast-days was still an ecclesiastical offence, punishable in ecclesiastical courts.

The power of excommunication, with all its civil penalties, still remained. An act of Charles II still made any peer who went to Court, or remained in the King's presence without having taken the Oath of Supremacy and Declaration against popery, a popish recusant, although it had become so perfectly obsolete that, as Stanhope observed, the whole bench of Protestant Bishops had violated it. The Canons of 1663, breathing a spirit of implacable intolerance, were still believed to be binding on the clergy, and any writing which impugned the supernatural character of the Christian creed was a criminal offence. Though the greater part of this legislation had become inoperative, it might be set in motion by individual fanaticism or private malevolence. He was able to cite more than thirty cases in which persecuting laws had been put in force during the preceding twenty-six years, sometimes against Roman Catholics, sometimes against Protestant Dissenters, sometimes against persons who simply abstained from going to church.

The main object of the Bill was to improve the condition of Protestant Dissenters. Among his friends Stanhope numbered

CHAP, many Nonconformists, including the famous scientist, Joseph V. Priestley, the equally celebrated Dr. Price, the literary Kippis and Towers. Dissenters were conspicuous in various branches of science, philosophy, and literature, and they were an order-loving and law-abiding people; but the Established Church was jealous of its prerogative, and the advanced views of many Nonconformists made them obnoxious to the Government. Moreover, the French Revolution was already beginning to cast its shadow over English politics. The Bishops united against any encroachment on the privileges of the Establishment. The Archbishop of Canterbury contended that, if unrestrained speaking, writing, printing, and publishing of religious opinions were permitted, there was scarcely a mischief to the Church or to civil society that imagination could form an idea of which might not be effected. ' Such a measure said Bishop Horsley, ' would leave our mutilated Constitution a prodigy in politics, a civil polity without any public religion for its basis."

Though the Bill was thrown out in the Lords on the second reading, Stanhope was determined to persevere. ' If the right reverend bench would not suffer him to load away their rubbish by cartfuls, he would endeavour to carry it off in wheelbarrows; and if that mode of removal was resisted, he would take it away with a spade, a little at a time 1 He immediately moved to introduce another Bill ' to repeal an Act of the 27th of Henry VIII, to prevent vexatious suits relative to Quakers." This provoked an altercation with the Lord Chancellor, which Stanhope ended by saying, ' On another occasion I shall teach the noble and learned lord law, as I have to-day taught the bench of bishops religion." The religious scruples of Quakers prevented their paying tithes, which rendered them liable first to excommunication, then to be cited in a spiritual court, and then to be handed over to justices of the peace and cast into prison. Some most respectable Quakers were now confined in common gaols for paltry sums. It was the extreme of absurdity as well as of oppression, he declared, to deprive men of their liberty for these petty causes. He considers it ' wonderfully absurd, too, in the ecclesiastical law which enacts the same punishment for various offences. Men are forbidden to marry their mothers or grandmothers. If any man offend against this law his punishment would be excommunication with all its civil consequences. So that a man's marrying his mother or grandmother is the same offence in the eye of the ecclesiastical law as owing two-pence or three-pence to any minister of the church." He contended CHAP, against the right of the clergy to excommunicate for civil causes, v-and he proposed to enact that no suit should hereafter be brought or maintainable in any ecclesiastical court for the recovery of any tithes, dues, or other spiritual profit. 1 The Bishops did not relish Stanhope's Erastian doctrines, and this Bill was also rejected.

CHAP. ' IN every great revolution some petty incident becomes sym-VI. bolical, and thenceforward holds in the imagination of mankind a place altogether disproportionate. The Bastille was of slight strategic consequence; its capture was not a brilliant exploit, and it was dishonoured by infamous cruelty. Only seven prisoners, most of them detained for good reason, were found within its walls. But to popular feeling, both in France and abroad, it was the embodiment of all that was most hateful in arbitrary power; and its fall seemed to announce a new age of freedom, justice, and humanity." 1 As such, it was regarded by most of the friends of liberty in England; and Stanhope shared the view of Fox that it was much the best and happiest event that had ever happened.

The fall of despotic government was celebrated by the Revolution Society at its annual meeting on November 4. 2 In the forenoon the members assembled at the Old Jewry, and listened to a sermon by Dr. Richard Price on ' The Love of our Country In the convulsions in France he discovered a repetition of our own revolution of 1688. ' I could almost say, "Lord, now lettest Thou Thy servant depart in peace, for mine eyes have seen Thy salvation." After sharing in the benefits of one revolution, I have been spared to witness two others, both glorious." This celebrated discourse was the proximate cause of Burke's ' Reflections on the French Revolution." The report of the Committee congratulated the members as Men, Britons, and Citizens of the l Cambridge Modern History, viii. 167.

3 The following pages are based on The Correspondence of the Revolution Society with the National Assembly, and with various Societies of the Friends of Liberty in France and England. London, 1792.

World, on that noble spirit of civil and religious liberty which CHAP, had since the last meeting so conspicuously shone forth on the V I-Continent, more especially on the glorious success of the French Revolution; and they expressed their ardent wishes that the influence of so glorious an example might be felt by all mankind, till tyranny and despotism should be swept from the face of the globe, and universal liberty and happiness should prevail. Dr. Price then moved the famous address to the National Assembly, which stirred Burke to fury. ' The Society for commemorating the Revolution in Great Britain, disdaining national partialities and rejoicing at every triumph of liberty and justice over arbitrary power, offer to the National Assembly of France their congratulations on the revolution in that country and on the prospect it gives to the two first kingdoms of the world of a common participation in the blessings of civil and religious liberty. They cannot help adding their ardent wishes of a happy settlement of so important a revolution, and at the same time expressing the particular satisfaction with which they reflect on the tendency of the glorious example given in France to encourage other nations to assert the inalienable rights of mankind, and thereby to introduce a general reformation in the government of Europe, and to make the world free and happy At the unanimous wish of the meeting the signature of Stanhope, who acted as Chairman, was affixed to the address, which was forwarded to the Due de la Rochefoucauld with a letter requesting him to present it to the National Assembly. The Duke informed Price that the address forwarded by Earl Stanhope had been received by the Assembly with lively applause. They had directed their President to write, but as he had not yet found time to do so, he had not delayed his reply to Dr. Price. On the receipt of the letter the General Committee of the Society met, with Stanhope in the chair, and passed a vote of thanks to the Duke for presenting their address and for sending them a copy of his speeches.

Shortly after, the official reply of the Assembly arrived from the Archbishop of Aix, the President, dated December 5. The National Assembly, he wrote, discovered in the address of the Revolution Society the principles of universal benevolence, which ought to bind together the true friends to the liberty and happiness of mankind in every country. The Revolution Society at once dispatched a reply, signed by Stanhope and the Secretary, cordially thanking the President for his letter. ' The members of the Society runs the communication, ' feel particularly the justice which the august Assembly has done them by imputing

CHAP, their Address to those principles of universal benevolence which VI. ought in all countries to bind together the friends of human liberty and happiness. Their hearts are warmed with these principles; and they desire nothing so earnestly as that the time may soon come when they shall so possess every human heart as to put an end to all jealousies between nations, exterminate oppression and slavery, and cause wars, those dreadful errors of governments, to cease in all the earth. They exult in the prospect of such a time, which seems to be opening, and with which the proceedings of the National Assembly of France promise to bless mankind." The letter concludes with an eulogium on constitutional monarchy. The Revolution Society ' learns with pleasure that the people of France are happy in a King who has encouraged them by his virtues in recovering their rights, and been on this account justly crowned with the title of restorer of French liberty. This elevates him to the highest pinnacle of glory. The despots of the world must now see their folly. This example must shew them that they can never be so great, or happy, or truly powerful, as by renouncing despotic power, and being placed (like the Kings of France and England) at the head of an enlightened people and free constitutions of government."

A letter from Baudouin, a member of and printer to the National Assembly, to Stanhope informs him that he was present at the reading of the address of the Revolution Society and shared in the transports of gratitude and admiration which it evoked. ' I have the honour he added, ' to present to you, from the Revolution Society, a copy of the " Proceedings " of our Assembly, the continuation to be sent every week. May this feeble tribute of a mind penetrated with the most sincere attachment for the English nation, the Revolution Society, and its illustrious Chairman, whose name is as much revered among us as that of Mably, be a pledge to them of the inexpressible satisfaction which their address afforded me." To this letter Stanhope and the Secretary replied that no present could have been more agreeable to them than the ' Proceedings." The Patriotic societies of Dijon and Lille also wrote expressing their gratitude for the address to the National Assembly, and declaring that they had long regarded England as the model of a constitutional monarchy which it was their ambition France should imitate. Suitable replies were dispatched in Stanhope's name. To the Abbe Volpius, President of the Patriotic Club of Dijon, he wrote: ' Sir, I hasten to inform you that I have received the letter you did me the honour to write me, and I shall not fail to present to the Revolution Society the resolution of your worthy Patriotic

Club, with the excellent address of Navier. Friends as we are CHAP, of the indefeasible rights of man, we desire that England should VI. remain at peace with France, that the French should enjoy the happiness of which they have shewn themselves worthy, and that the world should be free." 1 The address of November had echoed through France, and had carried the name of Stanhope into its remotest corners.

Early in 1790 Stanhope addressed a Letter to Burke, provoked by one of his speeches on the Revolution. 2 Though it appeared several months before the ' Reflections it answers by anticipation many of the arguments of that work. The ' Letter a pamphlet of thirty pages, is not destitute of literary merit, and its author was better acquainted than Burke with the state of France. Burke had said that the French had made their way through the destruction of their country to a bad constitution, when they were in possession of a good one, the time of which he fixed as 1 the day the Estates met in separate orders ' You know, Sir replied Stanhope, ' that at that time the Bastille existed, the practice of arbitrary imprisonment existed, no Habeas Corpus was established, no trial by jury was then known in that country, nor had it ever been moved for in the National Assembly. There was then no Declaration of Rights, no liberty of the press; nor had the nation even the semblance of a free constitution. May, such was the horrid extent of despotic power and so numerous were the persons who had been its victims, that it was not till several months after the happy period you allude to that the National Assembly could find out the multitude of persons arbitrarily imprisoned throughout the kingdom nor even the places of confinement; nor could this discovery be made till the National Assembly, on the second of last month, voted that all Governors of prisons and all persons charged with the custody of persons imprisoned by lettres de cachet should give a full and true account of all persons in their charge. Such were the blessed effects of that good constitution, of which you say the French were at that time in absolute possession

Of the oppressed condition of the people Stanhope was peculiarly qualified to speak, for in his journeys backwards and forwards to Geneva he must often have been a witness of their intolerable hardships. ' The common people he exclaims," were borne down by oppressive services and by unequal and galling taxes, from which the opulent were free. Feudal tyranny 1 Moniteur, iii. 191, January 24, 1790.

2 A Letter from Earl Stanhope to the Rt. Hon. Edmund Burke. Dated February 24, 1790.

CHAP, existed, and the abject state of vassalage existed also. A nest VI. of Government spies swarmed throughout the country, and in Paris they were stationed even in private houses. The people saw their fellow-citizens (and often their best fellow-citizens) thrown into dungeons and kept in chains, detained in those solitary and dark cells of despotism, without any public accusation, without the possibility of obtaining any trial or of procuring any redress, and even without being informed of the supposed offences of which they were basely and secretly accused, or of the names of their accusers. The people, moreover, from the great scarcity of corn, were then literally starving for want of bread." Without attempting to condone such tumults as had already taken place, he excuses them as incidental to all explosions of popular feeling. ' The nation saw their capital surrounded by foreign mercenaries joined to their standing army, who had been ordered thither to overawe the National Assembly and to intimidate the people. Was it to be supposed that under such circumstances an oppressed, a threatened and a famished people would proceed upon abstract ideas of Metaphysics, or would even act in all respects with that perfect temper and moderation which under other circumstances they might have done? Any man who could expect this must know but little of human nature." The Revolution arose in large measure from poverty, which had been produced by their former detestable and arbitrary government and by their mad wars, occasioned not by the wishes of the people but by bad administration. The explosions of popular desperation and the misfortunes to individuals which the Friends of Humanity lament, were exclusively due to that execrable and wicked Government. ' Those insurrections are themselves the strongest proof of the necessity there was for the people to throw off their yoke and to break asunder the chains of tyranny. The change of government was an unparalleled example of public spirit to other enslaved nations on the Continent. The Revolution Society in London have, therefore, with heartfelt satisfaction rejoiced at this great event."

A further reason for our rejoicing was that it promised the continuance of peace between the two countries. ' Every observant person must have perceived how much this country was sinking at the time of the accursed American War, and also how rapidly it has been rising since. It is to the timely making of peace more than to any other cause or united causes that our present prosperity is to be ascribed." The unreliability of the Government had led France to be considered as a restless and perfidious neighbour ' not because individuals in France are more treacherously inclined than individuals in this country, CHAP, but because a government constituted as theirs could never VI-be relied on longer than from day to day. When that country was governed one hour by a mistress, and the next by any artful sycophant at Court, their administration could only be capricious. It appeared treacherous because it was versatile; and it was versatile because it was guided by intrigue. An absolute government is generally proud, captious, and quarrelsome. A despotic Minister is generally ambitious. Consequently we cannot wonder at the former empty projects of ambition of the Court of France. Whereas, since the Revolution, in that Kingdom there is far less danger of their making wars from motives of ambition. It is not for the interest of the people of France to go to war with Great Britain any more than it is for the interest of the people of this country to go to war with them. It is therefore to be expected that under their new form of government, in which the people have so much weight, the representatives of that people will neither dare nor be inclined to adopt a system of politics that would be evidently contrary to the interests of the majority and to their wishes also." Moreover the desire for the friendship of great Britain had been recently manifested in many parts of France. ' They consider the people of England as men who profess the same political truths with themselves, and who, in the last century, set them the glorious example which they follow at present. I trust that this favourable disposition of the patriots in France towards this country will not be in the least altered by any of the declamatory speeches you may ever make or by all the speculative pamphlets you can ever publish."

Stanhope then proceeds to defend the ' wicked persons ' who had shown a disposition to imitate the French spirit of reform, and quotes the resolution moved by Dr. Price at the London Tavern and transmitted to the National Assembly. ' This he cries, ' was that abominable resolution which those wicked persons voted, and which, as their Chairman for the day, I had the honour to sign. It is fit, Sir, that you should learn that the members of the Revolution Society are men who are friends to liberty, and that they are therefore firm friends to our free and excellent constitution. They meet to commemorate the passing of the Bill of Rights and the glorious Revolution, the true principles of which they will ever be ready to defend. They know that the rights of the illustrious family upon the throne are founded upon those sacred principles; and every Whig feels a warm constitutional attachment to that family,

CHAP, because their rights depend upon the people's rights, which they VI- were brought to this country to maintain. Nor has the Revolution Society ever shewn itself deficient in the respect due to his Majesty himself. No member of the Revolution Society was ever heard to say " the King had been hurled by Providence from his throne" because our gracious sovereign had the misfortune to labour, for a time, under bodily infirmity

Whether the French had gone too far in their constitutional changes could only be determined by those who had witnessed the events and knew the opinions of the French people. ' On those topics the Revolution Society pronounced nothing. But as Whigs they exulted over the demolition of the Bastille and the downfall of systematic tyranny. That Revolution has given a wholesome lesson to Tories and a salutary lesson to tyrants by teaching them that men by becoming soldiers cease not to be citizens, and that no length of oppression can ever eradicate from the human heart the immutable principles of natural justice. All warrantable political power is derived mediately or immediately from the people. The natural rights of the people are sacred and inalienable, rights of which despotism may rob them for a time, but which it is not in the power of tyranny to annihilate. We therefore commemorate with rapture the glorious era when the army of England nobly refused to overturn our free constitution, and we exult with Mr. Fox that the army of France last year followed that glorious example." Burke had described the Declaration of the Rights of Man as a Digest of Anarchy. In it, declared Stanhope, were contained the fundamental principles of a free government and the noblest assertions of the rights of men and citizens. ' I have read that Declaration often, but never without peculiar satisfaction, since it is superior in some respects even to our admirable Bill of Rights."

Turning to the complaint that the danger from France was no longer from intolerance but from atheism, he quotes two ' incomparable resolutions of the Assembly opening all political, civil, and military posts to non-Catholics. They have thereby united and consolidated their citizens, and set an example of wisdom and liberality worthy of the imitation of all their neighbours." In France they had abolished tithes; and so ought the English Parliament to do, ' substituting another mode for providing for the clergy, less vexatious, less detrimental to agriculture, more convenient for the clergy, and less injurious to the cause of religion." They had dissolved the monasteries, as we had done long ago. They had reduced the unreasonable revenues of the superior clergy and of the drones, while increasing the hard-earned stipends of the inferior clergy. ' If the information I have received be correct, five parts out of six of the whole clergy have been gainers by the late Revolution. Is this what you call atheism? I call it an act of justice, as well as a fine stroke of policy. The Revolution in France concludes the pamphlet, ' is one of the most memorable pages in history, and no political event was, perhaps, ever more pregnant with good consequences to future ages. That great and glorious Revolution will, in time, disseminate throughout Europe liberality of sentiment and a just regard for political, civil and religious liberty. It will, in all probability, make the world for centuries prosperous, free and happy, when the author of The Sublime and Beautiful shall be no more."

The ' Letter to Burke ' enjoyed remarkable success. Three English editions are known to have been printed, and a number of French translations quickly appeared. Two were printed at Paris in 1790; and in 1791 the pamphlet appeared under the title of ' Apologie de la Revolution francaise." The publisher's preface declares that the brilliant and rapid success of Priestley's ' Letters to Burke ' suggested that the French public would accept with equal eagerness Lord Stanhope's reply to the great enemy of the Revolution. ' My correspondents in England and elsewhere," he proceeds, ' have asked for it." In addition to the Paris editions, we possess a translation which appeared at Dijon in 1790. ' The author having sent a copy of his work to the Patriotic Club of Dijon, this society believes that a translation will be both interesting and useful." There can be no doubt that Stanhope sent copies to other cities, and it is not unlikely that other clubs and societies followed the example of Dijon by circulating this resounding testimonial to the wisdom and necessity of the Revolution.

On July 14, 1790, the first anniversary of the fall of the Bastille, upwards of 600 gentlemen met at the Crown and Anchor Tavern and partook of ' a most elegant dinner with excellent wines." Stanhope presided, and delivered ' a pointed speech." ' The French," he said, ' have even improved on our constitution, for they have not only civil but religious liberty. They had no laws to complain of such as disgraced our Statute-book. They did not restrain their women from going out of the kingdom lest they should be converted from their religion, nor had they a law by which their clergy by fasting and prayer were enabled to cast out devils. They had abolished tithes, and they had made a provision that no description of men should be driven from offices of trust because they had the bad or good fortune to differ from the Established Church." He concluded with the toast, ' To the extinction of all jealousy between France and England, and may they vie with each other in seeking to extend the benefits of peace, liberty, and virtue throughout the world." Dr. Price pronounced the French system of government ' a union between philosophy and politics." Sheridan then rose to move, ' That it be resolved that this meeting does most cordially rejoice in the establishment and confirmation of liberty in France, and that it beholds with peculiar satisfaction the sentiments of amity and goodwill which appear to pervade that country towards this." This resolution, records the Public Advertiser, was received by the most vehement acclamations of applause, which were damped only for a time by Home Tooke. '

They should," he said, ' mark the distinction between this Government and that of France. They had to build a ship from the keel. We had a ship with a sound bottom, but which had only gathered some concretions and wanted to be docked." Tooke was ' so interrupted from all sides of the room' that he was compelled to sit down. Whereupon Stanhope pointed out that he had misrepresented the resolution, which made no allusion whatever to the difference between the two systems, nor set up one for a model to the other.

The proceedings had opened as usual with ' short invocations made to the Supreme Being by Drs. Kippis and Towers," and a song composed for the occasion. All the gentlemen present wore cockades, and a stone from the Bastille decorated the table. Stanhope proposed seven toasts, and Sheridan gave ' Earl Stanhope," ' which was drunk with great joy." The rest of the evening, say the newspapers, was ' spent in the highest conviviality." 1 The resolutions of this meeting were sent to France, not, as the St. James's Chronicle ironically suggests, in one of Stanhope's new boats, but in the form of a letter to the Due de la Rochefoucauld. ' Sir wrote Stanhope, ' it is with extreme satisfaction that I have the honour to inform you that yesterday, July 14, we, to the number of 652 friends of liberty, celebrated your glorious Revolution and the establishment and confirmation of your free constitution. Mr. Sheridan proposed the enclosed resolution, which was received with !â l Public Advertiser, July 16, 1790; London Chronicle, July 13 and 14; Stephens, Life of Home Tooke, ii. 112; Life of Priestley, ii. 79; Camille Desmoulins, Revolutions de France et de Brabant, iii. 525-9.

repeated acclamations and with all the warmth which character- CHAP. ises free and independent men. May I ask you, on. behalf of VI. this assembly, to present it to the National Assembly of France? It is as their President of the day that I ask this favour. Soon we hope that men will cease to regard themselves under the odious aspect of tyrants and slaves, and that, following your example, they will look on each other as equals and learn to love one another as free men, friends, and brothers." The President read the letter, which was received by the Assembly with applause. Charles Lameth proposed that it should be printed and that the President should send a reply. A jarring note was struck by a member named Foucault. ' The sentiments of Lord Stanhope are shared by every friend of peace; but I do not think a private society can enter into correspondence with a National Assembly. Moreover, I do not believe that two nations unhappily rivals ' The speaker was not allowed to finish his sentence. When the uproar subsided, he remarked that it was prudence to be distrustful, and that the Club of 1789 should reply. The Assembly took no notice of Foucault, and ordered Stanhope's letter to be printed and answered. 1 The matter was considered of sufficient importance by the British ambassador to be reported. ' I take the liberty of informing your Grace wrote Earl Gower on July 23, ' that a letter of compliment was read from Lord Stanhope, as president of a society in London who call themselves Friends of the French Revolution, merely to shew what effect the reading of it had on the Assembly. Lameth moved that it should be printed, and also that the President should be ordered to write an answer to the society, and declared that in his opinion it might tend to the tranquillity of Europe. Another member opposed it, and whenever he spoke of the two nations as rivals, he was called to order with much clamour. Lameth's motion was carried." 2

The banquet and the resolutions brought a new crop of letters from France. On July 28, Treilhard, President of the National Assembly, wrote to Stanhope, on behalf of the Assembly, thanking him for the resolutions. ' It is fitting, my Lord, in a country in which liberty may be said to be naturalised that the French Revolution should be rightly judged. When shall we see that happy day in which governments will be distinguished only by their humanity and good faith? It is to men like you, my Lord, and to the worthy members of your Society that it is reserved to hasten this new revolution. Your benevolence will 1 Moniteur, v. 187.

Despatches of Lord Gower, 1790-2, ed. O. Browning, p. 18.

CHAP, then encircle the whole surface of the globe." Other letters VI. to Stanhope arrived from societies of the Friends of the Constitution in Cherbourg and many other cities. ' A Stanhope, a Fox wrote Toulouse, ' eulogising our laws to the English, what a triumph for the Revolution! ' That from Vire declared that the names of Stanhope, Price, and Sheridan were repeated with emotion in every part of France. Such was the zeal of the Reformers of Nantes that they dispatched M. Frangais, their President, and one of their members to London, with instructions to call on Lord Stanhope and ask permission to be presented to the Revolution Society, to which they would present a report of the Anglo-French fete given in that city on August 23. They were to remain in London long enough to cultivate the friendship of the sages who composed the Society. Frangais and his colleague were the guests of Lord Stanhope in Mansfield Street, and addressed the Committee on September 29 at the London Tavern. Universal brotherhood, they declared, was not a speculative dogma but had been reduced to practice. The Secretary wrote to thank the Society of Nantes for sending gentlemen of such merit and amiability.

While Stanhope's championship of the Revolution naturally excited the ardent gratitude of France, the more conservative of his countrymen watched his conduct with growing indignation. ' We are at peace at home, I thank God, pour le moment' wrote George Selwyn to Lady Carlisle on November 19, 1789. ' I hope that it will continue, and that no Lord Stanhope or Dr. Priestley will think a change of government will make us happier." 1 A week later Horace Walpole, now a trembling reactionary, wrote in stronger terms. ' The horrors make one abhor Lord Stanhope and his priestly firebrands, who would raise Presbyterian conflagrations here." 2 After reading Burke's 'Reflections," he remarks: ' Every page shews how sincerely he is in earnest. That cordiality, like a phial of spirits, will preserve his book when some of his doctrines have evaporated in fume. Lord Stanhope's were the ravings of a lunatic, imagining he could set the world on fire with phosphorus." 3 ' What say you to that mischievous lunatic, Lord Stanhope he wrote to Mary Berry on July 12, ' who is to celebrate the French Jubilee at the Crown and Anchor? ' 4 Five days later, when the fete was over, he wrote to the same fair correspondent: ' I go into Kent to-morrow; how you will envy me if I meet a detachment of poissardes on the road to Chevening to create Earl Stanhope no peer!" 5 He 1 MSS. of the Earl of Carlisle, p. 678. 2 Letters, xiv. 237.

thus described his journey: ' My journey delighted me; such CHAP, a face of plenty and beauty. All the farms and lodges so tight VI. and neat, and such rows of houses tacking themselves on to every town, that every five miles were an answer to Dr. Price and Lord Stanhope." x ' I must not pretend any longer, my dear Lord he wrote to the Earl of Strafford on August 12, ' that this region is devoid of news and diversions. Oh! we can innovate as well as neighbouring nations. If an Earl Stanhope, though he cannot be a tribune, is ambitious of being a plebeian, he may without a law be as vulgar as heart can wish; and though we have not a National Assembly to lay the axe to the root of nobility, the peerage have got a precedent for laying themselves in the kennel." 2 Walpole's detestation of the Jacobin Earl was widely shared. ' Hitherto," wrote Lord Auckland from the Hague to Grenville, on May 13, 1791, ' the French madness does not seem to make much progress in England, and the prosperity of our country will perhaps avert it; but the late debates in the House of Commons and the nonsense talked by Lord Lansdowne and Lord Stanhope are of a dangerous tendency." 3

In the summer of 1790 Stanhope withdrew from the Revolution Society. 'The stock of the National Assembly," wrote Horace Walpole gleefully, ' is fallen down to bankruptcy. Their only renegade aristocrat, Earl Stanhope, has scratched his name out of the Revolution Club." 4 The step is explained in the following letter to Cooper, the Secretary 5:â 'Mansfield Street: August 12, 1790.

' Sir,â I have received from you a printed paper containing resolutions said to have been passed at the General Meeting of the Revolution Society on July 20, by which it appears that members may be rendered responsible for resolutions of other members, though they may possibly not approve thereof. This appears to me so extremely improper that I judged it right to take my name yesterday out of the list of members. Having taken this step I think it proper to inform you, as their Secretary, of my reasons. I cannot, however, help expressing at the same time the very great esteem I shall always have for many worthy members of that Society. ' I am, Sir, ' Your most obedient, humble servant, ' STANHOPE."

1 Letters, xiv. 271. 2 Ibid., xiv. 282. 3 Fortescue MSS., ii. 73. 4 Letters, xiv. 313. 5 Chevening MSS.

CHAP. The resignation was due to no change in his political con- VI. victions, and was followed by no slackening in his activity. 1 Regarding Burke as the high priest of reaction, he lost no opportunity of striking at his principles and his influence; and about this time he discovered that one of his propositions infringed a statute. ' Lord Stanhope can hardly be serious in his design to impeach Mr. Burke of high treason wrote Priestley to his brother Minister, Lindsey, on N ovember 26, 1790; ' however, it will make the subject talked of." 2 The situation is explained in Priestley's ' Fourth Letter to Burke." The great Whig publicist had denied that the Revolution of 1688 gave England a right to elect her kings, asserting that if we had ever possessed the right, we then renounced it for ever. This was not the case, replied Priestley, referring his antagonist to the sixth of Anne, 'pointed out to Dr. Price by Lord Stanhope. From which it appears that your assertion is nothing less than high treason. The words of the Act are as follows: "If any person shall maintain that the Kings or Queens of this realm, with and by the authority of Parliament, are not able to make laws of sufficient validity to limit the Crown and the inheritance thereof, every such person shall be guilty of high treason." Far am I from wishing to bring you into any serious inconvenience by representing you as having offended against the laws of your country; but I wish it may serve as a hint to you to pay more attention to the great principles of our constitution." 3

Parliament met on November 26. The King's speech made no mention of the state of France, and there was no debate on the Address, except that Stanhope called attention to a work of Calonne, which he termed ' a libel on the French Revolution, a libel on justice and human reason, a libel on the majesty of the French nation." The late Minister had announced that if an attempt were made to effect a counter-revolution in France, such an attempt would be assisted by all the powers of Europe. This, he cried, was a libel on his Majesty of Great Britain, and it should be publicly repudiated. He pointed out that the pamphlet was much more dangerous in France than in England; 1 It was at this time that Mrs. Macaulay, famous for her democratic History of England, published anonymously her Observations on the Reflections of Edmund Burke on the Revolution in France, in a Letter to the Rt. Hon. the Earl of Stanhope. The pamphlet opens with a tribute to the position which Stanhope had won for himself. ' My Lord, your Lordship's character as a patriot, a philosopher, and the firm friend of the general rights of man, encourages me to present to you the following observations."

2 Rutt's Life of Priestley, ii, 97, 3 Works, xxii. 175, for there it was believed, and in consequence many British CHAP. residents and travellers experienced much inconvenience. He VI. concluded with a thrust at his old enemy, Lord Thurlow. ' The House of Lords should defend their Sovereign from those base imputations, particularly the noble and learned lord (the Chancellor) who, on a very serious occasion, had said he would never forget his King." No one supported the protest, and it was left to Mackintosh, in his masterly treatise, ' Vindiciae Gallicae," to refute Calonne's argument and assumptions. An exaggerated version of the debate was sent by Walpole to Agnes Berry. ' Earl Stanhope made a most frantic speech on the National Assembly and against Calonne's book, which he wanted to have taken up for high treason. He was every minute interrupted by loud bursts of laughter, which was all the answer he received or deserved. His suffragan Price has published a short, sneaking, equivocal answer to Burke." 1 But neither Price nor Stanhope allowed themselves to be deflected from their support of what seemed to them a holy cause by the sneers and misrepresentations of men with a less generous faith in humanity.

1 Letters, xiv, 326,

CHAPTER VII

THE RIGHTS OF JURIES, 1791-1792

CHAP. THOUGH the French Revolution claimed a large share of Stan-VII. hope's attention, he was not unmindful of his responsibilities nearer home. The following letters from Wyvill, his old associate in the cause of Parliamentary Reform, show how the Reformers outside Parliament looked up to him as their leader and spokesman. Wyvill was collecting material for the six precious volumes of documents and correspondence which enshrine the early history of the movement, and asked his friend for a copy of the papers of the Kent meeting of 1782, on which the important Yorkshire petition to Parliament was based.

' November 25, 1791, ' My dear Lord,â I think your Lordship will not dislike the use I shall make of some of these papers; nor, though I have unavoidably published several in which Mr. Burke is commended, will you have any reason to think, when my collection shall appear, that it has any tendency to revive the credit of that name. Be assured, my dear Lord, that though it has been my lot to remain in silent obscurity for so many years, my zeal in the public cause is as warm as ever; and that, feeling an entire confidence in the integrity and public spirit which govern your conduct in all your various enterprises for the good of the country, I have constantly wished your success with the most friendly zeal. I hope you enjoy your accustomed health and ability to bear fatigue, for which it seems not improbable that you will have great occasion at no very distant period. Thank God, by quiet and regularity I have rather improved than weakened my constitution; and should the time for exertion come soon, I shall not be afraid to wear every fibre of it out to promote the cause of liberty and benevolence.

' I am ever, my dear Lord, with great regard, ' Most sincerely yours, 'C. WYVILL."

A month later (December 24) he again wrote in reference CHAP, to the events of 1782, and concluded thus:â V H- ' I wish you all success in the prosecution of philosophical studies. Though it seems scarcely possible that a ship should be moved forward in opposition to wind and tide, yet the powers of machinery are very great and may afford you a means of effecting your purpose. I know you are accustomed to overcome great difficulties. I fear, however, the conclusion to be drawn from engaging in philosophical disquisitions of so much difficulty and abstruseness is that you see little prospect of doing good at this time in the political field.

' I am with great regard most truly and sincerely yours, 'C. WYVILL."

Wyvill was for once mistaken. Though his friend was grappling with the thorny problems of steam navigation, he had plenty of energy to spare for political work. Never, indeed, did he labour more assiduously in the public service than during the next three years. He took his duties as a peer in the trial of Warren Hastings very seriously, and did his utmost to secure fair play for the defendant. He also kept vigilant watch and ward over the Government's handling of the great drama. On May 16 a debate arose in the House of Lords in reference to the effect of a dissolution on the impeachment. 1 If an impeachment could be stopped by a dissolution, he pointed out, the remedy given to the people against the use of power would be destroyed. A Minister might at any moment screen himself or his instruments from public justice, when the hue and cry became too hot. A fortnight later 2 the case again came up in the form of a request that Parliament should not be prorogued till the trial was finished. Grenville's reply that such a demand would be an infringement of the royal prerogative brought Stanhope to his feet. The extraordinary doctrine laid down by his noble relative would not, he declared, permit him to remain silent. He would never hear with patience that Parliament had not a right to advise the King on the exercise of any of his prerogativesâ a doctrine of the most mischievous tendency, which ought no sooner to be heard than reprobated. His protest was echoed by Lans-downe, who expressed amazement at Grenville's doctrine, and added that if Ministers were allowed to use such arguments it was useless to meet, since all matters of importance could be connected with the royal prerogative.

1 Parl. Hist., xxix. 527-8. 2 Ibid., pp. 662-3,

CHAP. Stanhope was not sorry to have the opportunity of counter-VII. working Hastings's great antagonist on the neutral ground of Westminster Hall, and friction with Burke on the admissibility of evidence was not infrequent. When in May, 1792, Hastings's counsel produced a letter with extracts from other letters referred to therein, he supported the Lord Chancellor in ruling that they might be read, regardless of Burke's protest that there was no proof of them being the documents mentioned. Early in the following year he denounced the action of the Managers in prolonging the cross-examination as a scandal. A few weeks later he supported the admission of additional evidence for the defendant. On May 27 he interrupted Burke while cross-examining a witness on the opium contract, remarking that it was impossible to permit parole evidence of matters of fact recorded in the books of the Company, and that the books themselves ought to be produced. At this Burke flared up, and, before dealing with the objection, made a formal protest to the Court. ' On behalf of the Managers we demand of your Lordships that any censure of the Managers shall be the act of the House, to which, and not to any individuals of it, we are subject. Nothing can lead to more unpleasantness and disagreeable altercation with individual members than the kind of observation that is made by the noble Lord." In the following year he took part in the cross-examination of Cornwallis, questioning him on the efforts of the Governor-General to cope with the native coalition. On April 30 he brought before the House of Lords some words of Burke reflecting on the Judges. He moved that the shorthand writers be summoned to the bar to read their notes; but as other Peers had heard nothing derogatory to the Bench the motion was negatived without a division. When at length the end was reached in 1795, Stanhope had already withdrawn from all part or lot in the proceedings. ' The most noteworthy of the absentees from the verdict and the most regretted was Earl Stanhope. From the commencement till the end of May 1794 he had never been absent for an hour. He had taken notes of the evidence, and had always shewn candour and impartiality in dealing with the difficult questions arising. But, in consequence of the suspension of the Habeas Corpus Act, he declined further attendance on the ground that the Courts of Justice had lost their dignity." 1

The close of the Hastings trial, falling in the era of reaction, has led us to anticipate; but before that melancholy period 1 See Bond's prefaces to Speeches in the Trial of Warren Hastings, vols. iii. and iv.

was reached, Stanhope was privileged to take a leading share in CHAP. erecting one of the landmarks on the track of British liberty. y IL It was natural that Fox's Libel Bill should find an enthusiastic advocate in his old antagonist, and some of his most earnest speeches were delivered in its support. His motion for the second reading on June 8,1791, was met by the Lord Chancellor with the plea that the session was too far advanced to discuss such an important measure. He replied that its importance was an argument for its discussion, not for its postponement. It was their duty to protect the people from the arrogance and usurpation frequently shown by judges to juries in the directions they presumed to give them. He was censuring not the present judges, who thought it their duty to follow precedents, but those who had made them; though, were he a judge, he should not think himself bound to follow precedents which appeared to him unjust and profligate. Were they to have trial by jury or a jurisdiction as detestable as the Star Chamber? To confine the juror's duty to the fact of publication was to destroy trial by jury root and branch. There could be no libel without criminal intention, on which the jury must decide. This alone constituted a difference between free and despotic countries. When the Chancellor's dilatory motion was carried, Stanhope drew up one of the protests in which reforming Peers have often sought consolation in defeat. ' We hold it to be an inalienable right of the people that in cases of libel, as in all criminal cases, the jury should decide upon the whole matter that may constitute the guilt or innocence of the person accused, and we conceive that the said right of the people is of the utmost consequence to the freedom of the nation and to that bulwark of its rights, the liberty of the press." 1 The protest was also signed by Lord Radnor; and a somewhat similar declaration was drawn up by Fitzwilliam, Lauderdale, and Portland. Two days later the session of 1791 came to an end.

On March 20 in the following year the Bill was again brought before the House by Lord Fitzwilliam, and the chief speech in its support was contributed by Stanhope. 2 It was as plain as noonday that the Bill merely restored to juries the function with which the constitution had originally invested them. The constitution was founded on five clear and solid principles. The first was the civil liberty of the subject, his security as to his personal freedom and property. The second was the liberty of the press, which might be considered as the main pillar of 1 Parl. Hist. 9 xxix. 727-8. " Ibid. y pp. 1042-6,

CHAP, the constitutionâ the right of freely investigating every public VII. transaction. The third was the right of the people to arm in their own defence. Had this been observed we should have been spared the disgrace of 1780, ' and the more recent shame of July last in the infamous riots at Birmingham." The fourth was the principle of representation. The fifth was trial by jury. As the people were governed by laws of their own making, so they reserved to themselves the right of interpreting those laws; and this was precisely the function of the jury. So intimately were these principles connected that if one were touched the others were shaken. ' Invade the privilege of a jury, you silence the press, you silence the people; their arms drop to the ground, personal liberty and property take their flight together." Why should the judges attempt to filch from the jury the most important part of their jurisdiction? The press was like an alarm bell. A noble lord had complained that libels appeared almost daily against the constitution. ' I reply, Do justice and fear no libels." Where the constitution was free, no danger was to be apprehended. Every government rested on public opinion. He had seen the strongest of them collapse when that opinion was lost, and rightly so. He concluded his speech by an eloquent peroration. ' The law is above the judges. The constitution is above your Lordships. Justice is above us all."

On May 16 the debate on the motion to commit the Bill was opened by Lord Camden. Stanhope followed with an attack on Lord Kenyon, whose direction to the jury in the case of Stockdale had, he declared, been the immediate occasion of the Bill. 1 Defendants had the right to reject any juryman, and he regretted that judges also could not be challenged. He proceeded to quote what the reporter describes as ' an infinite variety of authorities," proving the power of juries to determine cases as a whole. He concluded a long speech by an eulogy of the constitution, properly understood and loyally maintained. 'We once had judges like Jefferies, that abominable monster, that bloody and brutal executioner, that murderer of Algernon Sydney. We have known tyrants on the throne, like Henry VIII, Charles I and II, James I and that English Tarquin, James II. If we are the most happy and prosperous people on the face of the globe, it is owing to that impregnable fortress, that stronghold of the constitution, Trial by Jury." Kenyon followed with a protest against the ' unprovoked attack' that had been made upon him, and denounced the harangue as 1 Pavl. Hist;, xxix. 1409-14, calculated to inflame the lowest dregs of the people and put CHAP, them out of humour with the administration of justice. But VI1-though Stanhope's speeches were couched in more forcible language than the Peers were accustomed to hear, the success of the Bill was in large measure due to his unwearying championship,

Not content with supporting the measure at every stage in the Legislature, he composed a substantial pamphlet in order to reach a wider audience. 1 ' The Rights of Juries defended and the objections to Mr. Fox's Libel Bill refuted ' 2 repeated the arguments and illustrations which he had employed in the House of Lords. Those invaluable rights of the people, he declares, Trial by Jury and the Liberty of the Press, had been in imminent danger, and it had been deemed necessary to secure them. The Act did not alter but confirm the law, by condemning an illegal species of direction to a jury. Juries were not so illiterate or incompetent as their enemies had been pleased to suggest; and a long array of witnesses, including Blackstone, is cited on behalf of their rights and authority. ' If we are still a free nation," concludes the pamphleteer, ' if the kingdom is the richest and most prosperous in Europe, we owe it to that stronghold, the impregnable Gibraltar of the English Constitution, Trial by Jury. This is that invaluable bulwark of liberty which Parliament has lately protected, and will I trust ever continue to protect. At least I shall consider it as one of my most essential duties to defend it steadily to the last hour of my life." We might be listening to the fervent accents of Erskine.

Stanhope sent copies of the work or a notification of its appearance to many of his personal and political friends, and received a number of hearty congratulations on his achievement. Among the first to write was his old patron, Lord Lansdowne.

' Bowood Park: September 24, 1792.

' My dear Lord,â I deferred acknowledging your letter till I received your book which I sent for to town. I have now read it, and must thank you for both. I make no doubt but the public and posterity will do the same. I was under no anxiety 1 In answer to an inquiry about Bentham's views, Dumont wrote (in French) from Lansdowne House on June 29: ' My Lord, Mr. Bentham has not published his views on Juries, and I have only gathered them in conversation. It is his opinion on the Circuits that he has printed in a work on judiciary organisation, which he addressed to the Constitutional Committee of the National Assembly." Dumont then proceeds to summarise his objections to the Circuit system.

2 By Charles, Earl Stanhope, F. R. S., and of the Society of Arts, and Member of the American Philosophical Society at Philadelphia. 1792.

CHAP, except as to the legal part, as there were some points which the VII. lawyers on both sides seemed to agree in thinking you had misconceived. I look upon the law to be the worst of all the professions, far more unprincipled than any army and more corrupt even than the Church; and as you have abilities, which few men have, to watch and to expose them, I think it a pity that you should ever give them the least advantage.

But, after what you say, I am persuaded that you stand throughout secure as to your legal ground, and as to every other there cannot be a doubt that you are invulnerable. I am very sorry for what has lately passed in France, as no good can come of it. I beg to offer my respects to Lady Stanhope and to be remembered to all your Lordship's family.

' I am, my dear Lord, most cordially yours, ' LANSDOWNE."

Wyvill wrote with his usual warmth from Hartlepool.

' October 16, 1792.

' My dear Lord,â At this place I have very lately received from your bookseller a copy of your excellent pamphlet, which I lost no time to read. I thank your Lordship for it most cordially, as a publication which defends in a manner that is completely satisfactory that part of our constitution which is perhaps the most important, and the only part which exists as perfect in practice as it appears in theory. I wish your Lordship's book were in the hands of every juryman in England, for as long as they are not ignorant of their rights they cannot lose them. I think it not improbable that the Court may wish to join the confederacy against the liberties of France. It would evidently be a more objectionable measure than the American War,â more foolish, more unjust, and more contrary to the general sense of the nation, and it would be, I think, the direct road to that revolution which the Court wishes to avoid. The nation, I am persuaded, would not submit to it; and the Ministers are too well acquainted with the discontents of the country to venture upon any breach of their promised neutrality. I wish, however, to have early information of any steps taken with a view to bring on hostilities, as you may be assured that this part of the country would give every possible regular opposition.

1 I am, my dear Lord, most cordially yours, ' C. WYVILL."

Joseph Towers, the friend and coadjutor of Price, sent congratulations from Clerkenwell.

' St. John's Square: October 30, 1792. CHAP. ' My Lord,â I trouble your Lordship with a few lines to return my thanks for the obliging present of your very spirited and satisfactory defence of the Rights of Juries. I have so long been convinced of the importance of the subject that I have had the honour to be a fellow labourer in the same cause in more than one publication. I wish your Lordship a continuance of health to prosecute your laudable Parliamentary efforts for the benefit of the public, in a House in which the interests of the people are certainly not too much considered."

Congratulations also arrived from Watson, Bishop of Llandaff, the only Liberal member of the episcopal bench.

' November 23, 1792.

' My dear Lord,â Allow me to return you a thousand thanks, and you deserve the thanks of your country, for your excellent tract on the Rights of Juries, which I have received and read with the greatest pleasure. While the House of Peers has in it men of talents, of independence and of liberal notions with respect to the rights of their fellow-citizens, every moderate man will contribute to its preservation. May your Lordship's example have more followers in the next age than it has in the present. 1

During the same session a forward step was taken in a cause which was not less dear to Stanhope's heart. On April 2 Wilberforce proposed and carried a motion for the gradual abolition of the slave trade, after a debate in which Pitt delivered perhaps the greatest of his speeches. Stanhope communicated the glad tidings to Condorcet in a letter of lyrical enthusiasm, which was at once reproduced in the Moniteur. 1 No one could foresee how many years were to elapse or how many obstacles needed to be overcome before the will of the House of Commons was translated into legislation.

' London: April 3, 1792.

' It is with extreme pleasure that I inform you that the House of Commons, where I have passed the whole night, has just decreed the abolition of the slave trade. The friends of the natives, with Fox, Pitt, and Wilberforce at their head, pressed for immediate abolition j but they lost the motion by 193 to 125, and the Chamber has postponed the fixing of the date.

1 XII. 89. April IT, 1792. My translation.

CHAP. But the vital point,â that the trade shall be abolished,â has VII. been carried by a very large majority. You will not fail in France, I hope, to follow the lead of Denmark and England, and you will shew thereby that you deserve to be free yourselves. The glorious moment is at hand when philosophy and justice will everywhere ensure the triumph of justice, and when the friends of the rights of man will destroy every abuse and every tyranny. Be good enough to send this letter to my respected friend M. la Rochefoucauld, and ask him to forward it to the worthy M. Petion. There have been about 500 petitions against the slave trade

On the following day he wrote to Dundas, exhorting him to follow up the victory:â

' April 4, 1792.

' Dear Sir,â I congratulate you on your division against the Slavers. When you draw up your ideas in writing, I hope you will attend to the following circumstances.

' i. That the grandchildren of negroes should be as free as white men from the time of their birth and not apprentices.

' 2. That your idea of gradual abolition be confined to the negroes for our own islands; but that the abolition be immediate as far as it relates to the French, Spanish, and other foreign dominions. There is not the shadow of a pretence for gradual abolition in these cases.

'3. No master should be the person to punish his slaves, but all punishments should be inflicted by the law only. They should also be permitted to give evidence, without which they can never be under the protection of the law.

1 4. To do what the French have now done, namely, to put all people of colour and all free blacks exactly on the same footing as white people.

' Believe me ever, with great respect, sincerely yours, ' STANHOPE."

It was even more the triumph of Granville Sharp and Clark-son, who had inaugurated the anti-slave trade movement in the country, than of Wilberforce, who joined it later. Among Stanhope's papers there is nothing more curious than a letter of portentous length from Clarkson, dated August 28, 1793, asking advice as to whether he should retire from the movement to which he had devoted himself without respite for seven years, and in which he had spent Â 1500 and ruined his health. ' I shall take the liberty of waiting on your Lordship in December,"

he concludes, ' to ask you the result of your deliberation on the CHAP, question, How far ought I or ought I not to go into retirement VII. at Christmas, and how far would the world have any just reason to censure me for such conduct? I feel the strongest bias to be guided by the majority of the opinions I solicit There can be no doubt into which scale Stanhope's influence was cast, and Clarkson, though compelled by ill-health to withdraw for some years, returned to the fighting line as soon as he was able. The causes to which Stanhope dedicated himself in early manhood he pursued unfalteringly to the end; and it was his constant endeavour to inspire others with the same loyalty. He was soon to prove that neither the anger of his brother Peers nor the fury of the multitude could avail to turn him from the path which conscience and patriotism appeared to mark out for him in the crisis of his country's fate.

CHAP. STANHOPE'S interest in the mighty drama of the Revolution was VIII. intensified by the personal relations in which he stood to some of the principal actors. He had made the acquaintance of the leaders of thought during his sojourn in Paris in 1774, and his powerful championship of French principles in 1789 brought a large number of visitors and a still larger number of letters to his door. 1

Among these friendships the most intimate and the most cherished was that of Condorcet. Both were aristocrats by birth and democrats by conviction; both were at once scholars and men of action. On July 3,1791, Stanhope wrote to his friend a memorable letter in reference to the finances of France. ' Such is my disquietude for the most admirable of revolutions and such my desire for you to avoid all that may injure it that I feel obliged to indicate to you a means of guarding yourselves against a mortal blow. I refer to the fabrication of false assignats. I need not remind you of the terrible evils that would arise if large numbers found their way into circulation. This danger must be avoided, while retaining the immense advantages of assignats. The larger the number of assignats in circulation, the greater the danger of false issues." He then proceeds to describe the system by which British Consols are transferable by a stroke of the pen at the Bank of England. ' My advice, therefore, is that you should establish banks at Paris (and perhaps elsewhere, in daily communication with the capital) where every owner of 1 It is almost certain that Danton met Stanhope during his short visit to England in 1791; but no decisive evidence has been discovered. See Robinet, Danton Â migr6, p. 29.

THE OUTBREAK OF THE GREAT WAR, 1792-1795 in assignats may deposit them for the sum mentioned on the face CHAP, in the books kept by authority of the Assembly. The notifi- VIII. cation of the sum thus deposited would be better than assignats, as it would not be liable to be stolen or destroyed, and could be subdivided at will. You could thus reduce the assignats in circulation. This would save you from the only considerable, or at least the most imminent, danger of your actual position, almost without expense within three weeks. Think of the hopes among the friends of the old despotism inspired by the thought of false assignats." All payments on a considerable scale, whether between individuals or from the State, would be made by simple transfer in the books. ' Do this and you will destroy the hopes of your foes. They will not again be able to lift their heads, and you will kill with their own rage all these enemies, aristocratic or sacerdotal, of the most magnificent revolution recorded in history." Four days later he wrote a second and shorter letter, adding that the Bank of Amsterdam employed the system which he had recommended.

These letters, written in faultless French, were promptly published in pamphlet form at Paris. 1 Condorcet welcomed the idea of depositing assignats in public banks and drawing cheques upon the amount; for he was well aware of the critical nature of the situation. He repeatedly declared in the Assembly that finance was the danger, and that far too much paper-money was in circulation. But he failed to persuade his colleagues to undertake far-reaching reforms on the eve of war; and when the struggle began the possibility of amendment had vanished. 2 The friends continued to correspond, and in his will, drawn up in March 1794 under the shadow of death, the philosopher advised his daughter, in case of necessity, to seek refuge with Stanhope or Daer in England, or with Franklin's grandson or Jefferson in America. 3

Next to Condorcet Stanhope's most intimate friend in France was the Due de la Rochefoucauld; and the following letter of the Duke is a further proof that his sympathy took the wise form of friendly counsel and criticism.

' January 14, 1792.

' I recognise in your two letters of December 18 and 22 your unchanging support for the cause of liberty and humanity. On this double ground the French Revolution has aroused and deserved 1 Lettres de Milord Stanhope M. de Condorcet. Paris, 1791.

2 Cahen, Condorcet et la Revolution Francaise, pp. 306-15.

CHAP, your interest. You have followed its progress, and, if you have VIII. blamed some of the faults of the Assembly, its work as a whole has met with your approbation. You have been above all struck by the evils which religious intolerance might bring in its train; for, though our Assembly has not adopted that principle, it has been led away by the belief that it was thereby serving the cause of liberty. You have feared a regrettable fermentation, and have sought for means to appease it. You will soon hear all the details you can desire on this and many other subjects from Talleyrand, the bearer of this letter, who is anxious to make your acquaintance. He is a man whose talents have been of the greatest value to the Revolution. You will find him penetrated with the great truth, with which you are familiar, that the interests of England and France are not antagonistic, and that, at the moment when the policy of courts is giving way to the policy of nations, the two peoples will ally and by their alliance secure the peace of the world. M. Talleyrand will be a very suitable instrument of such negotiations if your Ministry is disposed to entertain the idea, and doubtless you would assist in such a good work if you believed it could be effectual. Many people here begin to believe it is not impossible."

A third correspondent was M. Fran9ais, who had been dispatched to London in 1790 by the Reformers of Nantes and had been warmly welcomed by Stanhope.

' February 23, 1792.

' My Lord,â I hope you received the reply I addressed to Sevenoaks. I have no doubt that our enemies greatly exaggerate the embarrassment of our position in order to thwart the propositions of our envoys to your Cabinet. The French nation is at the moment passing through a crisis â but such is the vigour of the sick man that I am sure that the first cannon shot will give him prodigious energy and unite all his limbs in a common effort. The people is exalted to such an altitude and is so penetrated with the dignity of its new existence that no human effort can force it back. We have at least a million soldiers. Our national property amounts to over three milliards, and practically covers our debt. The arrears in the recovery of taxation arise from the over complicated system adopted by the Constituent Assembly, and from the necessity of forming a new survey of the land. But where this has been done the taxes are paid, and amount to at least one third more than under the ancien 1 Stanhope Miscellanies, vol. ii.

regime. Our commerce, absolutely paralysed by the subversion CHAP, of our colonies, will revive directly the whites and the natives VIII. are reconciled. Finally, our troubles are merely momentary. They are the effect of the greatest political shock any nation has ever undergone; but the advantages will be durable, and they rest on the evident interest of nineteen-twentieths of the nation. Our general conviction is that it is better to die than to retreat; and the National Assembly will set the example. Be so good, my Lord, as to sustain the honour of our nation against its detractors, who judge us by your ministerial papers, which paint as cannibals the people who, surrounded by dangers and in the middle of the rage of its enemies, shews itself the most gentle in Europe."

To this letter Stanhope replied at immense length.

' London: March 6, 1792, ' Sir,â I was delighted to receive your letter of February 23. Nothing can give me greater pleasure than good news of your great and admirable revolution, and I shall always feel grateful to those who send it. I also received your earlier letter, and I am glad that my ideas on the priests have deserved the approbation of some of the most respected members of your worthy Assembly. Mr. Paine and some other writers have foolishly suggested that the success of your revolution would be the fall of our constitution, and have thereby created many enemies for you. I believe their notion to be without foundation, seeing that we are already free, and that England is now the richest, the most prosperous andâ climate apartâ the happiest country in Europe. Unlike Mr. Paine I explained that your revolution, followed by an alliance between France and England, would assure peace, augment our prosperity, and thus increase our content and tend to preserve our constitution. Indeed, it would be endangered if the old and absurd system of war was revived, and still more if a government was established in France under Austrian, Russian or other foreign auspices. I spoke of the desire of the friends of your new constitution to be united with the English, and said that an alliance would assure prosperity to both for centuries. This speech was received with loud applause in different parts of the Chamber. In spite of every obstacle, I hope to see our two nations one day united by indissoluble bonds, and I shall not cease to work towards that end.

' I notice that a member of the Assembly has proposed a national establishment for the deposit of assignats, and also of

CHAP, cash, specie and precious stones. The latter does not appear VIII. to me wise. Be good enough to remind him and M. Condorcet of the danger of thus creating a great temptation to the populace in a moment of crisis to attack and pillage the building. In my letter to M. Condorcet I proposed that only books should be stored there. There would be no harm, however, in keeping assignats, since they could be destroyed by fire or by some chemical means before the insurgents could seize them.

' Allow me to return once more to the nonjuring priests. No man in any country can respect or admire more than I the greater part of the astonishing achievements of the Constituent Assembly. What tyrannies have they not overthrown, in such a brief space and with such slender means! And what truths have they not proclaimed! They did almost everything for the establishment of a free constitution when they armed the patriots and enlightened the people on their rights and on the true interests of their country. In speaking of an Assembly which has deserved so well of France and of the world, allow me, however, to say that it has committed a serious fault which, however, can and should be corrected by its successor. Religious intolerance was not one of the principles of the Constituent, but, on the contrary, quite foreign to it; and if it has been adopted once and failed, the error should be corrected without delay, and a return made with confidence and certainty to the fundamental rules of justice. I have maintained in Parliament and will maintain everywhere the two following propositions, which are applicable to every country.

' i. That no Assembly can have any authority but that which flows from the nation which it represents.

' 2. That no nation, even acting directly, has the right to coerce its members except in respect to the purely civil and political objects which form part of the Social Contract. Thus no nation has the right to demand from any individual any act regarding religion contrary to his conscience. Japan and China are not more outside the limit of European jurisdiction than conscience in matters of faith is outside the jurisdiction of governments. At the end of the eighteenth century it is too late to doubt a truth so evident. Yet the Constituent decreed that the priests should swear to maintain the constitution, though there are things in it which affect their belief and to which, however absurdly, they object. Why should there be such an oath for priests? In my eyes it is sovereign folly. Happily the said decree is not part of the constitution, and I am delighted to learn that some influential nonjuring priests at Paris CHAP, have expressed their willingness to swear to obey it,â a passive VIII. obligation, instead of to maintain it,â an active one. If this is so, you should not hesitate to alter the oath. You have in your Assembly such men as M. Condorcet. Why not consult a dozen of them? The Veto has paralysed your decrees on the priests, but it would not touch the alteration I propose. The great advantage would be that you could thus distinguish the good priests who are only bigots from the bad, aristocratic malcontents who only employ religion as a mask to impose on the people. I tremble to think of the massacres which will occur in your ignorant parishes if you have war,â massacres of which the reason or the pretext will be religion.

' Begin by observing the most scrupulous justice. Take from the priests the right to register births, deaths and marriages. Separate religion from your political disputes, and then you will be able to act firmly against all the disturbers of the public peace. If you are the philosophers we believe you to be, you must know that a free constitution is never so strong as when civil liberty is separated from theological disputes. Your wish, like mine, is to strengthen your liberty. I must therefore tell you the truth freely, for it is only in so doing that I can shew the respect I feel for you.

' STANHOPE."

A further letter from Frangais concludes the correspondence that has been preserved. 1 ' April 3, 1792.

' I must thank you for the excellent treatise of Mackintosh, which has just been translated. I have read with much pleasure the second part of Paine's ' Rights of Man." Apart from his republicanism and his mistake in not allowing for the difference between the Americans and the French, I cannot help considering him one of the first geniuses of Europe. I have read with equal pleasure, in the Morning Chronicle, your opinions in the Upper House. We are convinced that, despite the intrigues of Courts, the force of things and the similarity of sentiments will one day secure the union of our peoples. We cannot understand in France how your Parliament can be so indulgent to the Ministers. Zeal for our Revolution has never been more marked nor more constant than to-day. Man feels his dignity, and you would be 1 These letters were printed by the fifth Earl in Stanhope Miscellanies, vol. ii.

CHAP, surprised to hear people of humble birth speak at the tribune VIII. with the pride and eloquence of Livy's Romans."

Stanhope was always ready to show kindness to French reformers, old or young, famous or obscure. In May 1792 Madame Jullien, a cultured bourgeoise who ardently supported the Revolution, informed her husband in the provinces that their eldest son, aged seventeen, on going to London to finish his education, had received letters of introduction from Petion, Dumouriez, Condorcet, and others 1 to such men as Dr. Priestley and Lord Stanhope, Talleyrand and Chauvelin. ' Jules did not see Lord Stanhope when he called on him in London she wrote. ' My Lord asked for his address and went to see him at M. de Meuse's; but Jules was not at home. Lord Stanhope politely asked Madame de Meuse to beg the young foreigner to come to his house. They talked French together for two hours, and the philosophic Peer overwhelmed the poor child with attentions. We French ladies were rather surprised at the terseness of his note, "I dine at home on Wednesdays"; but our Anglo-French friends assure us that it is a frank and cordial invitation." The lad quickly discovered that friendly faces were the exception. ' Our revolution is not liked in London reports Madame Jullien to her husband. ' The Court detests it, and the people are jealous of it, while the selfish party in the nation is afraid of its epidemic effects. The neutrality that has been observed is a political miracle that has been secured by a sacred league. Lord Stanhope has given him some hints, and it is only by exercising the greatest prudence that our young patriot is safe in England. He never goes to the club, and the French cafes are full of government spies ' I am filled with admiration of Lord Stanhope she wrote to her son. ' All you tell me of that great man proves to me that he is after your own heart. Try to cultivate his friendship; it is among such men as he that you should seek for your models A few days later she returned to the theme. ' I like your Lord Stanhope, and I advise you to cultivate to the utmost so valuable an acquaintance. Do not fail to present your mother's respects to him and to express the gratitude he has awakened in a maternal heart, deeply sensible of the kind interest he takes in you and full of profound veneration for his virtues The young man's letters are not preserved; but we gather that despite the kindness of distinguished friends he found the atmosphere somewhat chilly and was glad to return to his home.

1 The Great French Revolution narrated in the Letters of Madame Jullien, pp. 76-136.

On February 27, 1792, Stanhope expatiated in the House of Lords on the virtues of the British Constitution, and emphasised the necessity for friendly relations with France. He was not one of those, he declared, who held the mad and detestable doctrines of some wild enthusiasts who were for pulling down the constitution and building it up anew. It was not perhaps so entirely perfect as the mind of man could make it, but it was all that reasonable beings could expect or desire. All that was excellent in the French constitution had been copied from ours. France, he had the happiness to know, had for a long time felt a growing attachment to this country, and the name of Englishman had become popular. It was the undoubted policy of this country to cultivate her friendship. United with her we could preserve the balance of Europe and awe neighbouring states from projects of aggrandisement and ambition. Great Britain and France had too long considered themselves as natural enemies. It was on a continuance of peace that the increasing prosperity of the country depended. He spoke as an independent man, under the banner of no party. 1

Two months after this speech the situation suddenly changed for the worse. On April 20 France inaugurated the Great War by a declaration of hostilities against Austria, and the question of British intervention began to be agitated. While Burke and the extreme anti-Jacobins thirsted for a crusade against the Revolution, Pitt was in favour of standing aloof, though the rise to power of the bellicose Girondins rendered neutrality more difficult. Stanhope grasped the danger as early as any one, and devoted his whole energies to avert what appeared to him the unspeakable shame of taking arms against the Revolution. To keep the peace with England was also the desire of the cooler heads in France, and it was the object of Talleyrand's mission to London in 1792. ' I must inform you of all my own ideas and of those of men well disposed to our country wrote Talleyrand to Delessart on March 4. 2 'Here is one of the latter class, which belongs to Milord Stanhope and appears to M. Duroveray to have some value. They both know how the King is personally prejudiced against our Revolution; but they think that a very good way of bringing him nearer to us would be for the King to write to him as a friend and to suggest that an entente would 1 Park Hist., xxix. 901-3, - Pallain, La Mission de Talleyrand d, Londres en 1792, pp. 146-7,

be agreeable to himself personally and useful for both. The letter could be written with cordiality. If the King's mind could thus be influenced my task here would be three-quarters accomplished." Acting on this advice Dumouriez obtained a confidential letter from Louis XVI to George III, 1 thanking his royal brother for not joining the coalition against France, and declaring that the traces of the enmity between the two countries were disappearing day by day. ' It is the duty of two Kings who have signalised their reign by a continual desire for the happiness of their peoples to form bonds which would become more permanent as the interest of the two nations becomes more obvious. United we ought to assure the peace of Europe." But Louis XVI was no longer master in his own house, and all the world knew it. The following remarkable letter, written many years later to Major Cartwright, throws further light on Stanhope's relations with Talleyrand. 2 ' Berner's Street: January 3, 1809.

' Dear Sir,â You desire my testimony on an important subject, and you have a right to it. After the French Revolution and previously to the first war between France and Austria, I remember expressing my regret to M. Talleyrand that two such great and enlightened nations should cut each others' throats for such small objects as those which were then the ostensible pretexts for hostility. He expressed with great warmth and eloquence-how totally he coincided with me upon the folly and immorality of unnecessary wars; and he said that the French nation wished to avoid a war with Austria as much as he did. He assured me that the French nation had so high a respect for the English nation, as the only free nation in Europe except France, that the new Government in France would willingly leave to the King of Great Britain, or to any Commissioner he should be pleased to appoint, the settling the points then in dispute between France and Austria. I felt, I must confess, great pride and pleasure, as an Englishman, at this idea of a reference to the first magistrate of my country as a free country, so honourable to us in that respect, so handsome on the part of the friends of liberty in France, and, by preserving peace in Europe, so beneficial to humanity. I asked M. Talleyrand whether it was their intention to propose to our Government such an arbitration. He told me, if they were sure it would be accepted by our Government, the offer would be made formally; but that they

1 Pallain, La Mission de Talleyrand a Londres en 1792, pp. 215-19.- Cartwright, Reasons for Reformation, pp. 17-18, did not think it right to make such an offer if they were not CHAP, certain it would be accepted here. He then said that, as I had VIII. several near relations in the British Cabinet, he should be much obliged to me to endeavour to find it out. I replied that I would do it with great pleasure. I went to Lord Grenville, though I did not obtain any satisfactory answer. He told me generally that he was only one, and that he must consult others. I then went to my brother-in-law, Mr. Pitt. I made a full communication of what had passed between M. Talleyrand and myself, and I expressed the high satisfaction I felt at my having it in my power to give him such pleasing information. Mr. Pitt, without a moment's hesitation, rejected the idea totally. I urged with great earnestness every argument which occurred to me in favour of the proposal, but wholly without effect. I received his answer with sensations more painful than I have any words to express. 1 Believe me, dear Sir, most sincerely yours, ' STANHOPE."

The storming of the Tuileries on August 10 and the fall of the Monarchy rendered the relations of England and France still more strained; and the problem of saving the Royal Family occupied the thoughts of all parties. The method adopted by the Bishop of Llandaff was to implore Stanhope to approach his friends in Paris. ' Soon after the dissolution of the Constituent Assembly wrote Bishop Watson in his Autobiography, 1 ' I dined at Lord Stanhope's (it was the only time I ever had the honour) in company with the Bishop of Autun and several other principal Frenchmen who had been members of that Assembly. Having witnessed the respect with which Lord Stanhope treated these gentlemen and with which he was treated by them, I was induced to write the following letter to him in the autumn of 1792 after the king of France had been committed to the Temple. I had no great expectation of success attending the application of an individual buried in the wilds of Westmoreland; yet I was determined to make an effort to prevent that horrid butchery of the Royal Family which afterwards took place.

' " My Lord,â Your opinion will have great weight with the National Assembly. I wish you could persuade them to do an act which would throw a veil over the late brutality of their populace, establish their new Republic on a solid foundation, and transmit their names with immortal honour to posterity. Instead of bringing their King to trial, let them give him his

CHAP, liberty, assign him one of his palaces, settle on him and his VIII. posterity Â 100,000 a year, subject to forfeiture on any act of treason against the Republic. Such an act of magnanimity, justice and humanity would conciliate the minds of all men to what appears to me an axiom, that the majority of every nation has at all times a right to change their civil government." Whether Lord Stanhope ever troubled himself to suggest this hint to any of the National Assembly adds the Bishop, ' I know not. His answer to me was that new discoveries of the treachery, perfidy and duplicity of Louis XVI had within these few days rendered the resentment against him more violent."

While Watson was imploring him to exert his influence at Paris to save the King, an Englishman named Stephen Sayre, who had become a French citizen and was now a trusted agent of the French Government, was exhorting him to intercede with Pitt in London to avert a war. 1 ' Paris: October 28, 1792.

' My Lord,â I was ordered to return here a few days after I had received your note. It was my wish to have had an interview when I should have explained my motives and my objects. They were such as ought not to have been trusted to paper. My visit was ostensibly to purchase arms for this nation. I have done so, to the number of about 10,000. I had other matters of much higher import; but the moment was unfavourable, for just as I reached London the news of the massacres came also. This is now a great and powerful nation, a more formidable Republic than the Romans at any period. The object of this letter is to request your Lordship, if you have no particular objections, to take the trouble of sounding Mr. Pitt or my Lord Grenville as to their disposition towards this country. They have refused to communicate with the present Government; they may not at this moment, perhaps, be persuaded to send back their Minister or another; but I wish to know whether they would have any objection to a cool and friendly deliberation with me. My visits will give no suspicion or offence; if no good should arise out of it, no injury can be done. I will answer for this Government that they would meet you on the most friendly ground; but they are not to be intimidated. Let me request you, my Lord, as a friend to mankind to take the trouble of visiting the Minister or the Secretary of State, and let me know if he 1 Alger (Englishmen in the French Revolution, p. 99) mentions Sayre or Sayer as a member of an English club in Paris.

will hear me. I have more to offer than he may suppose; CHAP, a private interview may lead to public arrangements, peace VIII. and happiness.

' I am with great respect, yours, ' STEPHEN SAYRE."

A fortnight later Sayre made an alternative proposal:â ' Paris: November 12 (1792), (First year of the Republic.) ' My Lord,â I wish your Lordship could come over here for some ten or twenty days, after seeing the proper people; I cannot venture to write upon the matter to be thought of and considered. If you do resolve to come, please to give me notice. I have a part of White's Hotelâ his first floor is yet unoccupied. As I wish to see you often without appearing to do so, let me engage the apartments for you. You will be well received here by all the leading characters, you will return with accurate information, may meet Parliament with advantage and confidence, and render service to the world.

' STEPHEN SAYRE."

The suggestion of a visit to Paris was attractive; but Stanhope felt that he could be more useful at home. The following letters to Wyvill show how the dread of a war with France came to submerge for the time every other emotion. 1 To cry for Parliamentary reform seemed futile at a moment when every nerve had to be strained to prevent the consummation of a colossal crime.

' Chevening: September 18,1792.

' Dear Mr. Wyvill,â In consequence of what you tell me in your last respecting the idea of calling a meeting this winter in Yorkshire upon the subject of Parliamentary Reform, I think it right to tell you frankly my opinion about it, having invariably been a warm friend to that measure. The French Revolution has frightened some weak minds, Mr. Paine's works others. And the late events in France have intimidated many. However despicable such feelings may be, abstractly considered, yet, when they are pretty general, they must be treated with some respect. I am clear that no attempt at present for a Parliamentary Reform can produce any good, but, on the contrary, shews weakness in the end. Consult your friends about

CHAP, the idea of eventually petitioning the King and Parliament VIII. against war, should any Ministers be mad enough to involve this country in a war against the liberties of France. I hope we shall keep at peace. But the very thought of a war so impolitic, so rash and unjust fills the mind with horror, and the friends of liberty should endeavour to prevent it.

1 Ever most cordially and sincerely yours, ' STANHOPE."

' Chevening: October 21, 1792.

' Dear Sir,â I am happy to hear from you that a war against the liberties of France would be received with such marked disapprobation in your part of the country. The late signal successes of that nation will, I trust, prevent it from happening. Other motives will, no doubt, co-operate strongly to prevent it, but let us be upon the watch.

' Sincerely and truly yours, ' STANHOPE."

' Chevening: December 30, 1792.

' You would do me a great favour if you would have the goodness to inform me soon what you have lately found to be the opinions of persons of different descriptions in your county with respect to a war with France. To me it appears that it would be madness. I wish you many happy new years, and as many as your upright conduct makes you deserve.

' With great esteem, dear Sir, ever cordially yours, ' STANHOPE."

On January 10 Wyvill wrote that war if it took place would be more generally odious than that with America at its commencement, and would excite much more dangerous discontents in its progress. He added that Wilberforce deprecated war as much as his correspondent, who replied by return of post.

' Chevening: January 13, 1793.

' Dear Mr. Wyvill,â I canot delay a moment returning you my most hearty thanks for the important information it contains. Let us wait to see what ministers do. After that, as you have had the infinite merit to stop one ruinous war, you may be able to stop another.

' I am ever, my dear Sir, ' Most affectionately and cordially yours, ' STANHOPE."

When the new session opened in December, Stanhope pursued CHAP, his efforts for peace in the House of Lords; but his speech VIII. on the Address was little calculated to serve the cause which he had at heart. He once more eulogised the British Constitution as excelling all others, ancient and modern, and rendering revolutions unnecessary. 1 In early life, he added, he had pursued philosophical researches and been introduced to the most learned men on the Continent. Among others he had contracted an intimacy with M. Condorcet, whose reputation he wished to rescue from the aspersions thrown out against him. He then read a letter from the philosopher, declaring that it was the height of folly for the English to attempt to subvert their Constitution, which embodied the wisdom of the ages. As a citizen of the world and a friend to mankind, concluded the speaker, he expressed the most heartfelt satisfaction that the officious interference of the confederacy against the liberty of France had been frustrated. That monster, the Duke of Brunswick, merited the execrations of every man of feeling for publishing a manifesto of his intention to put half a million of his fellow-creatures to the sword. Had he realised this pious resolution, it would have exceeded the wanton ferocity of Nero and Caligula. The massacres in Paris were the result of this declaration.

Stanhope was still on friendly terms with Grenville, through whom alone he could hope to influence the policy of the Cabinet. On December 18 he implored him to see one of the numerous Englishmen who had thrown in their lot with the Revolution and were employed on semi-official missions.

' My dear Lord,â A respectable person of my acquaintance (Mr. Stone) is lately come from France and has got a Decree of the National Convention and also questions from the Committee for the Colonies, which he has been requested to bring to this country, and he wishes to shew them to your Lordship. ' Believe me ever, my dear Lord, with great truth, 1 Most sincerely yours, ' STANHOPE 2

Grenville coldly replied the same day that until he knew of the subject of the papers in question he could not grant Mr. Stone an interview. On the next day, December 19, Stanhope wrote again in more urgent terms.

1 Parl. Hist., xxix. 1573-4.

2 Foreign Office, France, No. 40. This letter was discovered and copied for Miss Stanhope by Dr. Holland Rose.

CHAP. ' My dear Lord,â I have written to Mr. Stone to send you VIII. a copy of the Decree of the National Convention, and also of the questions of the Committee for the Colonies. Mr. Stone is an Englishman well acquainted with the Ministers and leading men in France, and whom your Lordship will do well at least to see, as he can convince you of their friendly disposition towards this country. Good God! my dear Lord, you have no conception of the misfortunes you may bring upon England by going to war with France. For as to France, I believe all Europe cannot subdue them, whatever efforts may be made. It will only rouse them worse.

' Believe me ever, my dear Lord, ' STANHOPE

This letter is endorsed in Grenville's hand ' To be circulated and must therefore have come before Pitt. 1

During January a final attempt to prevent war was made by Maret, afterwards Due de Bassano, one of Napoleon's most trusted and honourable servants. Arriving in London on January 3, he sought out the friends of France. ' Lord Stanhope was announced to Maret last night about half-past eight wrote Miles on February 4. ' I was in close conversation with him at the time, and, as he was on the eve of his departure, he made no difficulty in receiving his Lordship. I was much pressed to stay; but as it is my unalterable resolution, under present circumstances, to have no communication on public matters with any members of the Opposition nor even to be present at any such conversation, I withdrew at the same instant that Lord Stanhope entered the room 2 The mission was, however, too late, for Pitt refused to see the envoy.

The execution of Louis XVI was followed by the expulsion of the French ambassador. On February i Grenville opened a debate on the royal message for an increase of the forces in a speech warmly eulogising the late King, and expressing horror of the men and the principles which had brought him to his doom. ' We may see the same scenes here; we may see them crowned by the same terrible and atrocious act The British Government had manifested the most scrupulous neutrality through- 1 Stanhope, Life of Pitt, ii. 180-1,

Miles, Correspondence on the French Revolution, ii. 60; and Ernouf, Vie de Maret.

out the Revolution; but it was impossible for such an attitude CHAP, to continue after the French intervention in Holland and the VIII. open manifestation of aggressive principles. The British ambassador had been recalled from Paris, and official communication with Chauvelin, the French Minister in London, had ceased.

When Grenville sat down, Stanhope rose and delivered a speech of passionate conviction. 1 It was, he declared, the most important occasion in his life. The approaching calamity of war, pregnant with ruin to England, had been caused by the Ministry, not by French aggression. England had neither been injured nor insulted. Even now war might by avoided if we would act with candour. He then read a letter from Condorcet, expressing the anxious desire of the French to maintain friendly relations with England. This friendship, he added, might have been maintained, had we not irritated a galled people, insulted their distress and provoked their pride. We had broken our neutrality, demanding that the French should quit Brabant but not that the Kings should desist from their attack. ' You will not make this a war of the people of Great Britain he cried. ' It is a war of the Government against her best and dearest interests. Its real motive is that you dislike the principles of the French Revolution. If those principles are good, your war will not extinguish them." He concluded by moving an amendment praying the King to exert every means to avert the calamities of war.

When the amendment was negatived without a division, Lansdowne, Lauderdale, and Derby recorded a Protest in the journals, declaring that they knew of no danger to Great Britain rendering war necessary. Their phraseology was too restrained to suit the taste of Stanhope, who drew up a protest reflecting his burning emotions. 2 War, he declared, is so unnatural, so barbarous, so calamitous, so immoral when unnecessary and so atrocious when unjust, that every friend of humanity should endeavour to avoid it. Peace is always for the interest of the common people in all countries. It is a well-known fact that the people in France, in general, are extremely desirous to maintain and strengthen the bonds of friendship with Great Britain. Peace would be the constant object of their Government, if not first provoked by our ministers by such acts as refusing to acknowledge their new government and sending away the French ambassador. The old despotic and detestable government in France, from its secrecy, perfidy and restless ambition, has been

CHAP, the fatal cause of many wars in Europe for centuries. Therefore any assistance to restore that tyrannical form of government is injurious to the true interests of this country. The people of France, moreover, have as much right to enjoy civil liberty as ourselves.

On the same day France declared war against Great Britain, and on February 12 a full-dress debate took place in both Houses In the Commons, Pitt, Dundas, and Burke supported the war which Fox and Sheridan attacked. In the Lords the Government was supported by Portland, and condemned by Lauderdale and Lansdowne. Stanhope pronounced the conflict to have been begun by the British Cabinet, when they dismissed Chauvelin. 1 He was aware that he should be unpopular during the present frenzy; but he could not agree to sanction a struggle where we were the sole aggressors. Moreover, the resources of France were enormous. They had rightly declared the Crown lands and the Church lands the property of the nation, and confiscated the estates of the emigres. He did not again challenge the majority till June, when he attacked Auckland's memorial to the States-General. The document presented by the British Minister at the Hague, inviting the Dutch Government to put to death the regicides who had fallen into their power owing to the treachery of Dumouriez, had been hotly condemned by Sheridan in the Commons; but his motion, for which he and Grey were the Tellers, only secured 36 votes. 2 Stanhope had waited till Auckland could be present, and he now denounced the ' most ferocious' manifesto to his face. 3 However they might differ about the objects of the war, he declared, they would all agree that it should not be carried on with savage barbarity. Such horrible menaces were as impolitic as they were wicked, as the experience of Burgoyne and Brunswick had shown. He concluded by moving that the King should be asked publicly to disavow the memorial. Grenville approved the declaration as in accordance with the spirit of his instructions, and after Auckland had defended himself, the motion was negatived without a division. 4 The diplomat remained wholly impenitent. 'When I contemplate the fate of Marat, Brissot, Vergniaud and above fourscore others of the regicides he wrote to Grenville, ' I continue, in spite of Lord Stanhope, to see traces of the Divine vengeance." 5

On January 23, 1794, a year after the outbreak of war, 1 Parl. Hist., xxx. 414-17. 2 Ibid,, 702-25. 3 Ibid., 1035-43.

4 Cp. Auckland's Correspondence, iii. 74-6.,.

5 Fortescue MSS., ii. 445. October 13, 1793.

Stanhope moved to acknowledge the French Republic. 1 In CHAP, scathing terms he accused Ministers of misleading opinion in VIII. regard to the strength and resources of the French armies, and their lack of ammunition and food, clothing and money. England had been led to believe that the French were a disordered rabble; but the Republic had already proved itself equal in discipline and superior in bravery to its enemies. Enthusiasm made them bear the evils of war not merely without a murmur, but in many cases with enthusiasm. Such were the men whom mercenary troops were attempting to conquer. The French were indeed invincible. Was there any of this zeal in the mass of our people? As far as he could judge, there was no desire to prolong the war, which was being waged to impose a certain form of government on an independent State. ' I am ready to be hanged or guillotined for the cause of liberty cried the speaker; ' it is not what I wish or call for, but I hope if it became necessary I should not shrink from it." He made no attempt to defend what he described as the provisional government of France. The constitution, on the other hand, was fixed and definite, and was based on the Declaration of the Rights of Man, which was so excellent that he defied all the philosophers on earth to improve it. After reading it to the House he declared that its basis was liberty, of which equality was part. Equality meant not that all should be equal in property, which was impossible, but that all should have an equal right to gain and keep their property, to equal laws and impartial justice. What security, he might be asked, could we have for a faithful observance of a treaty? He answered, the French constitution, which was better security than any other power in Europe could give, since it was the act of almost the whole people. The provisional government was erected for the purpose of repelling the invaders, and the sanguinary decrees of the Convention might be repealed at a breath. Turning to the common charge of atheism, he declared that the religion of other countries was no concern of ours. Moreover, there were plenty of aristocratic atheists before the Revolution, and he recalled an occasion in a Parisian drawing-room when he had been present at a debate on the existence of God. In France as elsewhere there was more religion among the lower and middle classes. If it had been often treated with levity, this was mainly due to the clergy who made a trade of it and performed barefaced tricks to delude the populace.

The speech was eloquent and sincere; but its weakness lay CHAP, in refusing to recognise that the Revolution had ceased to be VIII. defensive and had become aggressive. He quoted the decisive article of the French constitution by which they renounced, solemnly and for ever, all thought of interfering with any government but their own. But while he appealed to their words, his opponents appealed to their deeds. Of the two speakers who followed, the first brutally declared that his arguments were best answered by a good loud horse-laugh, while the second maintained that any minister who proposed or accepted peace with the French Government deserved to lose his head. Thus the debate flickered out, and the motion was negatived without a division. ' Lord Stanhope wrote Lord Sheffield's clever daughter, ' should certainly be sent as a handsome present to the Convention." 1 On the other hand, the London Corresponding Society resolved to print and circulate the speech. 2

Undeterred by his rebuff, Stanhope came down to the Lords a week later on an errand which required scarcely less courage. 3 The trials of the Scottish reformers had recently taken place, and the brutality of the Judge and the severity of the sentences had created disgust and indignation. One of the victims, Palmer, a cultured clergyman, had addressed a piteous appeal to him from the dark recesses of the Tolbooth.

' November n, 1793.

' My Lord,â Your public and parliamentary conduct is such a convincing testimony that you are a friend to the liberties of your country that I trust an obscure individual crushed by the tyrannical hand of government will not apply to you in vain. My oppression is not isolated. It may be that of every man who condemns the measures of administration, who lays open the consequences of this disastrous war, or who endeavours after a reform in Parliament. For these are the only objects of the handbill for printing and publishing which I am condemned to seven years' transportation. If the servants of the Crown can three times pack the jury, if they have the dreadful power of any punishment short of death, and if from their sentence no appeal lies, a despotism prevails in Scotland equal to that of the Stuarts. If you should think proper to endeavour to get a Bill passed to put a stop to this despotism, to restore to the 1 Girlhood of Maria Josepha Holroyd, p. 268.

2 Hardy's History of the London Corresponding Society. (Add. MSS., 27814, f. 49.) 3 Parl. Hist., xxx. 1298-1301.

Scots a trial by jury and the privileges of British subjects, I CHAP, hope that from the illegality of the proceedings and the enormous VIII. disproportion of the punishment to the offence (if any) that you will see it just to have my sentence reversed by a clause restoring me to the rights and emoluments I before enjoyed; for I fear that by this disgraceful sentence I shall lose my senior fellowship of Queen's College, Cambridge, and half of my small fortune."

In calling attention to the case, Stanhope declared the proceedings to be the most unjustifiable that ever came before a court of justice. He complained that fresh charges were made in the trial not mentioned in the indictment, which he had no time or opportunity to rebut by witnesses. If this was the law of Scotland, there was no more liberty than under the Stuarts. After quoting a number of precedents he demanded the postponement of the sentences till an inquiry had taken place. Mansfield, Thurlow, and the Chancellor replied that the law of Scotland was not the law of England, and that if a revision of the sentence was desired it could be secured by a petition. Lauderdale, who alone sympathised with the motion, declared that it was no wonder that these trials had excited surprise, since men in Scotland were transported to Botany Bay for what in England had raised others to the highest situations. He had, however, endeavoured to dissuade Stanhope from raising the question in this manner, and even now he hoped that he would withdraw it, so that it might be brought forward in a more regular way. The friendly appeal was in vain. The motion was lost by 49 to i, after which Stanhope, as usual, entered a protest in the journals.

His next intervention in debate was on February 2I, 1 when the landing of foreign troops without consent of Parliament was discussed. A few Hanoverian and Hessian battalions had come ashore in Hampshire as a temporary measure before their transfer to other ships. Fox and his friends had raised a protest in the Lower House, but Pitt refused to accept a Bill of indemnity for his action. Stanhope repudiated the monstrous doctrine that the King might land as many armed foreigners in peace or war as he pleased. If any Minister tried to practise such a doctrine, he hoped it would be resisted by force. He supported the proposal for a Bill of indemnity, in order to register the unconstitutional character of the occurrence. When the motion was rejected, he repeated the substance of

CHAP, his speech in a Protest. 'It is a most dangerous doctrine VIII. he declared, ' that the Crown has a right to do any act which is not warranted either by common or statute law, under the frivolous pretence of its appearing useful to ministers. A prerogative in the executive power to introduce any number of armed foreign hirelings into the country, without the previous express consent of the legislature, is totally incompatible with a free constitution." His conduct met with warm approval in the radical camp. The Society for Constitutional Information resolved, ' That the protest of Earl Stanhope respecting the landing of foreign troops in this country be entered on the books of this society; and that its warmest gratitude is due for his exertions on a subject in which the dearest interests of Englishmen are involved." 1 A month later the London Corresponding Society, at a meeting at Chalk Farm, resolved, ' That the thanks of this meeting be given to Earl Stanhope for his manly and patriotic conduct during the last sessionâ a conduct which (unsupported as it has been in the Senate of which he is so truly honourable a member) has, together with the timely interference of certain spirited and patriotic Associations, been productive of chasing the Hanoverian and Hessian troops from our coasts." 2 A somewhat similar problem arose on March 28. The Government had applied to the Lords-Lieutenant to organise a voluntary subscription throughout the country to augment the national forces. The question was raised in the Commons by Sheridan and Fox, who pronounced it dangerous and unconstitutional for the executive to raise money and maintain a force without consent of Parliament. On the same day Lauderdale initiated a debate in the Lords. He was supported by Stanhope, who contended that the Crown could not maintain a single man without the sanction of the legislature, and therefore that it was illegal to contribute to the support of that man. 3 If a section of the people was to be armed, he would urge that the whole people should have arms. A partial army might endanger every man suspected of being a warm friend to liberty, and one part of the nation would be set against the other. If Ministers were allowed to go on with their prerogative doctrines, we should soon have subscriptions of Austrian troops and money to take care of us.

In April Stanhope administered an unusually severe shock 1 Newspaper cutting, endorsed by Stanhope.

2 Hardy's History of the London Corresponding Society. (Add. MSB., 27814, f. 70.) 3 Par. Hist., xxxi. 133-4.

to the nerves of his brother Peers by a motion condemning CHAP, interference in the internal affairs of France. 1 As an Englishman VIII. supporting the honour of his country and a Christian maintaining the principles of his religion, he protested against the proposal to foment a civil war in France in order to restore a government directly in opposition to the will of the majority. At the commencement of the war Ministers had disclaimed any desire to settle the constitution; but they were now openly fighting to restore monarchy. Turning to the bench of Bishops he read the passage from the Book of Samuel in which the people were rebuked for asking for a King and punished when their wish was fulfilled. ' We, on the contrary, profess to know better than the Deity what is good for the French and are resolved to force upon them a King against their consent. I shall be happy to-night in having brought forward this motion and cleared myself from the imputation of agreeing with such sentiments This uncompromising utterance stung the Peers to anger.

I confess I never heard any speech," cried Grenville, ' with such indignation. Sorry I am to see the noble mover suffering his passions to get the better of his reason. I will not insult your understandings by replying. He will see the entire House against him, and the people throughout the country will equally condemn his resolution He advised the Lords to refuse to allow the resolution to be entered in the journals. The Lord Chancellor agreed, and believed that they would be equally averse to hearing it read from the Woolsack. He then read the resolution without the preamble, which led Stanhope to complain that his motion was being presented in a mangled shape. When it had been negatived, Grenville moved and carried that the entry of the motion should be expunged from the journals. At the next sitting of the House Lauderdale raised the question of the Chancellor's procedure. 2 If the forms of the House were not observed, there was an end to the freedom of debate. ' Were it the most absurd that human fancy could suggest, the motion should be submitted to the House in the precise language of the mover Stanhope protested both against the mutilation of his motion and the expunging of all reference to the debate from the journals. Had a Speaker of the House of Commons acted thus, he would have had his wig pulled over his ears and his gown stripped from his shoulders. But these heated protests fell on deaf ears.

It was in recognition of his courage in these fierce and unequal i Parl. Hist., xxxi. 141-7. a Ibid., 198-205.

CHAP, encounters that the London Corresponding Society drew up the VIII. following letter x:â ' April 28, 1794.

' My Lord,â I am directed by the London Corresponding Society to forward you their unanimous resolution passed at a general meeting on Monday the I4th instant on the Green at Chalk Farm, to which place they were obliged to retire as they were prevented from assembling at the room they had hired for the purpose by the intimidation of the owner of it. The object of this letter is in a great measure novel to the Society. To have an opportunity of declaring their approbation of the measures adopted by Parliament, as it is now constituted, is almost beyond their hope and certainly beyond their expectation. To have found it in the conduct of individuals of that body they might have had some reasonable expectation, if the professions of men could be depended upon. But that they cannot, the history of the world furnishes us examples sufficiently notorious. They have, however, on some particular questions been afforded a few solitary instances, and the pleasure they receive in bestowing just praise cannot be more fully evinced than by the avidity with which they have publicly avowed it. But it has remained to you, my Lord, and to you alone, to call forth our warmest applause, our full and entire approbation of the whole of your parliamentary conduct during the present session, a conduct which we trust will have considerable effect in opening the eyes of the people to a sense of their true interests at this momentous crisis, and in rousing their just indignation against any attempts that may be made to deprive them of that portion of those long boasted liberties which yet remain to them; while by its firm and decided character it reflects as much honour on your manly feelings as it does contempt and infamy on the venality of its adversaries.

'T. HARDY, Sec."

Stanhope replied as follows 2:â ' Mansfield Street: May i, 1794.

' Sir,â I return you a great many thanks for your very obliging letter of the 28th of April last; and I feel myself highly honoured by the distinguished approbation which the London 1 Morning Post, May 7, 1794.

- Treasury Solicitor's Papers, General Series, No, 3510 B. I owe this reference to the kindness of Mr. P. A. Brown.

Corresponding Society has been pleased to give to my Parlia- CHAP, mentary conduct this session. I pledge myself that the same VIII. principles of justice and liberty that have guided my conduct hitherto in Parliament shall continue to guide it to the last hour of my life.

' I remain, Sir, with great esteem, ' Your faithful Fellow-Citizen, ' STANHOPE."

War and repression, as usual, went hand in hand. On May 22 Grenville moved the suspension of Habeas Corpus in order to deal with the British ' Jacobins." When he sat down, Stanhope rose in wrath to oppose the measure. 1 The Bill was designed to set up a Bastille and to introduce lettres de cachet, by which any man might be imprisoned for any length of time at the will of Ministers, without proof, without reason, without trial, and without redress. The excuse was the summoning of a convention, which was designed to usurp the functions of Parliament. He spoke the more freely as he had never belonged to any of these societies and did not approve of the meeting of a convention, because, however legal, it was not likely to be effectual. But the legality of an attempt to secure Parliamentary reform without applying to Parliament was clear. If it was said that these men had extravagant ideas of reform such as annual Parliaments and universal suffrage, he would remind their Lordships that the Duke of Richmond and other distinguished men had openly expressed the same views. They all knew the record of Mr. Pitt on Parliamentary reform. Sir George Savile, that great and good man whom to know was to esteem, had made use of harsher words in regard to Parliament than these societies had employed in their resolutions. He quoted the Duke of Richmond's declaration that he had no hope of any reform from Parliament and that the people must do everything for themselves. If their lordships were to send to prison any member of the societies for disrespectful expressions to Parliament, they must send with them, for the same offence, Citizen Richmond. ' Let us do justice and give the people peace," he concluded, ' and then we may be able to guide their reasoning." When the Bill had been carried through all its stages on the same day, he entered the following protest on the journals. ' Dissentient, because I abhor the idea of establishing a dangerous and unconstitutional system of lettres de cachet in this country."

That Stanhope continued to correspond with France long after the outbreak of war is evident from two reports found in Lord Grenville's papers. Writing from Milan on June 10, 1794, Francis Drake encloses two letters in French from an anonymous correspondent believed by him to be closely connected with the Comte d'Artois and the Vendee leaders. ' On May 7," ran the first bulletin, ' a memorable thing occurred in the Committee of Public Safety. St. Just reproached Robespierre for having in his speech on the restoration of religion named Lord Stanhope, though he had been expressly urged not to compromise him. Robespierre denied that anything of this character had been said to him. Barere then maintained to his face not only that he had told him, but that he had actually read to him Lord Stanhope's letter on the subject.

Whence it clearly results that Barere is his correspondent at Paris." 1 A further bulletin described the events of the sitting of May 30. ' Barere informed the Committee that his friend Stanhope recommended to them a Colonel Hamilton, a member of the Scottish Convention, who had taken refuge in France." It would be interesting to know more of his relations with one of the most worthless of the revolutionary leaders; but the letters have disappeared and there is nothing to take their place. The Frenchman makes no mention of his distinguished correspondent in his ' Memoirs and Stanhope never referred to Barere in his speeches. 2

Remaining thus in close touch with Paris he realised more clearly than the Ministry that behind the red pageantry of horror lay an unconquerable resolve to defend the conquests of the Revolution and the integrity of French soil against all comers. At this time, moreover, he began to detect signs that his own coutrymen were beginning to weary of the war, and accordingly redoubled his exertions. The following letter to Lansdowne urges him to resist the blandishments of Pitt, who had recently swallowed the Portland Whigs and thereby immensely strengthened his Parliamentary position. 3 ' Mansfield Street: November 23, 1794.

1 My dear Lord, â Before your Lordship receives this, I shall get into my post-chaise to go to Chevening House, therefore pray send me no answer as I dislike the post. I have been reflecting 1 Fortescue MSS., ii. 570. 2 Ibid., ii. 582.

on the things your Lordship's (well-placed) confidence induced CHAP, you to mention to me. And I have thought upon that subject VII. with all that anxiety which my duty to the public in the present alarming and unexampled situation and which also my personal affection for your Lordship, as an old, well-tried friend, have naturally excited in my mind. The result is that I am clear that you ought, on no account, to commit yourself with Pitt, Loughborough, Grenville, Buckingham, or any man whom the public (no matter why) never will trust, and whom other nations may abhor. Mr. Pitt has several valuable friends,â I speak not of them, but of him and of such men as are above mentioned. May all success attend your Lordship's efforts for the public good! But there are two things I recommend to your Lordship to attend to, and never to lose sight of for an instant; or I foresee you may bitterly repent it. I say bitterly on account of the high ground on which you now stand, if you preserve it. Those two things are:â ' i. To recollect that public opinion on political subjects is changing in a manner unparalleled, and not slowly, but silently, and with an increase; and increasing certainly and in a ratio which will be continuously increasing.

' 2. Distrust all men (whoever they may be) who have cold hearts, not capable of friendship to others, nor of real zeal for the public.

' Speaking of cold hearts, I will tell you an amiable instance of hearts of an opposite description. Before I left the country my daughters requested of me as a favour, if (from any foul practices) the jury should convict Mr. Tooke, that I would voluntarily stand forth and offer myself as guardian to his two daughters. I confess such a sentiment, originating entirely with themselves, gave me great pleasure. I have written to the Citizen and have mentioned, in a kind way, your Lordship's regret at not having been asked to speak in his favour.

' Believe me, my dear Lord, with cordiality and truth, ' Your Lordship's faithful and affectionate Fellow-Citizen."

A long and earnest letter to Wilberforce, written a few days later, travels more directly to the goal at which he was aiming. 1 ' Chevening House: December 5, 1794.

' Dear Mr. Wilberforce,â The personal regard I have for you, and the motives which induce me to write you this letter, will make you, I am sure, excuse the liberty I take. The day of the meeting of Parliament draws nigh; the awful question of blood-shed and war, or of peace, will be agitated. You, of course, must make up your mind on that momentous subject. You can do much; it is therefore the more essential that you should do right. However much I approve your general conduct and admire some sublime parts of it, I must tell you, with all the sincerity of a friend, that your conduct on the above-mentioned subject is not what I expected from you. When a man votes for war, for the destruction of hundreds of thousands, for the laying waste of countries, he heaps indeed a dreadful responsibility on his head. For it is not to you, dear Citizen, that I need observe that this life is no other than a journey; the being unavoidable is the necessary requisite in order to reconcile any war to a religious mind. You cannot say that it would not have been possible to have avoided the present one, nor that it is not possible to put an end to it. That alone might decide the question. But when you reflect on the situation of things, the events abroad and those likely to happen, the change of the public mind at home, and the greater change that will probably take place as taxes and difficulties increase, you would do well to ask yourself this question, namely, Whether by voting to continue the war you may not finally bring this country into such a situation that peace may not be possible to be obtained. Possibly you may never have put to yourself that question.

' It is not sufficient for a man of your description not to vote for the projected carnage; but as an individual who has attracted the attention of the public, and as the representative of our largest county, it is your duty, both in Parliament and in private, to do everything in your power to prevent it. Do you not remember when the House of Lords was told, and I believe the House of Commons also, that the French had but few arms, no clothes, no stock of ammunition, no real enthusiasm, no discipline in their armies, not provisions enough to prevent their starving, no means of cultivating their lands, no money, no credit, no resources; and when I stated, in every one of these respects, directly the reverse? I mention not this to recall to your recollection the odious and infamous reflections cast out against me for having dared to do my duty (though often single), and to speak the truth; but I do it to show you, from what is now notorious, that those who ought to have been well and officially informed had no good information, or did not think it proper to lay it before Parliament. Suffer not therefore your honourable mind to be misled by pretended official information. I have no doubt but that the resources of the French (if properly brought forth) are greater at this moment than when I stated them in the House to be greater than those of all their enemies combined.

' On the contrary this country, Great Britain, is vulnerable in so many ways that the picture is horrid. By letter I will say nothing upon that subject. One instance I will however state, because it is information you cannot, as yet, receive from any other quarter. I know (and in a few weeks shall prove) that ships of any size may be navigated in any narrow or other sea without sails, so as to go without wind and even directly against both wind and waves. The consequences I draw are as follows. First, that all the principal reasons against the French having the ports of Ostend, c. cease; inasmuch as a French fleet, composed of ships of the above-mentioned description, would come out at all times from Cherbourg, Dunkirk, c. as well as from Ostend, c. and appear in the same seas. The French having Ostend ought not therefore, under this new revolution in naval affairs (for it will be complete revolution), to be a bar to peace. But the most important consequence which I draw from this stupendous fact is that it will very shortly render all the existing navies of the world (I mean military navies) no better than lumber. For what can ships do that are dependent upon wind and weather against fleets wholly independent of either? Therefore the boasted superiority of the English navy is no more! We must have a new one. The French and other nations will, for the same reason, have their new ones. Now, do you seriously mean, or can you as an honest man (which you are), reconcile it to your conscience to place the very existence of your native land on this miserable foundation: namely, on the circumstance of which of the European nations can build new ships fastest? Recollect, I pray you, that the French, according to Dr. Price's calculations, independent of their new acquisitions were upwards of thirty millions, and that England and Wales together do not contain five.

' Having now received the above information, what answer, nay what excuse, can you make to your constituents and to your country should you not oppose the war; and, above all, what excuse can you make to that Being, infinitely high, who is the Creator of us all? Reason, temper, foresight, and justice can alone save us. I send you enclosed a literal translation of the n8th and ngih Articles of the French Constitution in case you should not have seen it, as it completely refutes the nonsense we daily hear about their supposed intended interference in our internal concerns. It is not a simple decree nor a mere law, but a

CHAP, fundamental article of the last constitution. I shall be ever happy VIII. to hear you are well, though I neither wish nor expect you to reply to this; I shall be glad merely to know it is received. I am quite sure at least you cannot answer my arguments. Possibly I may not have the pleasure of seeing you in the winter, as I shall be almost entirely at this place. Whilst I had a prospect of opening men's minds, I was anxious to attend the House. That time is past; events I believe either have or will open them shortly. Till then I shall be more happy at a distance from the disgusting scene, from which I wish my duty would allow me to be wholly absent.

' Dear Sir, believe me, with great regard and truth, and as an Englishman, 1 Your sincere and faithful Fellow-Citizen, ' STANHOPE."

To some extent Stanhope was forcing an open door. Wilber-force had not been satisfied with Pitt's handling of the negotiations with France before war broke out, and after the fall of Robespierre he believed peace to be possible. But it is not unlikely that the earnest appeal from Chevening determined or helped to determine him to take overt action. In the debate on the Address, December 30, he moved an amendment in favour of peace, and supported Grey's motion a month later. Pitt was deeply chagrined by the opposition of his greatest friend, and for once lost his sleep; but he declined to modify his policy. On the same day that Wilberforce was pleading for peace in the Commons, Stanhope renewed his protest in the Lords. 1 Events, he declared, spoke for themselves, and the disasters of this accursed war were the best answers to the arguments of its defenders. The French had no antipathy to the people of this country, and only detested the Government. A week later, on January 6, 1795, he once again moved to refrain from interference in the internal affairs of France. 2 The opinion of the country, he began, had entirely altered. It was now obvious that it was impossible to exhaust the finances of France, and that her army was the best in Europe. Her naval force was equal or superior to ours. The French could neither be conquered nor starved. Her successes had been ascribed to chance; but he could not help considering them as proofs of the wisdom of their Government. If he were asked with whom we were to make peace, he replied with the Republic, one and indivisible, with those men whose republican constancy, courage and ardour 1 Parl. Hist., xxxi. 986-7. 2 Ibid., 1130-43.

had made victory the order of the day. We had lost lives and CHAP, trade, and, what was more important, our character as the VIII. friends of liberty and peace. The debate pursued its usual course. Lord Abingdon, who, on another occasion, had described the conflict as a war with original sin, declared that Jacobinism had robbed the Earl of his politics as an Englishman and had deprived him of his senses. Auckland, his old enemy, admitted that the armies and the councils of France had displayed great energy and ability; but it was less their merits than the disagreements of the allies which had led to the present situation. He was prepared to acknowledge a republic if France would surrender her aggressive designs. Mansfield declared that the war was purely defensive. Lansdowne, while glad that the motion had been brought forward, declared that he could not support it at the present juncture. In the division that followed Stanhope found himself alone. 1

Once more he entered an elaborate protest in the journals. After enumerating fifteen reasons for his motion he added these striking words: ' Having upon this most momentous subject frequently stood alone, and having been now totally unsupported in the division, if I should therefore cease at present to attend this House (where I have been placed by mere accident of birth), such of my fellow-citizens as are friends to freedom and who may chance to read this my solemn protest will find that I have not altered my opinions; for my principles never can be changed. And these fellow-citizens will also find that I hereby pledge myself to my country that I shall continue a zealous and unshaken friend to peace, justice and liberty, political, civil and religious; and that I am determined to die, as I have lived, a firm and steady supporter of the inalienable rights and of the happiness of all mankind." With these words of proud defiance, which he proceeded to publish, Stanhope withdrew from the Chamber which he had lectured and shocked for a decade. A medal was struck in his honour, with the motto, ' The Minority of One, 1795." 2 But, while not afraid of standing alone, he rejoiced to 1 ' The motion was not directly negatived," wrote the Duke of Leeds, ' but on a division on the adjournment the numbers were 60 to i. I stayed but a short time, and should not have attended but under the idea that Lord Stanhope might have called upon me in consequence of what I had formerly said, that in case France was satisfied with her Government I cared not of what nature it was, so long as the safety of this country was provided for."â Political Memoranda, 213-14.

2 The Duchess of Cleveland gives no authority for the story that Stanhope once rebuffed a supporter in the lobby with the words, ' You spoiled that division."

CHAP, receive support or approval from within or without the House. VIII. The London Corresponding Society once more hastened to express its admiration of his conduct. 1 ' February 3, 1795.

' My Lord,â We think it a point of duty to our country that we should offer to your Lordship our thanks for your Protest against the motion of adjournment which was passed in the House of Lords on the 6th of January, and we trust they will not be the less acceptable to your Lordship because they come from men who have long suffered reproaches from various combinations. It were forming an ill opinion of our country were we to suppose the approbation of your Loidship's sentiments, and the spirited and explicit manner in which they have been delivered, was confined to this Society. We are persuaded there are many thousands to whom their merits are equally obvious, but who, from the prevalence of factious practices and the depraved state of the constituted bodies and the want of association among themselves, have no means of collecting each others' opinions. But if ever that equal representation which is the great object of this Society should be attained, and the influence of party consequently annihilated, we are assured it will not be in the power of sophistry, even in appearance, to depreciate the integrity and sound judgment which do honour to your Lordship's sentiments."

The reply was brief but forcible.

' Mansfield Street: February 14, 1795.

' Citizens,â I beg leave to return you my most cordial thanks for the very honourable and marked approbation which you have given to the principles contained in my Protest. I no longer regret having stood alone upon that occasion, since my conduct is approved by my fellow-citizens. I have put my foot on the rock of liberty and justice, and from that rock I never will depart. Believe me, Citizens, with the greatest sincerity and truth, ' Your most faithful Fellow-Citizen, ' STANHOPE."

Stanhope's secession was announced in the columns of the Moniteur in words which he must have read with peculiar gratification. ' Le Comte de Stanhope, ce genereux ami de la liberte, ce philanthrope aussi recommandable par ses lumieres que par 1 Newspaper cutting preserved at Chevening.

la droiture de son coeur, ayant la douloureuse conviction qu'il CHAP, ne pouvait plus faire aucun bien dans la Chambre haute, a pris VIII. le parti de se retirer." 1 The question whether the British Ministry did all that could be done to keep England out of the tornado of the Revolutionary Wars is still unsettled, and there is no need to argue it afresh in this biography. It is clear that Stanhope under-estimated both the volume of aggressive feeling in France and the desire of Pitt to preserve peace. On the other hand, whatever may be thought of his political judgment, his courage in proclaiming unpopular views and his unflagging efforts to avert a war which he believed to be a crime and a blunder entitle him to the respect which political sincerity deserves and in the long run obtains at the bar of history.

CHAP. AT the time of his secession from Parliament Stanhope's repu-IX. tation as a champion of liberty had spread throughout Europe. In France he had long been a hero, and his speeches were reported at length in the Moniteur. He was scarcely less

known in the provinces than at Paris, and in the spring of 1794 the Republican Society of Rochefort addressed to him the following resonant expression of its homage:â '
Rochefort: le 21 Ventose, l'an 2,

Ta voix tonnante pour la liberte" a retenti jusque dans les ateliers ou nous forgeons les foudres contre les tyrans. Nous t'avons entendu; nos bras sont restes leves; nous avons dit, "Celui-la meriterait d'etre citoyen fran?ais"; et les enclumes ont gemi sous nos coups redoubles.

' LEBAS, President, ' BARBAULT-ROYER, Secretaire." x

In the same year Lewis Goldsmith, an enthusiast for the Revolution who spent his time travelling through Europe, wrote from Poland, at the instigation of Kosciusko, urging British intervention on behalf of the Nationalists. Stanhope expressed sympathy with the hero, but stated that the Anglo-Prussian alliance debarred him from bringing the Polish cause before Parliament. 2

His courage and energy naturally made him the idol of young men of radical sympathies in his own country. In 1795, the year of his withdrawal from Parliament, Landor, then aged 1 Moniteur, xix. 736.

2 Alger, Napoleon's British Visitors and Captives, p. 105.

twenty, published an anonymous poem in his honour. The CHAP. Oxford undergraduate had pronounced himself a Republican, IX. written an ode to Washington, and passed for ' a mad Jacobin." For firing a gun at the shutters of a Tory and refusing to give explanations, he was sent down. He then wrote ' A Moral Epistle to Lord Stanhope in which he attacked Pitt in the style of Pope. He contrasts the republican Earl with the Tory premier, whose love of the bottle and system of espionage are sharply castigated. He despises the title as much as he admires the virtues of the patriot Stanhope. Fortune, he cries, was blind or insulting when it placed on his brow the tinsel coronet instead of the civic wreath. 1

The youthful Coleridge expressed his admiration in impassioned accents in a well-known sonnet. 2 'To EARL STANHOPE.

'Not, Stanhope, with the patriot's doubtful name

I mock thy worthâ Friend of the human race Since scorning Faction's law and partial aim,

Aloof thou wendest in thy stately pace, Thyself redeeming from that leprous stain,

Nobility: and aye unterrified, Pourest thine Abdiel warnings on the train

That sit complotting with rebellious pride 'Gainst her, 3 who from the Almighty's bosom leapt

With whirlwind arm, first Minister of Love! Wherefore, ere Virtue o'er thy tomb hath wept,

Angels shall lead thee to the throne above; And thou from forth its clouds shall hear the voice,

Champion of Freedom and her God! rejoice!"

Of inferior poetic merit but of equal intensity of feeling was the homage of Rutt, then well known as an active politician, now chiefly remembered as the friend and biographer of Priestley.

'To EARL STANHOPE, ' ON HIS LATE MOTIONS IN THE HOUSE OF LORDS.

' Stanhope! let rival statesmen loudly plead

Their fond attachment to the public weal;
In vain they seek the patriot's honour'd mead,
Who rest supine till rous'd by party zeal.
1 Forster's Life of Landor, i. 68-71.
2 Coleridge's political sonnets appeared during December 1794 and January 1795 in the Morning Chronicle.
3 Gallic Liberty.
CHAP. 'Twas thine for man the generous pang to feel, I As late each courtly peer and prelate stood,
Heedless of wounded Pity's meek appeal,
Unmov'd, though Peace the lovely matron sued! With Truth's strong pencil dipp'd in human blood, 'Twas thine to picture Europe's new crusade; Thine ere the bark of vengeance pass'd our flood,
Alone to rise in suffering virtue's aid. Scora'd by the great, yet honour'd by the good,
Who for the Patriot twine a wreath that ne'er shall fade

Stanhope, who appears to have had no special taste for belles-lettres, was probably more gratified by the following address from Alnwick, accompanied by over 300 signatures x:â ' My Lord,â We whose names are hereunto annexed, residing in the town and neighbourhood of Alnwick, in Northumberland, have presumed to address your Lordship on the very patriotic exertions you have lately made in the House of Lords. Without a perfect acquaintance with your Lordship's personal character, we are emboldened by congenial sentiments to offer you our united and most sincere thanks for having dared to stand alone in what we think a good cause. When a man steps forward boldly in the cause of suffering virtue, the conscious rectitude of his intentions affords him the highest gratification. But we think it a duty incumbent upon us, if possible, to add to your satisfaction by thus openly expressing our gratitude. We are not, it is true, among the great ones of the earth; we are not men high in power or in office; but we are Britons, who think for ourselves without bias, and, we trust, without prejudice. Merit and an upright heart constitute the true basis of distinction among mankind: and we therefore esteem public characters in proportion as they approach to that eminent station your Lordship posesses in our minds. Far removed from vile flattery and adulation, accept of this our address as a genuine token of our well-founded regard, which we feel more powerfully than we are able to express. That your Lordship may long live to run your glorious career, and finally behold your zealous efforts crowned with success, is our sincere and heartfelt wish."

Still more precious were the unfailing support and encouragement extended to him by the democratic societies which had sprung up shortly before or shortly after the commencement of the Revolution, in one or other of which most of his old colleagues in the Reform Movement were enrolled. 2 1 Newspaper cutting, endorsed by Stanhope, March 13, 1794.

2 ' My friend Mr. Joyce," wrote Hardy in his manuscript history of

Far more numerous than the tributes of admiration were the attacks on his opinions and influence. His ardent championship of the Revolution and his passionate opposition to the war rendered him in the eyes of the majority the typical Jacobin. We have seen the angry disgust which he inspired in the breast of Horace Walpole during the early phases of the crisis in France. But it was no longer the governing class alone with which he found himself in conflict. The nation had been thoroughly scared by the sanguinary drama enacted in Paris, and the sense of perspective disappeared from British politics for a generation. Moderate and familiar demands for Parliamentary reform were denounced as Jacobinism, and their authors were suspected of having entered into an unholy alliance with foreign revolutionaries to overturn the throne and altar. A tornado of savage invective blew round the head of the Peer, whose offence was deepened by his high rank and celebrity. After the meeting of the Corresponding Society at Chalk Farm on April 14, 1794, which expressed its lively gratitude to Stanhope, William Miles addressed to him an open letter, which embodied the opinions of most of his contemporaries. 1 The following abridgment will suffice to indicate the character of the attack.

' London: April 12, 1794.

' My Lord,â If I have dispensed with forms I can plead the example of your Lordship; and the occasion not only justifies the irregularity of a public address from a man who has not the honour of your acquaintance but supersedes the necessity of an excuse. I do not mean to dispute but to remonstrate with your Lordship. I feel sure that you will on reflection become sensible of the mischiefs that may eventually result to your rank, your character and fortune if the principles you admire and the doctrines you recommend should ever be in a condition to dispute the sovereignty of the laws. I am weary of recurring perpetually to the French Revolution. The intimacy in which the London Corresponding Society, ' has promised me a copy of all the motions, resolutions and letters of approbation from the Society to Earl Stanhope, Citizen, if there should be any occasion to publish the narrative of this Society. They were all cut out of my Minute-book and destroyed by some of my friends after I was arrested, fearful probably that the book might fall into the hands of some of the Government sharks." Add. MSS., 27814, f. 49, Several of the Society's resolutions are, however, fortunately preserved among Stanhope's newspaper cuttings. 1 A Letter to Earl Stanhope from Mr. Miles, 1794. (158 pages.)

CHAP. I have lived with some of the principal actors in that great event, IX. most of whom have been butchered or banished, and the recollection of Paris in its splendour and Paris in blood impress my mind with a train of awful reflections. What have the French done but change from bad to worse?

' Do the men, my Lord, who look up to you as their chief wish for a total change in the Government? Do they wish for the destruction of monarchy, or titles, of the House of Lords? The Dissenters are a numerous, learned and very respectable body of men; but they do not perceive that they are in danger of being made the tools of faction. I wish all good and conscientious men to reflect seriously on the blessings they enjoy at present in this happy country. It is not freedom but free quarter and free booty that they seek. Such are the designs of the men whom your Lordship affects to patronise. In the name of heaven, my Lord, what frenzy is this that stimulates you to qualify as improvement what has proved fatal to millions? Whichever way you direct your attention, you find affluence and content, freedom and happiness. In France every tree is a gibbet and every other man you meet a hangman. Yet your Lordship stands forth avowedly an admirer of crimes which desolate the earth and dishonour humanity. A peace with France, for which you seem so indecently anxious, can be obtained on no other terms than by a war with reason and humanity. I would entreat you to excuse the freedom with which I have addressed you; but I am unwilling to believe that you can be offended with a man who has no other object but to revive in your breast that ardent zeal for the interest of your country which marked the infancy of your Parliamentary career. It was reasonable to suppose that the multiplied excesses of the French would have convinced your Lordship; but the lessons of experience only serve to animate you, it seems, to a more violent opposition. Is it to enjoy a triumph over our subverted constitution that you pay court to the reptiles who, driven from house to house, assembled last week in the fields to flatter you into a participation of their crimes? It is incumbent on you to reject the vote of thanks which they have had the insolence to propose and which it would be infamy to accept. Your character is at stake. You must decide not deliberate, or the world will think worse of your principles than it does of your understanding."

The mob employed other and more forcible methods of conversionâ the same that it had applied to Priestley in 1791.

On June n, 1794, Lord Howe's victory was celebrated with great CHAP, enthusiasm, and the streets were illuminated. We learn from Ix-one of the spies who had been sent to join the London Corresponding Society that in the course of a meeting held that night people came in with news of the attack on Hardy's house in Piccadilly and crowds parading outside Stanhope's residence in Mansfield Street. It was proposed to go thither in a body and give him three cheers; but it was decided to go by twos and threes to avoid arousing the temper of the crowd. 1 But the mob required no inducement to riot, for they attacked the house and set it on fire. If Lady Hester's memory is to be trusted, her father was obliged to make his escape over the roof. 2 His wrath was deepened by the conviction that the malefactors had been incited by persons of high rank. On the next day he inserted the following advertisement in the newspapers: ' Outrage in Mansfield Street. Whereas an hired band of ruffians attacked my house in Mansfield Street, in the dead of night, and set it on fire at different times; and whereas a gentleman's carriage passed several times to and fro in front of my house, and the aristocrat, or other person who was in the same carriage, gave money to the people in the street to encourage them; this is to request the Friends of Liberty and Good Order to send me any authentic information they can procure respecting the name and place of abode of the said aristocrat or other person, in order that he may be made amenable to the law." The culprit, however, was never discovered.

Another blow was struck almost at the same moment when his private secretary and the tutor of his sons was arrested at Chevening on a charge of treasonable practices. Like the majority of Unitarian ministers, Jeremiah Joyce eagerly welcomed the French Revolution, joining the Society for Constitutional Information and the London Corresponding Society. ' He was a man of great worth," testifies Hardy, ' and highly esteemed by all who knew him." 3 His arrest was described by Lady Hester many years later in a conversation with Meryon. ' He was just coming down to breakfast when a single knock came at the door, and in bolted two officers with a warrant, and took him off without even my father's knowledge." 4 It was believed in certain quarters that Pitt ordered the arrest in order to annoy his brother-in-law; but there is no ground for this supposition.

1 Treasury Solicitor's Papers, General Series, No. 3510 A. I owe this reference to the kindness of Mr. P. A. Brown.

2 Meryon, ii. 21-2. 3 Hardy's Autobiography, p. 48. 4 Meryon, ii. 21-2.

CHAP. The Government was frightened by the discovery of the Ix- following letter to Home Tooke:â ' Dear Citizen,â This morning, at six o'clock, Citizen Hardy was taken away by order from the Secretary of State's office. They seized everything they could lay hands on. Query, is it possible to get ready by Thursday?

' Yours, ' J. JOYCE." 1

As Joyce was known to visit Wimbledon, the Government believed that the closing words referred to the outbreak of an insurrection, and at once arrested Home Tooke and his correspondent. It was established on the trial of the former that the mysterious query only related to a promise to select from the Court calendar a list of all places held by the Grenvilles, in order to cast odium on Pitt and his relatives. 2

Joyce's own account of his arrest appeared as an appendix to a political sermon preached in February, 1794, which closed with a reference to the transportation of the Scottish reformers. 3 The times, he had declared, were solemn and awful. ' We are not ignorant that some are already suffering from their attachment to principles which some twelve years since would have led to honours instead of exile. It may be reserved for us to follow them in similar or even severer trials." When he wrote the preface to the publication on October 23, ' Being the twenty-third week of my close imprisonment in the Tower it seemed likely that the prophecy might be fulfilled. ' I look back on my political life," he concluded, ' with complete satisfaction, and am prepared, if need be, cheerfully to lay down my life." But from this consummation he was saved by the genius of Erskine and the courage of a British jury.

On Monday, May 12, relates Joyce, Hardy and Adams, Secretary of the Society for Constitutional Information, were arrested. ' It was immediately rumoured that other persons would be favoured with domiciliary visits and that I must not expect to escape. Conscious of never having offended against the laws of my country I continued undisturbed the exercise of my business. On Wednesday about 8 in the morning, while I was conversing with Lord Mahon and his two brothers, Mr. King, Under-Secretary of State, and Mr. Ross, one of his Majesty's messengers, were introduced to me as having some private business 1 Stephens, Life of Home Tooke, ii. 119. 2 Ibid., ii. 144.

3 A copy is in the British Museum.

to communicate. When the young gentlemen had left the room, CHAP. Mr. Ross produced a warrant against me for 'Treasonable Ix-Practices by which he was authorised to seize my person and all books and papers connected with the Society for Constitutional Information and the London Corresponding Society. He demanded my keys, and after having searched my pockets and bed-chamber, they selected from my drawers and bookcase whatever they pleased." Driven to London, he was brought before the Privy Council the same day at one o'clock, and examined for about three-quarters of an hour. After declaring that he lived with Lord Stanhope and had care of his two elder sons, he refused to answer questions as to his membership of societies or his political activities. Bidden to withdraw, he remained till five o'clock, when he was informed that he was to be in Mr. Ross's custody till further orders, without pen, ink or paper. ' I signified an earnest desire that I might be indulged with the sight of Lord Mahon and his brother, concluding from their tender age that no objection could have been made, but I was informed that I could have no communication with any of the family of Earl Stanhope." On the following Monday he was lodged in the Tower.

The Grand Jury of Middlesex found a true Bill against the prisoners; but on the trial of Hardy it soon became clear that the Government possessed no real evidence. When he was acquitted it was scarcely probable that Home Tooke, a man of far more moderate opinions, would be condemned. But the prosecution once more strained every nerve to secure a conviction. The prisoner conducted his own defence, and called in evidence a number of distinguished politicians, among them Pitt and Sheridan, Stanhope and Wyvill. Stanhope was examined by Erskine, who inquired as to the meeting of July 14, 1790, at which he presided. 1 ' I perfectly recollect the meeting," he replied, ' one year after the Bastille had been pulled down, and we met to celebrate that glorious event." He then recalled the substance of Tooke's speech. ' He did not speak so respectfully of the resolution moved by Sheridan as, I confess, I wished. It was with some difficulty I could procure him a hearing, for they seemed very angry at him. He proposed as an amendment that something should be added about our own constitution. I think I recollect an expression that all our timbers were sound." He was then asked if he had seen Tooke at other meetings for Parliamentary Reform, and replied that he had seen him in 1 Howell's State Trials, xxv. 394-9.

CHAP, company with other Reformers such as Pitt and the Duke of IX. Richmond. Asked if he had ever seen him in private life, he replied, ' No, I have never been in habits of intimacy with Mr. Tooke in private life." Cross-examined by Scott, the Attorney-General, afterwards Lord Eldon, he deposed that he had not seen the defendant at any public or private meetings subsequent to 1790.

On the acquittal of Home Tooke, the Attorney-General announced that he would not call evidence against the other prisoners, who were accordingly found not guilty and released. The result was extremely gratifying to Stanhope, who celebrated the event by a fete at Chevening, which was thus described in the Gentleman's Magazine. 1 ' Lord Stanhope gave a grand entertainment at his villa in Kent to his neighbours and tenants, to celebrate the honourable acquittal of the Rev. Mr. Joyce. Besides near four hundred gentlemen and ladies in the neighbourhood who received cards of invitation, a number of his Lordship's friends from several distant parts were assembled. At eight o'clock the company were introduced into the ball-room. In the centre of a large group of emblematic figures was displayed, in large characters, the Rights of Juries. After the ball near two hundred persons, of both sexes, withdrew to partake of every delicacy that Chevening Hall, or the season, could afford; and after a number of appropriate toasts and songs retired to give place to others at the tables. The dancing was resumed and continued till six o'clock next morning, when the company separated, enraptured with the harmony and hilarity which distinguished the banquet, and considered it a display of Old English hospitality, revived with the best characteristic of Englishmen, the love of liberty. The acquittals they assembled to celebrate they considered as the triumph of truth and innocence, as an event which would give the people confidence in the justice of our laws, the integrity of our juries, and the independence of our judges, as an event which would perpetuate the rights of Englishmen and give vigour and stability to the Constitution in King, Lords and Commons, as by law established." 2

A great meeting, estimated at 1300, was also held at the Crown and Anchor taverná the scene of many memorable political gatheringsá on February 4, 1795. Stanhope was unanimously 1795, i- 73- 2 After leaving the service of Lord Stanhope Joyce became secretary of the Unitarian Society and minister of a chapel at Hampstead. His later years were devoted to the popularisation of natural science.

voted to the chair and delivered a stirring speech, which was CHAP, afterwards published. 1 'Worthy and Independent Citizens," IX. he began, ' we are met to rejoice at the vindication of innocence, at the grand victory lately obtained by patriotism, at the detection of plots, not supposed and visionary but real and substantial, formed against the liberties of the people. We have heard of the existence of strange laws not to be found amongst our statutes and of maxims which could never have taken root but in the heads or the hearts of despotic Tories." After condemning various features of the trial, he proceeded, ' We have seen several of our best-intentioned fellow-citizens immured for many months in close confinement for crimes they never did commit nor dream of. We have seen several of them afterwards dismissed without a single fact being produced against them, without any species of indemnity and without any punishment on their accusers. Are certain courtly aristocrats and apostates never to cease trampling under-foot the rights of their fellow-citizens and the liberties of their country? 2 would much rather be one of those honest " acquitted felons " I than be tormented for one hour with the unquiet reflections of some of their accusers. That they called one another citizens was termed an indication of an evil intent. It is a very proper word, and I confess that I am very happy it is growing into common use."

The speaker then dilated on the blessings of printing, liberty of the press, and trial by jury. ' There are certain fundamental principles which I have adopted as essential to freedom, and to which I pledge myself uniformly to adhere. First, a fair, free and equal representation of the people. Secondly, the ancient law of short, and even annual Parliaments. Thirdly, the Habeas Corpus Act, which was (and I wish I could say, which is) the safeguard of the personal liberty of the citizen. Fourthly, the sacred liberty of the press. Fifthly, the inestimable trial by jury." After this confession of faith he declared trial by jury to be in the greatest peril, and urged his hearers to urge the exclusion of contractors, revenue officers and tradesmen dealing with the Royal Family, and other reforms designed to safeguard men charged with treason against an unfair trial. 'Trial by jury," he concluded, f will not be attacked by men of aristocratic principles either by siege or storm. That citadel of the people can never be injured but by treacherous undermining. Let us 1 Substance of Earl Stanhope's speech, delivered from the Chair at a meeting of citizens at the Crown and Anchor.

2 A description applied to them by Windham.

CHAP, then, Citizens, be upon our guard, and while your Tory enemies IX. are awake, let the true friends of liberty not slumber." At the dinner which followed, no less than twenty-seven toasts were on the list, among them, 'Trial by Jury 'Thomas Erskine," 'The Cause of Liberty throughout the World,"' The Brave Kosciusko," ' The

Swinish Multitude and may the Honest Hogs never cease to Grunt till their Wrongs are Righted

The significance of the acquittal was in no way exaggerated by the jubilant Reformers. ' In my conscience," wrote Lord Holland many years later, ' I believe that had Home Tooke and his associates fallen victims to a charge of constructive treason, it would not have been long ere the first men in the country would have followed their fate. From such scenes I believe we were protected chiefly by the genius of Erskine." 1 The recent researches of Mr. Veitch 2 have established the moderation of the British Reformers, who emerge as upright and patriotic men, and who refused to discontinue their demand for Parliamentary reform because feudalism had been overthrown on the other side of the Channel. The only plot discovered during the years of excitement and repression was the work of Watt, a spy and agent provocateur.

Though the State trials of 1794 decreed that blood was not to flow, the Government pursued its policy of repression, and opposition became increasingly difficult and dangerous. Newspapers and sermons continued to lash the crimes of the French and to denounce the wickedness of Englishmen who were believed to be desirous of following their example. The most potent influence in scaring his countrymen was Gillray, who poured an unceasing stream of vitriol on the Whigs and democrats. If Fox naturally incurs the deadliest hatred of the great Tory caricaturist, Stanhope and Sheridan, Lansdowne and Priestley are not far behind. A glance at some of the principal pictures in his gallery suggests the prominent position occupied by Stanhope in the political life of the time. 3

On July 4, 1791, a picture of Alecto and her train at the gate of Pandemonium, or the Recruiting-Sergeant enlisting John Bull into the Revolution service, paints Stanhope stealing off 1 Further Memoirs of the Whig Party, p. 296.

2 The Genesis of Parliamentary Reform, 1913. For further discussion of their character see Laprade, England and the French Revolution, and W. P. Hall, British Radicalism, 1791-7.

3 Works of Gillray, ed. by Thomas Wright, pp. 130-355 passim. Miss Stanhope made a large collection of prints, of which only a few can be reproduced.

from the recruiting-party under the influence of a threatening CHAP, letter from Pitt. In suggesting that he was hesitating as to IX. which side he should embrace, Gillray showed himself singularly blind to the character of one of the most fearless politicians of his age. A second scene, two years later, is equally inexact. On June 12, 1793, he appears in company with Sheridan, Priestley, Home Tooke, and others, at a meeting at the Crown and Anchor to consider the pressing financial needs of Fox. Though Stanhope now supported and opposed the same causes as the great Whig leader, there is no evidence of any personal friendliness. A year later ' Citizen Don Quixotte ' fills the stage as ' The Champion of French Principles which include atheism, rapine and murder, and are symbolised by blood-stained axes and daggers. On May 3, 1794, a broadside, entitled ' The Noble Sans-culotte represents him with a cap of liberty on his head dancing on his coronet. In his hand he holds a stick with the head of an ass, attached to a flag bearing the legend Vive l'Egalite. The following stanzas suggest the character of a satire too coarse to print in full 1:â 'Rank, character, distinction, fame,

And noble birth forgot, Hear Stanhope, modest Earl, proclaim Himself a Sans-Culotte!
'Of pomp and splendid circumstance
The vanity he teaches; And spurns, like citizen of France, Both coronet and breeches.
'But thrown away on lordly ears
His counsel none attend: No pattern take his brother Peers By Stanhope's latter end.
' "At one end," says a noble Peer,
"No breeches I retain; " From this confession we infer
At t'other end no brain.
'Nay, what if brains and breeches fail,
Pray, say no more about 'em; Since Stanhope, ay, and Lauderdale,
Can make a shift without 'em."

On July 25 Stanhope appears with the Duke of Norfolk, Derby, Michael Angelo Taylor, General Fox, Lauderdale, and Sheridan 1 A copy is in the British Museum.

CHAP, among the lazzaroni following the lead of Fox as St. Januarius. IX. The cartoon of February 2, 1795, The Genius of France Triumphant, or Britannia petitioning for peace, vide the proposals of Opposition, depicts Britannia sacrificing her shield and spear, crown and sceptre at the feet of a sans-culotte monster. Fox tenders the keys of the Bank of England, Sheridan promises allegiance, and Stanhope's figure bears ' the destruction of Parliament."

His withdrawal from the House of Lords in no way diminished the hostility of the satirist. In a sketch entitled ' Patriotic Regeneration, namely, Parliament Reformed fi la Frangaise, that is, Honest Men (i. e. the Opposition) in the Seat of Justice," Parliamentary Reform is supposed to have been carried. Fox occupies the presidential chair, while Sheridan and Erskine are at the clerks' table. Pitt, with a halter round his neck, is brought to the bar in the custody of Lauderdale, the public executioner. Stanhope, as the Fouquier-Tinville of the Assembly, is denouncing his brother-in-law for opposing the rights of subjects to dethrone their King, of sans-culottes to equalise property and annihilate nobility, of freemen to extirpate religion and divide the estates of the Church. On April 14 Gillray launched ' The Stanhope Republican Gunboat constructed to sail against Wind and Tide." Stanhope bears the boat on his back, while a hideous ogre prods him with a trident. The vessel has to struggle against ' the current of public opinion' in the water and the furious blasts of ' Loyalty ' in the air. On April 30 Pitt appears as ' Phoebus Apollo, or the Sun of the Constitution rising superior to the clouds of opposition." The thick clouds display the features of Sheridan, Fox, and Stanhope dropping their daggers. On May n he appears steering the barge which carries English cattle to a French ship lying off the shore. On November I he joins in the attack on the State coach, a sketch inspired by the hustling of the King on his way to and from the opening of Parliament. One of the most elaborate of the cartoons, entitled ' Promised Horrors of the French Invasion," appeared in the autumn of 1796. The French soldiers, having burned St. James's Palace, march up St. James's Street, slaying as they advance. While Pitt, Burke, Dundas, Windham, and other Ministerialists are dead or about to die, the Opposition assist the invaders in their work of slaughter. Among the seething crowd is Stanhope, who holds aloft a pair of scales in which the severed head of Grenville is weighed against the trunk. In the spring of 1797 he assists the Opposition leaders in endeavouring to dissuade John Bull from accepting the paper-money which became legal tender when cash payments were suspended. A year later Gillray commenced CHAP, a series of the Whig leaders under the title of ' French Habits." Ix-The third plate, ' Les Membres du Conseil des Cinq Cents," represents Stanhope, followed by Lauderdale, Derby, Byng, and Michael Angelo Taylor. Thus a month seldom elapsed in which Gillray's coarse but powerful brush did not hold him up to the detestation of his countrymen.

After celebrating the acquittal of the reformers in the State Trials of 1794 Stanhope virtually withdrew from active politics for some years, and devoted himself to his scientific pursuits. From time to time, however, he emerged from his retirement to plead for peace. On December 5, 1795, ' a most numerous and respectable meeting of many thousands of the nobility, clergy, yeomen, freeholders, and other inhabitants of the county of Kent was held at Maidstone, 1 and Stanhope moved the following address:â ' To THE KING'S MOST EXCELLENT MAJESTY.

' THE HUMBLE ADDRESS OF THE FREEHOLDERS AND ' INHABITANTS OF THE COUNTY OF KENT.

' May it please your Majesty,â WE, the underwritten Freeholders and Inhabitants of the County of Kent, beg leave to approach your Majesty with sentiments of sincere concern for the late outrage and attack made against your Majesty's person, on the day your Majesty went to the Parliament House, and to express the happiness we feel at your Majesty not having received any personal injury therefrom. We must, in duty to ourselves and to our country, avail ourselves of this opportunity humbly to request your Majesty to take into consideration the present critical situation of this nation occasioned by the present disastrous war and the dangers which may result from impending scarcity, and speedily to adopt the most effectual mode of averting calamities so dreadful. And we earnestly entreat your Majesty immediately to set on foot a negotiation in order to procure for this country a speedy, honourable and lasting peace."

A year later he delivered an address at the celebration of the landing of William III. He gave his audience the new name of citizens, and proposed the following toast, which was adopted with applause. 'To the eighty thousand incorrigible 1 A printed report is at Chevening.

CHAP, citizens who are friends of liberty, humanity, justice and peace, IX. and who, for this reason, are regarded by Edmund Burke as incapable of amendment 1 In 1797 he drew up yet another strongly worded petition for peace. 2 ' To THE KING'S MOST EXCELLENT MAJESTY.

' THE HUMBLE PETITION OF THE NOBLEMEN, GENTLEMEN, FREE-HOLDERS AND INHABITANTS OF THE COUNTY OF KENT, APRIL 19, 1797.

' That this nation is now unfortunately involved in a war the most bloody as well as the most expensive which perhaps ever existed, and that suffering humanity calls aloud for peace.

' That the said war has been solely occasioned by the hostility of your Majesty's Ministers to the sacred and inalienable Rights of Man.

' And that, if the present ruinous war were to continue, it must prove fatal to the commerce, manufactures, credit and remaining prosperity of this nation.

' Your Majesty's petitioners further shew that this bloody war has been unnecessarily protracted, because your Majesty's Ministers, who have been at last obliged formally to acknowledge the French Republic, did wantonly refuse to make such acknowledgment at a time when peace, founded on good will and confidence, would have been obtained thereby.

' Your Majesty's petitioners further shew that last year Lord Malmesbury did agree with the French Republic that " proportionable restitutions " should be adopted as the basis of peace. But that, notwithstanding such actual agreement so made, your Majesty's Ministers, contrary to their duty and in defiance to the national faith thus solemnly pledged, did instruct your Majesty's Ambassador to depart from such agreement by proposing terms of peace utterly inconsistent therewith.

' Your Majesty's petitioners therefore humbly pray that your Majesty will take speedy measures to make an honourable, sincere and lasting peace; and that all these men who either have acted in the unjustifiable manner above described or are systematically hostile to a sincere, durable and cordial peace, be excluded from your Majesty's councils for ever."

Friends and foes alike knew that his sentiments were, unchanged. In 1797 an anonymous pamphlet appeared, entitled 1 Moniteur, xxviii. 504. In The First Letter on a Regicide Peace Burke had estimated the ' pure Jacobins' of Great Britain at about 80,000.

2 Chevening Papers, in his handwriting.

' Vindiciae Regis, or a Defence of the Kingly Office: In Two CHAP. Letters to Earl Stanhope." A manuscript note on a copy of the IX. second edition in the British Museum declares it to be the work of ' the Rev. Mr. Ireland of Croydon." ' You have at length gained a proselyte writes the aggrieved cleric, ' to one of the most pernicious of your opinions in the bosom of my parish. While your principles were known to the nation at large, I lamented, but did not take upon me to confute them. While you addressed them to the House, I pitied the peers but held my tongue. Now I find you within my proper boundary. You have recently declared, and my parishioners believe you, that the kingly office is forbidden by the Scriptures." The author refers to the speech in which he quoted Samuel, and points out that the passage only had reference to a vindictive King, acting on a special commission. Scripture, he adds, is full of passages inculcating obedience to governments. ' Hitherto, I fear, the Scriptures have obtained but little of your attention." The second letter compares the Jacobins with the Puritans, and denounces both as the enemies of throne and altar. ' Be a dignified and enlightened Peer," he concludes. ' Reform your duty to the Constitution, and look with due reverence to the throne." The pamphlet is conspicuous neither for argument nor for ability; but it is of interest as expressing the feelings of anger and contempt which champions of the established order in Church and State entertained for the high-born iconoclast. 1 On the other hand his old fellow-workers still sought his encouragement and advice. The indefatigable Cartwright had proposed a meeting for Parliamentary Reform at Boston; but the room was no sooner granted by the Mayor than recalled. The Major forwarded the resolutions he intended to move to Fox and Stanhope. The latter replied from Chevening, January 19, 1798.

' My dear Friend,â I return you a great many thanks for the very excellent resolutions which you have had the goodness to send me, and which you intended to be moved at Boston in favour of Parliamentary Reform. You know I have long been of opinion that a substantial reform and annual elections are 1 Among Grenville's papers is one dated January 1798, which declares the fixed plan of the rulers of France only to make peace with a British Republic. The Directory was to include Paine, Tooke, Thelwall, and Lansdowne, while Stanhope was to be ambassador at Paris. As the paper bears neither name nor address, it probably represents nothing more substantial than a jeu d'esprit. â Dropmore Papers, iv. 70,

CHAP, indispensable to preserve the liberty and prevent the ruin of the x- nation. Every day confirms me in that opinion. It is one which it is impossible not to be rooted in the mind of every man of sense who means well; and especially after what we have seen of late!!!

' Ever your most faithful ' STANHOPE."

After several years' absence from Parliament Stanhope began to pine for a return to active political life. He had strongly supported the concession of legislative independence to Ireland in 1782, and, when the Union loomed in sight, he issued a vigorous protest. His main argument was that there was no security for the rights of the Irish people in an Imperial Parliament. The pamphlet was reproduced in the newspapers of London and Dublin, and naturally met with a mixed reception. 2 ' EARL STANHOPE'S ADDRESS TO THE PEOPLE OF GREAT BRITAIN ' AND IRELAND ON THE INTENDED UNION.

' FELLOW CITIZENS, â At this time of danger more than alarm it is the duty of an honest man to address you on the state of public affairs; and it is precisely because the danger is greater than your apprehension of it, that I deem it more incumbent upon me to call your attention to one of the most extraordinary and unconstitutional measures that ever has been agitated in this or in any other country which has any pretence to term itself a free nation.

' It is now publicly avowed that an attempt is to be made by the Minister of the Crown to deprive the people of Ireland of their separate legislature, by substituting for that national Parliament, to which they have a right, a few votes in a foreign Parliament, which can never be equally acquainted with their dearest interests. A foreign Parliament which can never be equally apprized of their feelings, of the sentiments and the wishes of the Irish nation. A foreign'Parliament which we, who live under it, have already been insolently told is " The Parliament of the King, and not the Parliament of the people "! That Parliament, which is and ever must be foreign to the local concerns of Ireland, will probably not become more the Parlia- 1 Cartwright's Life, i. 247.

See ' Memoirs of Holcroft," in Hazlitt's Collected Works, ii. 222.

ment of the people by having representatives from the boroughs CHAP, of Ireland added to the unequal representation which now exists IX. in Great Britain.

' The people of England and Scotland and of Ireland have moreover been impudently told that " The people have nothing to do with the laws but to obey them "! 1 The people of England, of Scotland, and of Ireland are however of a different opinion.

' The late aristocrat, Edmund Burke, even before it was known that this project of an union was in agitation, stated that there was amongst the thinking part of the English nation, without including those numerous, useful and industrious citizens who have been insulted as a " Swinish Multitude," no less a number than " eighty thousand incorrigible " citizens as he was pleased to term those most valuable men in this nation who are firm friends to the sacred cause of peace, of liberty, humanity and justice; and who are better friends to law and to order than those rash men, whose rash measures may hereafter precipitate this country into a state of ruin, misery, poverty and wretchedness, unexampled either in ancient or in modern history. This country is not like a mere agricultural nation without arts, without manufactures and industry. This country, on the contrary, depends upon all these sources of wealth, not only for its prosperity but likewise for its existence. It is a country depending upon credit and its paper currency, to which the whole coin of the nation bears a proportion insignificantly small. It is a country overwhelmed with public debt and almost borne down by public taxes. And one should have thought that if, there were in the whole world one country more than another where it was peculiarly important not wantonly to wound the public mind and exasperate the public feeling, Britain was that country, where the dictators of wisdom should prevent, where discretion and sober council should not give way either to precipitancy or violence. Yet it is in this very country that we have heard the most liberticidal and audacious doctrines broached and the most unprincipled and wicked language held upon subjects the nearest to the people's hearts. For of what other description is the profligate language of those men who talk of " vigour beyond the law," that is to say, of arbitrary power and pure despotism? or of what other description is the abandoned language of those men who have written and published that " the kingly government may go on in all its 1 A memorable utterance of Bishop Horsley in the House of Lords.

CHAP, functions, without Lords or Commons "? and that " they may IX. be lopped off and the tree be a tree still; shorn indeed of its honours, but not, like them, cast into the fire "? Such men should, at least, have had a little prudence and discretion. Such men, at least, should not have published and proclaimed their criminal designs until they had obtained the Union.

' A measure which is an insult even to those men in Ireland who have supported this very administration. A measure of inj ustice to the people of that generous and warm-hearted nation, who are now represented by venal tongues as men unworthy of any public duty, and as men not fit to be trusted with a separate or independent Parliament.

' The Protestant in Ireland and the Catholic, the Protestant Dissenter and the Freethinker, the Tory and the Whig, the Aristocrat and the Democrat, the Yeoman and the United Irishman, ought all, as one man, to be averse to that measure of national ruin and disfranchisement, to that measure of national degradation and national contempt.

' I should be glad to know what possible security the people of Ireland can have for the future performance of such articles of the treaty of Union as the majority in the new Imperial Parliament (or whatever other whimsical name it is to have) may choose at any time hereafter to infringe? My question is, Where is the remedy? And to what other, or third tribunal, are the two islands to appeal?

' I will suppose a case:â ' So long as Ireland retains her Parliament and so long as that Parliament shall sit at Dublin, it is quite out of the question to suppose that the Irish Parliament ever would or ever could consent, for instance, to permit that a body of fifty or sixty thousand foreign mercenaries, either from Germany or from Russia, be landed in the island of Ireland in order to be there permanently kept in garrison. The Irish Parliament never would sanction such a project. The thing is morally impossible.

' But let the Union take place. What is to prevent a Parliament voting in Westminster, at any time hereafter, to come to a vote to that effect, in order to render such a measure legal which is now notoriously against law?

' And if the Westminster Parliament should be disposed to pass such a vote; what means will the Irish nation have, from a distance, to persuade the Westminster Parliament not to adopt a measure of that description?

' And if such a vote were to pass; in what would then consist the future liberty, or the future hopes of liberty, of the Irish people? Does not the mind of every man who has either a CHAP. British or an Irish heart revolt at such an idea and at such a IX. possibility? And any man who may, moreover, believe that such an event is probable is neither a Briton, nor an Irishman, nor an honest man, if such an idea does not harrow up his soul.

' The time is come for every man frankly and publicly to declare his sentiments. I take pride in declaring mine.

' My opinion is that people of both nations ought to meet in order to discuss this important question of the Union. And then we shall see whether the very starting of such a proposition will or will not answer the purpose (whatever it may be) which is intended by those short-sighted men who have unwisely thought proper to propose it.

' My respectable friends, the patriots of property in Great Britain, will do themselves high honour if they will stand perspicuously forward to call together the people in county meetings.

But, if they do not do it, or neglect to do it speedily, then let other patriots of less property take the lead. And all men of integrity and public spirit will hail their honest and judicious efforts for the public good.

1 How insignificant are the opposers of the people's rights when they appear in the presence of that immense assemblage of resolute and sturdy citizens, who though resolved to be calm are determined to be free!

' The glorious and decisive victory obtained by the people of the county of Kent, at our last magnificent county meeting, ought to serve as an instructive example to the rest of the nation of the proper course for them to pursue.

' Not only all the freeholders, but all the inhabitants were called. The men of freehold property, who bear a very small proportion to the whole number, are not the only men who are interested in the public welfare. Is not the copyholder, is not the leaseholder, is not the merchant, is not the tradesman, is not the manufacturer, is not the citizen cultivator and the laborious and valuable artisan, deeply interested also in the property of his country? Let all these, therefore, together with the freeholders, be assembled. The legal forms, in the calling of the meeting, should be strictly complied with; but let the people meet.

' Let the meetings be called, openly and professedly, to reprobate the Union, to petition against the rapid increase of taxes, to petition against the English or Scotch Militia being sent to Ireland, and unequivocally to express the wish of the nation CHAP, for a speedy peace with the French Republic. For these objects IX- should the people meet.

The inhabitants should thus be assembled in all the counties, in all the cities, and in all the towns and various parts of the Metropolis. They should not only meet, but they should meet frequently. Repeated meetings of the people tend to instruct and to open the public mind. They are necessary in every free country to keep alive the public spirit.

' The quick steps of every species of collective violence are equally unnecessary and improper. But nothing is more easy than for the people, actuated by a strong and common feeling of their common interest and proceeding with a common impulse in the slow but steady pace of legal step, to defeat the puny handful of the opposers of their inalienable rights, and to trample all their impotent projects of innovation in the dust.

' Such is the plan (as yet unconcerned with any set of men) of an independent individual, who feels warmly for his country's welfare; who now lives as a man of science in honourable retirement; but who never will be wanting to the people when the people are not wanting to themselves.

' FELLOW CITIZENS, at this moment of crisis he deems it his duty to inform you of his opinion; and he is happy in this opportunity of declaring to the world at large the ever unchanging and unchangeable public principle of your faithful and devoted fellow-citizen, ' STANHOPE.

'Chevening House: January 21, 1799."

The Union was a war measure, and it was against the war still more than against the Union that Stanhope invited his fellow-citizens to meet in protest. But now, when Ajax was emerging from his tent, some of his most experienced comrades were for delay. Many members of the Opposition had ceased to believe in the utility of effort. ' The spirit of the Constitution is lost wrote Lady Holland in her ' Journal ' in 1798," and those who care about political liberty must be contented and no longer struggle for what the majority are disposed to yield up." 1 An active correspondence took place in the opening weeks of i8oo. 2 ' Lord Stanhope," wrote Polhill, a Kentish neighbour, to Wyvill, ' called here last night and brought a petition to our High Sheriff which I altered, and he agreed to. But then, not being quite satisfied with some part of his, I drew up this 1 Lady Holland's Journal, i. 203. 8 Wyvill, Political Papers, vi. 76-94.

morning the enclosed Address, 1 which, with some very immaterial CHAP, alterations, he did me the honour to approve of, and desired me I x-to send to you." Wyvill rejoined that he approved the Address, but that attempts by isolated counties were useless. On the same day he wrote to Stanhope expressing his doubts, and asking him to consult ' the principal friends of liberty in London and the neighbouring counties, and to concert with them what may best be done. We are now in the middle of winter; a new campaign cannot be opened for several months; there is time for counsel and previous arrangements He then wrote to a score of Yorkshire friends; but the replies were unfavourable to any action on the part of the county. With his own convictions thus strengthened he again urged delay. ' I hope that you he wrote to Polhill, ' Lord Stanhope and your friends in Kent will suspend your application to the Sheriff till there is a prospect of a powerful co-operation, first in London, then in Yorkshire and the other northern counties, who are only waiting for the proper moment to come forward." ' I received your wise and friendly letter," replied Polhill, ' and shall advise my Lord to stop. He is the man to bring, at a proper time, such a thing forward. We could not do anything without him." Meanwhile Stanhope had also been making inquiries.

' Chevening: February 4, 1800.

My dear Wyvill,â I have been in town and executed your commission; and the result is as follows. Some persons are very sanguine about county meetings on the subject of peace. Others are of a different opinion. One opinion, however, seems general, and that is a wish for the people to call the meetings themselves. Nor do I disagree with this idea, though I have set my name to the Kent requisition. I particularly asked Mr. Fox what he thought had best be done in Yorkshire as to calling the freeholders only or the other inhabitants also. He is most clearly for the latter mode. Perhaps your best way will be for you to ask him his opinion about it. There is a middle mode, and that is the calling the householders. To this I should have no objection if others do not. But as for calling the freeholders only, the idea is quite scouted here. Almost all think the public wish for peace, though now torpid. I never saw Mr. Fox so well in his health at any time as at present. I went over to Holland House on purpose to pass a morning with him and his excellent nephew. He told me he had heard from you. Some persons 1 See Wyvill, Political Papers, vi, ii-iii.

CHAP, in the City of Westminster wish for a meeting in Westminster.

IX. But what is of most consequence is that it is not quite unlikely that a measure will take effect which, if it should, will produce more union among the friends of peace than any which has been thought of yet.

' Most cordially and affectionately yours, ' STANHOPE."

Wyvill replied that the letter revived his hopes. Peace, however, was still far off, and Stanhope no longer hesitated to return to the Chamber where he could compel a hated government to listen, if not to obey. Before, however, we embark on the political struggles of his later life, we must study in some detail the scientific activities which had claimed the greater part of his time and thought during the years of his retirement from Parliament.

THE change from the metaphysical radicalism of the eighteenth CHAP, century to the more empirical methods of the Utilitarians was X. often accompanied by an ardour for the natural sciences. The Duke of Bridgewater, whose plainness of attire led him to be confused with his own workmen, aided Brindley to construct some of the principal canals in the kingdom. Lord Shelburne played Maecenas to a number of learned men, including Price, Bentham, and Priestleyâ the latter as notable for his radical opinions as for his services to English chemistry. Tom Paine, again, displayed considerable mechanical ingenuity in his designs for iron bridges. In Lord Stanhope advanced political views were joined to a sound knowledge of mechanics, based on his early training in ' practical' mathematics and his acquaintance with the fine machinery in use at Geneva; and, in middle life, he turned his mind to the application of the steam-engine to the purposes of navigation. His thoughts may have been directed to the subject by Symington's pamphlet published in 1777, or he may have heard, through his French friends, of the attempts of Jouffroy. As member of the Philosophical Society of Philadelphia he probably read Franklin's ' Maritime Observator printed among the ' Transactions."

Up to the year 1783 steam power had been limited to pumping, and consequently to the single industry of mining. Watt, who had been steadily working at perfecting the steam-engine, was resolved to adapt it to mill-work. The Albion Mills for grinding corn were erected at Blackfriars, and fitted with two double-acting engines, the most complete and powerful which he had until then turned out of the Soho manufactory. The gear of these celebrated mills was designed by John Rennie (afterwards CHAP, the engineer of Waterloo and London Bridges) and was a novelty, X. being made entirely of cast or wrought iron in place of wood. Delighting in the society of clever mechanics and attracted by Rennie's practical abilities, Stanhope frequently visited the works to see what was going on. He designed a boat and tried it on the small lake at Chevening. My father remembers a very old gardener who often referred to these steam-boat trials, which took place in his boyhood. The boat was apparently started into action by towing, and ' when his Lordship thought she was going all right, without warning he would cut the rope and let us all down." The anecdote is delightfully characteristic of the man, who was regardless of the comfort of individuals as compared with the advancement of science or the welfare of humanity.

On March 13, 1790, while Miller and Symington were still experimenting with the first steam-boat on the Scotch lochs and before Fulton had applied his mind to the subject, Stanhope took out a patent for ' constructing ships and vessels and moving them without help of sails, and against wind, waves, current or tide." x The invention was notable for the shape of the vessel, the manner of guiding it, and the mechanism by which it was moved. The shape of the boat is tapered to a fine point at the ends, these being ' for greater safety covered with iron or other metal." The length was three and half times the breadth. Its inventor wished to make it greater in length in proportion to breadth, but was prevented by the Act against smuggling (24 Geo. Ill), which forbade any of the King's subjects to own a ship whose proportions were in excess of these. As it could navigate either ' head foremost or stern foremost' and be impelled not only with the wind but against it, he described it as an ambi-navigator. His improvements in the rudder aimed at securing ' as nearly as possible an equal pressure from the water on both sides of its stern or axis, which contrivance the pilot may move or hold in any required position with much greater ease."

The most important factor is the mechanism for moving the ship. There is a slit in the centre of the vessel, and in this, on pivots, is suspended a long iron arm terminating in a hook, which Stanhope designates ' a vibrator." In a fixed space it moves backwards and forwards from head to stern, carrying with it an attached plate called ' a free operator." The ' free operator ' is a thin plate of iron of considerable size, having its edges turned up square and strengthened by ' bars and braces." Hinged on

pivots fixed in the hook of the ' vibrator," when it 1 Bennet Woodcroft's Specification of Patents, 1732.
is made to move in the direction from the head to the stern of CHAP.
the ship, it acts vertically with its whole surface against the X.
water; but when moving in the contrary direction, the water causes it to assume a horizontal position, in which it offers but little resistance. In order to cause the vibrator to move to and fro, ' the strength of men or of animals, or a steam-engine, or any forcible power whatever may be applied." To bring the ' vibrator ' and ' operator ' back in the direction from the stern towards the head of the ship, a weight may be fixed to the operator by means of a very strong iron arm which acts by its own weight like the pendulum of a clock. He also anticipates the invention for disconnecting the screw and shipping it when the vessel is under canvas, the method adopted by all the early screw steam-boats of the Government service.

Realising in 1790 ' what a material thing it is to prevent nuts from unscrewing he invented that ingenious little contrivance which is used to this day in every form of machinery, ' the split pin Cottier has given it the neatness of finish which was impossible when machinery was made by hand, but its invention we owe to Stanhope. ' There must be he says, ' a small slit in each bolt, and a hinch-pin should be put into the said small slit. It is split at one of its ends in order to be bent back both ways after it is put into the slit, in order to prevent it from starting out He spent the year in perfecting his mechanism, and took out another patent for having the slit' of a proper form, covered and made air-tight to prevent the water rising in the slit and obstructing the motion of the ' vibrator by which the vibration might be decreased. The principal improvement is the ' free operator which was to be of the shape and principle of a duck's foot, contracting by the force of the water as it moves from head to stern and expanding and ' acting violently against the water ' as it moves backwards. By this means the propulsion of the vessel is effected. It is generally supposed that Stanhope adopted the principle of the duck's-foot paddle from Genevois, who laid it before the Admiralty in 1760; but as all early steam navigators attempted in the first place to assimilate their inventions to the two propellers known to natureâ the duck's foot and the salmon's tailâ it was possible that he was not aware of this invention. In any case he gave it a more practical trial, and his method of employing it was quite different. His mode of propulsion was entirely new, and has been often copied since his time. Trevethick tried to employ it in I82Q, 1 and I believe i Life of Trevethick, ii. 369.

CHAP. Mr. Welton was the last to use it on a steam-boat exhibited at X. the Naval and Sub-marine Engineering Exhibition at the Royal Agricultural Hall, Islington, in I882. 1

In October 1789 Stanhope wrote to Boulton and Watt about a steam-engine for his ship.

' Chevening House: October 23, 1789.

Earl Stanhope presents his compliments to Mr. Bolton and should be much obliged to him to return this letter with full answers written under the following queries. Whatever expense may be occasioned by a clerk's making the calculations Lord Stanhope will readily defray.

' Qy. i. Would Mr. Bolton have any objection to make a very small fire engine (of any required dimensions) to serve as a model for a large one, by way of experiments?

' Qy. 2. Can Mr. Bolton make a fire engine to move in an horizontal instead of a perpendicular direction?

' Qy. 3. Is there any person in London who has any of Mr. Bolton's for sale ready-made; or are they always bespoke?

' Qy. 4. Is there any intelligent workman in London, connected with or employed by Mr. Bolton, who could make a small fire engine that would work well (as a model) according to directions to be given by Earl Stanhope?

' Qy. 5. Have Mr. Bolton's fire engines anything adjusted to them to make them work at any degree or scale of strength short of their full degree? And also stop them instantly?

' Qy. 6. Lord Stanhope would be glad to have one of the prints (or plans) of Mr. Bolton's best fire engines, and of his most simple construction if Mr. Bolton has any such prints.

' Qy. 7. When is Mr. Bolton to be in London, and where will he be to be met with?

' Qy. 8. Lord Stanhope would be glad to be informed whether Mr. Bolton has made any new discovery in respect to his fire engine since his patent, and what is the nature of such discoveries? ' 2

Stanhope invariably took counsel upon his schemes and inventions with Rennie, who made inquiries as to the cost of applying Boulton Watt's steam-engine to his ship, and reported the results. 3 1 Transactions of Mechanical Engineers for 1885, p. 126.

2 From Boulton and Watt MSS., in the possession of Messrs. Tangye.

3 Manuscript Life of John Rennie, by his son Sir John Rennie, at Institute of Civil Engineers; and Smiles' Lives of the Engineers, ii. 143.

1 My Lord,â I have seen Messrs. Boulton Watt, to whom CHAP. I put the following queries, which I think contain the substance X. of what your Lordship wished me to obtain.

' Query i. What are the terms B. W. will undertake to furnish steam-engines for working ships, to be applied to Earl Stanhope's new invented machine for making ships move through the water without sails?

' Answer. Â 5 per annum per horse power which is the country premium for rotation engine; the London premium is Â 6 6s. per horse power.

1 Query 2. Can a steam engine be made to work to advantage without throwing any cold water into the condenser?

' Answer. Yes. Messrs. B. W. have made an engine on this plan, but to work properly it requires the vessel to which cold is to be applied to be a very large size.

' Query 3. Will any material inconvenience arise from giving the cylinder of the engine a very small degree of inclination?

' Answer. The cylinder of an engine is best to be perpendicular, and the degree of inconvenience will be in proportion to the inclination.

' I am, my Lord, with respect, Yours most obtly., ' JOHN RENNIE.

-'April 27, 1790."

On this Stanhope wrote to Boulton Watt expressing certain views as to the manner in which the engine he required should be adapted to steam navigation; but these suggestions failed to commend themselves to the Soho firm. ' His Lordship wrote Watt, ' has applied to us for engines; but we believe we are not likely to agree with his, as he lays too much stress on his own ingenuity." 1 The following letter expresses the same sentiment in a more courteous form:â ' My Lord,â We are honoured with your Lordship's note of the 5th. When we are asked general questions we can only give general answers. If your Lordship had informed us what were your wishes and specific wants we should have been enabled to have given a suitable answer. From what Mr. Rennie said we certainly did not fully comprehend your Lordship's desires in respect to the engine wanted. It rarely happens that different men see the same object in the same point of view. As soon as one of us can come we shall do ourselves the honour of waiting 1 Watt to Cullen, April 24, 1790. B. Woodcraft's Collection at Patent Office,

CHAP, on your Lordship, not doubting but by conversation we shall X. settle such points as are in our department to satisfaction. ' In the interim we remain with great respect, ' My Lord, Your Lordship's most faithful and obedt. humble servants, ' BOULTON WATT.

'May n, 1790." i

The firm next submitted certain diagrams containing their notions of what a marine-engine should be. Stanhope's reply was to cover several large sheets with ' Objections to the plans of Boulton Watt'; and his engine was finally built from his own design by Rob. Walker Dewer. In 1795 he writes to his old Genevese tutor, Le Sage:â ' Depuis plusieurs annees je me suis occupe a analiser la theorie difficile de la navigation, et d'en reformer et totalement changer la pratique. J'y ai fait beaucoup de progres: et il resulte de mes decouverles que nous en sommes jusques ici non pas seulement a 1'A. B. C. de cette science, mais que nous en sommes encore a la lettre A." 2

From this time forward he built innumerable ships and boats. The large craft were on the Thames, and the smaller were kept for experimental purposes, either at the ' piece of water at my seat in Kent, or the Great Pond The Admiralty Warrant to the first Kent ambi-navigator vessel, dated April 26, 1790, informs us that she was 51 feet in length, 6 feet 2 inches in breadth, 3 feet 4 inches in depth. In this vessel the ' vibrators ' appear to have been worked ' by men with wooden handles," and it is evident that no steam-engine was on board, probably on account of her size and the immense weight of engines as then built. A vessel for conveying coals from Newcastle to London drew from Lord Holland the caustic remark that she would have consumed her entire cargo before she arrived. This was the very drawback Boulton Watt had predicted with any other engine than their own; but Stanhope invented a boiler to overcome the difficulty.

A letter to Condorcet written in May 1791 shows how closely his scientific activities were related to his political ideals. 3 ' I am too busy to follow the question of weights and measures as much as I should have wished. I am deeply occupied with my great project, of the success of which I have no doubt, of 1 Chevening MSS. Ibid. 3 Ibid.

making vessels move without sails against wind and waves. CHAP. I hope to make an experiment this year on a large scale with a x-vessel 100 feet long between Dover and Calais. I like to think that I shall thereby be drawing our countries nearer together, without regard to the seasons or storms. But I shall rejoice still more if I can contribute to unite their hearts. Since your happy and glorious Revolution you deserve the esteem and gratitude of the whole world.

' STANHOPE

Till 1832 the administration of the Admiralty was vested in the Navy Board and the Lords Commissioners of the Admiralty. The civil administration gave every opportunity for jobbery, peculation and waste; but the Navy Board were bitterly opposed to any plan which, in remedying it, would reveal the corrupt management of affairs. They were equally hostile to any exhaustive experiments in naval architecture, steam navigation or kindred subjects. 1 That the Admiralty Board were slightly more enlightened only led, in the words of the First Lord, ' to the Admiralty and the Navy Boards being at daggers drawn." 2 But it had dim, inchoate ideas that' something ought to be done," without knowing how to do it. Again and again did Bentham, their Inspector-General, recommend the use of steam-engines in the dock-yards. Again and again did Stanhope urge on them that experiments in steam navigation should be made. The Admiralty would have ignored the latter, like other inventors, but for special circumstances. In 1788 Lord Chatham, his brother-in-law, had been appointed First Lord; and, though Stanhope was not a man to exploit any relationship or connection, Chatham's indolent disposition made him willing to comply with any request when its insistence became tedious to him. Accordingly in October, 1792, Stanhope signed an agreement with the Admiralty that they should build a ship according to his plan, and if, after experiments under his direction, the Lords of the Admiralty should see fit to retain her for the Government service, they should bear all expenses.

1 They were no more enlightened than their inexperienced contemporaries. In 1794 John Whittaker, B. D., wrote of ' that wildly eccentric but vividly vigorous genius who professes to send a ship, by the force of steam, with all the velocity of a cannon ball, and who pretends by the power of his steam-impelled oars to beat the waters of the ocean into the hardness of adamant."â The Course of Hannibal, ii. 142.

2 Life of Sir 5. Bentham, p. 171.

CHAP. The Society for the Improvement of Naval Architecture, x- which had recently come into existence, was due to the European Magazine. Struck by the remark of several ship-builders ' that it would ever be the case, while that business was not studied as a science but carried on by precedent, that there had not been one improvement that did not originate with the French, where there were schools and seminaries instituted for the study of it, and that our ships were not a match for those of that nation either singly or as a fleet the publisher, Sewell, collected books on naval architecture and exhibited models of ships at his shop in Cornhill. 1 The Society was founded in 1791, at a meeting at the Crown and Anchor Tavern. It numbered over three hundred members, under the presidency of the Duke of Clarence (afterwards William IV), and distributed premiums and medals. To ascertain the laws of floating bodies and the resistance of fluids nearly 10,000 experiments took place at Greenland Dock between 1793 and 1798. Stanhope was one of the most active Vice-presidents, and lent three of his boats for experimental purposes.

The virtues of his methods of construction seem to have been eagerly canvassed by the members. One of them, John Leard, ' after very maturely considering the construction of your Lordship's vessel strongly advised that she be fitted with sails besides the machinery,' that she may be perfectly manageable in all cases 2 Stanhope agreed to the proposal, and was so much pleased with Leard, whom he calls ' an able and experienced officer that he desired him to command the Kent. Accordingly, in July, 1793, the Admiralty appointed him Master of the Ambi-navigator ship. He was one of the committee of the Society for the Improvement of Naval Architecture chosen to conduct experiments in Greenland Dock; but he was no scientist or mathematician. He does not hesitate to report when some one pronounces steam navigation ' a wild scheme '; to which the inventor replies that ' experience and experiments will open all men's eyes in due time

After six months' work the ship was ready. On March 31, 1793, the dowager Lady Stanhope writes to Lady Chatham: ' I with pleasure can acquaint you that the expected ship was launched yesterday with great success and named the Kent. The indefatigable inventor and constructor, Lady Stanhope, and all his young family were present, and all happy and pleasant.

1 Preface to a Collection of Papers on Naval Architecture, originally printed on the wrapper of the European Magazine. 9 Leard to Stanhope, November 12, 1792.

The prospect of its most probably being of great public use, the CHAP. great pleasure my son must feel after so many laborious experiments to find it answer his expectations, and that his health has not suffered, is indeed a very infinite satisfaction to me, and it makes up for many anxious moments. I always feared that even his strength could not stand the fatigue of both mind and body, the strongest men that were employed often complaining that it was too much for them. I fancy you'll easily suppose the joy of the young people; the show, their eagerness for its succeeding, having been witness to great part of the fatigue and trouble it had given their father, the being on the Thames in a boat down to Greenwich where he accompanied them after he had sailed in his ship, in short the whole may perhaps be marked in their calendar as one of the happiest days of their lives." 1 The Kent measured in feet, was about n feet deep, drew 7 feet odd inches of water and was over 200 tons without engines.

Stanhope's fame has been in large measure overshadowed by the world-wide celebrity of Robert Fulton. In the ' Annals of Philosophy for 1818 ' an anonymous writer says of the former and his steam-boats: ' He is understood to have constructed two or three kinds of apparatus which were adequate to the purpose; but in expectation of accomplishing something still more perfect he hesitated in making them public, and thus lost in a great measure the honour of the invention. Mr. Fulton, with less science but with more decision, has immortalised himself. It is well known that Lord Stanhope and Mr. Fulton were at one period in the habit of frequently meeting, and conversing on topics connected with the improvement of machinery and that of steam-vessels in particular." 2 Rennie unjustly dismissed the American as ' a quack who traded on the inventions of others'; 3 but it is indisputable that he learned a great deal from Stanhope, whom he met in 1793. The following letter, on which Fulton based the claims of priority for his inventions, merely proves that the two men were working independently at the problem. 4

My Lord,â I extremely regret not having received your Lordship's letter in time to have the pleasure of an interview at Exeter, as a mechanical conversation would have been infinitely 1 Lady Stanhope to Lady Chatham. Chevening MSS. ' 2 Annals of Philosophy, xi. 84.

3 Smiles' Lives of the Engineers, ii. 237.

4 Chevening MSS. It is not the original, but a copy sent by Fulto in 1811. It has been printed in Dickinson's admirable Life of Fulton, 1913.

CHAP, interesting to a young man. To atone for such a loss and conform X. with your Lordship's wish I have made some slight drawings of my ideas on the subject of the steam-ship. In June 1793 I began the experiments of the steam-ship. My first design was to imitate the spring in the tail of a salmon. For this purpose I supposed a large bow to be wound up by the steam-engine, and the collected force attached to the end of a paddle, as in No. i, to be let off which would urge the vessel forward. This model I have had made, of which No. I is an exact representation, and I found it to spring forward in proportion to the strength of the bow about 20 yards; but by the return of the paddle the continuity of the motion would be stopped. I then endeavoured to give a circular motion, which I effected by applying two paddles on an axis. Then the boat moved by jerks, as there was too great a space between the strokes. I then applied three paddles, forming an equilateral triangle, to which I gave a circular motion by winding up the bow. I then found it to move in a gradual and even motion 100 yards with the same bow which before drove it but 20 yards. No. 2 is the figure of my present model on which there are two equilateral triangles, one on each side of the boat acting on the same shaft which crosses the boat or ship and turns with the triangles. This, my lord, is the line of experiment which led me to the triangular paddles, which at first sight will convey the idea of a wheel on perpendicular oars which are no longer in the water than they are doing execution. I have found by repeated experiment that three or six answer better than any other number, as they do not counteract each other. By being hung a little above the water and allowing a short space for the delivery of one to the entrance of the other, it likewise enters the water more on a perpendicular. The dotted lines will shew its situation when it enters, and when it is covered the circular dots exhibit its passage through the water. Your Lordship will please to observe in the small wheel with a number of paddles, A, B, C, and D strike almost flat in the water and rise in the same situation, whilst E is the only one that pulls the others against it, which renders the purchase fruitless. While E is urging the ship forwards, B A is pressing her into the water and C D is pulling her out; but remove all the paddles except E and she moves on in a direct line. The perpendicular triangular paddles are supposed to be placed in a cast-iron wheel, which should ever hang above the water. It will answer as a fly and brace to the perpendicular oars. This boat I have repeatedly let go and ever found her to move in a steady direction in proportion to the original purchase. With regard to the formation of ships moved by steam I have been of opinion that they CHAP, should be long, narrow, and flat at bottom, with a broad keel, as a x-flat vessel will not occupy so much space in the water and consequently has not so much resistance. A letter containing your Lordship's opinion of this mode of gaining a purchase on the water and directed to me at the Post Office, Exeter, will much oblige ' Your Lordship's most obedient and ' Very humble servant, ' ROBERT FULTON. ' Tor Quay; November 4, 1793-'

Stanhope renewed his bond with the Admiralty on June 30, 1794; but towards the end of 1796 he desired a new arrangement. In November Lord Spencer, who had succeeded Lord Chatham at the Admiralty, wrote to him:â ' My Lord,â Some difficulties on the subject of the Kent have been started by the Navy Board; but if I am not deceived in my expectation of getting over them, it will be but a very few days longer before I shall be enabled to acquaint you that the business is put in the train you wish."

The Admiralty desired the Kent to have a sailing trial; but it had to be postponed, because Leard found that the ship must be recaulked, and could not be repaired without going into dock. When at last she was ready in February, 1797, the Navy Board saw their opportunity for another attempt to frustrate his plans. They had received directions from the Admiralty, ordering them to appoint a fast sailing-vessel to accompany the Kent from the Thames to Portsmouth. The experiment was to be made under the direction of Leard; but the Navy Board were to ' send a person properly qualified on board to see that such experiment be duly made, reporting to us the result thereof." 1 They appointed a Mr. Madgshon, Master Attendant of His Majesty's Yard at Chatham, and directed Leard ' to follow the directions of Mr. Madgshon in the said experiment." Leard naturally refused to be under the orders of a man ' who was not acquainted with the construction of the vessel; nor will I ever submit to be duped by the Navy Board." He appealed to Stanhope, and showed the order to one of the Lords of the Admiralty, 1 The Admiralty to the Navy Board, November 16, 1796.

CHAP, who assured him that the Admiralty did not approve of the x- Navy Board altering the spirit of their directions. 1

The Navy Board got wind of the fact that the Admiralty was displeased with them, and hurriedly wrote an unofficial letter to Leard, saying that their warrant to him was perfectly consistent with the order received from the Admiralty. They sign themselves ' your affectionate friends 2 but Leard knew better. ' I have two charges he writes," to shew their unwillingness to attend to anything belonging to the Kent. But it was all levelled at your Lordship. They are now afraid of you." 3 The Kent finally left Deptford on February 22, and arrived at Chatham on March I. ' We sailed with the Hilsborough, East Indiaman," reported Leard, ' which we beat considerably, and every other vessel except a Scotch smack which pretty near kept pace with us. She steers admirably and works well. The commissioners and officers of the dock-yard have been very kind, and readily supplied me with what I wanted. The commissioners have sent for me three times to ask questions. Mr. Madgshon comes on board this evening. He has three different orders, the last of which is that the whole is to be under my direction 4 The Raccoon, l a sloop of war rigged as a brig was ordered to accompany her. After a tedious passage with unfavourable winds they came to anchor at Spithead.

On the return passage Leard writes: ' I must congratulate your Lordship on the success of the principles on which the Kent is constructed. I have great reason to believe they will be very much adopted. I have seen enough to say for certain she is a most excellent construction, and every other person that has seen her sail is of the same opinion 5 He had reported that she was leaking when she came out of dock, and ' leaking considerably ' during most of the sailing trial. But being flat-bottomed and fitted with a sliding keel she was still able to sail well in conditions which would have been fatal to a sharp built ship. Neither Leard nor Stanhope express any suspicion as to the cause of this leak. The sudden conservatism, as Burke calls it, of the Navy Board made them bitterly opposed to innovations of any kind; and they were not above thwarting improvements by very questionable means, as Sir Samuel Bentham found in regard to his two experimental vessels, the Dart and the Arrow. Leaks were found on board the Arrow, 1 Leard to Lord Stanhope, February 19, 1797.

2 Navy Board to Leard, February 20, 1797. Chevening MSS.

3 Leard to Lord Stanhope, February 21, 1797.

4 Ibid., March I, 1797. 5 Ibid., March 22, 1797- and it was more than suspected that they were purposely caused CHAP. â to ' dish the vessel as a sailor was heard to declare. x-

On March 22 Captain Lloyd handed in his report to the Admiralty, and through them to Lord Stanhope.

' Raccoon in the Downs: March 22, 1797.

' Agreeable to your orders of the 5th instant, I weighed in his Majesty's sloop under my command, in company with the Kent Ambi-navigator, on her intended trial. I ran down Channel as far as Dungeness at the rate of seven knots and a half an hour: the Kent kept company under moderate sail, at near the same rate of sailing. The wind drawing round to the W. S. W. and blowing strong, with a heavy sea, the Kent weathered in a degree that far surpassed my expectation. I perceived her very easy and lively in a head sea. I thought it a good opportunity to give her a trial in stays, and had the satisfaction to see her come about without any apparent difficulty in hauling round the Owers with a strong wind to the north-east. It appeared by my log that she went seven knots and a half, but in light winds she does not bear the same equality in her sailing, in my opinion from her masts and sails not being in proportion to the hull, and cannot consider them as any other than jury masts. I am convinced, were she properly masted, and without the steam-house, vibrator ports, and shutters, which must of course act greatly to impede her sailing, she would be equal to any of His Majesty's frigates, and in her present state sails astonishingly well in every point."

On May 6 the Navy Board sent to the Admiralty their opinion on the Kent. They consider ' that she may be converted into a gunboat and employed as such in His Majesty's navy, and deem it advisable upon Lord Stanhope's delivering up the vessel that he should take away whatever part of the steam-engine or its apparatus which may have been put on board'; adding ' we are the more inclined to give this advice to their Lordships from a thorough conviction that an invention of this kind could never be applied to any advantageous purpose in His Majesty's navy." 1 This interesting document was transmitted by Mr. Nepean to Lord Stanhope. But the inventor had no intention of giving up without a struggle, being thoroughly 1 Navy Board's Report to Admiralty, May 6, 1797. Of course the wits made fun of the inventor:â ' Behold from Brobdignag that wondrous fleet With Stanhope keels of thrice three hundred feet! Be ships or politics, Great Earl, thy theme, Oh! first prepare the navigable stream."

â â Notes and Queries Second Series, iv. 265.

CHAP, convinced that ' the national importance of such investigation X. is almost beyond description." He accordingly wrote as follows to the Lords Commissioners of the Admiralty:â 'Chevening: May 22, 1797.

' My Lords,â I feel truly sensible of the very proper conduct of your Lordships in communicating to me one of the most extraordinary papers perhaps ever written by any public Board, in which they state that no attempt has during four years been made to put my plan into execution. To this unaccountable assertion I have to observe that the very first step proper to be taken, in order to ascertain experimentally the practicability of moving ships and vessels by means of steam, was to construct a vessel free from the various objections to which the vessels built by the Navy Board are liable, which are of a construction repugnant to the fundamental principles of mathematics and mechanics, and contrary to the unquestionable laws of naval architecture. It was not till about the middle of the year 1795 that the boiler (successfully invented by me for burning its own smoke and for saving a great part of the fuel) was fixed on board the vessel together with other parts belonging to the steam apparatus. So that instead of it being four years, it was the middle (or thereabouts) of 1795 that I had any opportunity of making any experiments with steam on board the said vessel. Instead of "No attempt " having been made to put my plan into execution, the number of experiments made on board the Kent have been very great and the results most conclusive and important. Most of the analytical experiments about steam are in the nature of things of a sort to be made with the vessel at anchor. It is only a different class of those experiments which require that the vessel should be taken to sea. And most certainly I have no idea of submitting to be censured by the Navy Board on account of the particular manner in which I have thought proper to conduct my own experiments relative to steam. There never was, I believe, any steam-engine ever invented which was calculated to work well in a very boisterous sea, until I made sundry new and valuable discoveries to overcome the difficulties upon the subject. All that can be expected from me (and more than ought to be expected from any individual) is to take the risk upon myself. With respect to the hasty and unspecific opinion of the Navy Board that a plan for moving vessels by means of steam " could never be applied to any advantageous purpose in His Majesty's Navy," I will condescend

1 Lord Stanhope to Mr. Nepean, October 9, 1796.

to make thereto only one remark: viz. that if I shall actually CHAP, succeed in producing sufficient velocity and in moving vessels X. without wind and against wind, those men who have never seen (or asked to see) any of the experiments and who have never received from me any explanation of what is intended either as to vessels in general or as to the navy in particular cannot possibly form any enlightened opinion upon the subject. If this explanation should not be deemed by your Lordships sufficiently satisfactory, I request that your Lordships will order the Navy Board (as an inferior Board) to appear before the Board of Admiralty, and to answer such proper nautical questions as I shall, in the presence of the Board of Admiralty, put to them.

' Your Lordships' most obedient ' and most humble servant, ' STANHOPE." 1

Meantime Leard went every day to the Admiralty to ascertain the progress of affairs, and his letters give a curious account of the relations between the Admiralty and Navy Boards. He had several interviews with Mr. Nepean, who told him that ' the Admiralty Board were perfectly satisfied with respect to the vessel'; 2 and he was informed that ' the Admiralty mean to build on the principle of the Kent immediately." 3 But on May 30 Nepean tells Leard ' the Navy Board are very stubborn and the delay do not rest with the Admiralty Board, which are dissatisfied with the Navy Board on account of the difficulties they have made." 4 The Board of Admiralty disregarded the N avy Board's advice, and determined that the experiments should proceed. On July 20 Stanhope was informed that the Lords of the Admiralty had directed the Navy Board to prepare a new bond in the manner proposed by him. The Navy Board had received instructions to this effect once before, but they had taken no notice; and they now procrastinated as long as possible. At last he wrote to Lord Spencer, saying that the affair of the Kent must be attended to. In August the Navy Board sulkily executed the bond by which the Government became sole owners of the vessel; but they revenged themselves by refusing to pay the bills which had been contracted by Leard under the distinct understanding that, the Kent being a Government vessel, all expenses incurred by her were to be defrayed. The creditors were clamorous, and threatened Leard with an action. H(?

1 Chevening MSS. 2 Leard to Lord Stanhope, April 14, 1797.
3 April i. 4 May 30.

CHAP, begged Stanhope to pay them, but in vain. A grave principle x- was involved, and he had his bond and the letters from the

Admiralty. The Navy Board again had to eat humble pie, for, some months later, Stanhope learned that the Admiralty had ordered the bills to be paid.

Up to 1797, though the Kent was practically a Government vessel and under the control of the Admiralty, the entire cost of the engines had been borne by Stanhope; but in the new bond of that year the steam-engines became the property of the Government. In January 1798 the Admiralty wrote to him 'acquainting him that experiments with steam on board the Kent should not proceed," 1 and in November they informed him that orders had been given to remove the steam-engine altogether. It was a severe blow. A steam-engine of 1300 men-power was on board her wrote the inventor, ' and she was to be tried with steam. I intended to take her, by means of that powerful agent, off a lee-shore in a tempest. I was about to make the experiments at my own risk and expense; but to my great surprise I was prevented by an official letter from the Board of Admiralty, when Mr. Pitt was Minister and Earl Spencer First Lord." 2 The vessel was re-named, not inaptly, the Contest. The Admiralty wished to refit her as a gun-vessel; but on the recommendation of her old enemy, the Navy Board, she was broken up. 3 It must have been with a sigh of relief that they saw her disposed of and the application of steam power to the Navy abandoned, at any rate, for the time.

Stanhope had none the less effected considerable improvements in the marine steam-engine, which are enumerated by himself in a letter to Boulton Watt. ' I have of late years theoretically and experimentally investigated the principles of the steam-engine and of its various parts with uncommon assiduity and attention. Your steam-engines in their present state are not fit to be sent to sea. Especially your boilers (surrounded by brick work) would not do in a violent storm. Your engines are not calculated to work well in a very inclined situation; in other words, they are not calculated to work well in a boisterous sea. I have for several years past made it my particular study, and at a large expense, to obviate all the aforesaid objections to your engines, by means both of new principles and new contrivances discovered 1 Digest of Admiralty Papers at Record Office.

2 Theo. Laurance, December 19, 1808. Chevening MSS.
8 Digest of Admiralty Papers, October 8, 1797 (59, c). Admiralty Letters to Navy Board, June 19, September 10, October 8, 1799 (2225). Public Record Office.

by me, and which are really admirable. I am proceeding rapidly. CHAP. Some of those contrivances, more especially those which relate x-to the boiler and its bars, are now on board the said ship in Greenland Dock. That boiler is near 12 feet long and near 8 feet wide. It has no door. And when the fire is properly conducted it yields no smoke whatever. It is perfectly safe and fit for sea, and no danger from fire can result from it. The quantity of water it evaporates in a given time, when compared with the fuel used, far exceeds I believe everything hitherto produced. I have improved the piston; I can save above two-thirds of its weight without injuring its strength. I can make it act in an inclined position. I have invented and executed new valves very far indeed preferable to any other whatsoever. I have also invented and executed a new safety-valve, a thing of great consequence at sea. I have formed a way of making much better joints and of saving certain parts. I have got a new mode of opening and shutting the valves. In short, I have made a regular and complete analysis of the steam-engine and of all its parts." He proposes to consolidate their different inventions, ' though I do not doubt but that I can, without any man's co-operation, perform what is highly useful to mankind. Your exclusive privileges are about to expire; but if you act as you ought to in this business I mean to stand your friend. For I bear you goodwill, both as brother mechanics and (as I understand) as worthy citizens."

Baffled in his attempts at steam navigation, Stanhope devoted his attention more exclusively to the important question of construction.

Scientific ship-building was practically non-existent in England, and the want of it was the cause of innumerable disasters. In 1807 he wrote that the average life of the ships of the navy was only about eleven years. 1 Nelson bitterly complained of the specimens built by the Navy Board which formed the fleet before Toulon. As to these crazy vessels," he wrote," only four were fit for winter cruising. It is not a store-ship a week that would keep them in repair." 2 Lord St. Vincent, before he was in office, declared that nothing but a radical sweep of our dockyards would do any good. 3 Even Gabriel Snodgrass 1 Earl Stanhope to Commissioners on the Weatherer, December 20, 1807. Printed by order of the Admiral in 1813.

2 Mahan's Life of Nelson, ii. 196. 3 Life, by Tucker, ii. 142.

CHAP. Surveyor to the East India Company (under whose superin-X- tendence were built more than 200,000 tons of shipping), ventured the pious opinion ' that the King's ships were not constructed in all respects as they ought to be." A large number of Government vessels were built in private dockyards, and it was a well-known fact that scarcely one did not require to be rebuilt in six or seven years, while many had to be paid off after four or five years' service. Not only were our ships at a disadvantage in time of war, but they were also dangerous to the lives of those on board.

To impress these facts on the Government Stanhope desired a conference with Lord Mulgrave, who became First Lord of the Admiralty in the Portland ministry. ' The preservation of the country and its commerce he declared, ' must infallibly depend on the security of the navy and its retaining the command of the seas 1 Believing that his method of construction might be of great value in the public service he showed models to Mulgrave, and asked him to appoint a committee to report. 2 Mulgrave finally appointed three Commissioners to report on the ' Stanhope Weather er." To assist them and to ' induce them to investigate the subject properly Stanhope sent them forty-one questions relating to his invention. The naval officers, without technical knowledge and opposed to innovation, drew up a report antagonistic to the Weather er before they had seen a single experiment. Stanhope loudly protested, and, after some discussion as to where the experiment should take place, His Majesty was graciously pleased to grant the use of the Round Pond contiguous to Kensington Palace The inventor desired certain persons to be present, ' among them Colonel Beaufoy and Mr. Scott, who were two of the principal persons who made the admirable set of experiments at Greenland Dock for the Society of Naval Architects 3 The experiments ' with the broad boat' took place on October 12, 1807, in Kensington Gardens, and some with â the narrow boat' on the Thames, January 8, 1808. The Commissioners reported unfavourably. Admitting the Weatherer's superiority as to speed, stability, stowage accommodation for the men, and manageability, they objected that the form of the vessel ' will tend to her collecting weeds

Small wonder that Stanhope described it as 'a puerile report and he wrote to the Admiralty demanding better qualified 1 April 28, 1808. Royal Institution MSS.

2 Correspondence with Lord Mulgrave. Royal Institution MSS.

3 Royal Institution MSS.

Commissioners. ' The plans of mine," he says, ' may be classed CHAP. under three general heads: ist. The form of the ship. 2nd. The x-mode of building her. 3rd. Certain machinery called gills for increasing her manageability. Upon the first two parts of this subject they report to you that they do not feel competent to give an opinion. I am not in the least inclined to controvert the truth of that proposition; and I fully agree with the Commissioners that " such questions as relate to shipbuilding can only properly be investigated and decided upon by men thoroughly versed in the science and practice of that profession." I am therefore under the necessity of requesting the Board of Admiralty to appoint a more numerous committee of men fully competent to mathematical, mechanical and nautical investigation. I ask distinctly whether objects of such unparalleled importance, and at such a critical time as this, are or are not to undergo some sort of regular and scientific investigation? On such scientific questions may probably depend the power of our navy, the existence of our commerce, the salvation of the State, the safety of his Majesty's crown, and the happiness of the people." 1 Five years passed without any action being taken; but in 1813 Stanhope wrote to Lord Melville requesting that if he should appoint a committee it might be formed of properly qualified persons. ' I have frequently informed your Lordship that the ships of this country are built contrary to the most obvious scientific principles, and in consequence they do not possess the properties which are of the very highest importance. Within six years upwards of one million sterling has been expended upon the navy, and your Lordship has the means of knowing what is the actual state of upwards of one half of the ships of the line." He catalogues their defects, enumerates the properties which a British ship should possess, and begs Melville to nominate a competent committee. She is to be built according to his plan, that is, with diagonally braced and trussed frame-timbers, and he makes a great point of her being constructed

' under cover." Melville appointed six persons, and did his best to fulfil Stanhope's requirements by choosing Colonel Mark Beaufoy, whose experience made his opinion of great value. A model of a single-deck 6o-gun frigate built according to Stanhope's plan was submitted to them, together with the most exact estimate of its cost and diagram of its proportions. Stanhope proposed that it should be 210 feet in length, 48 feet in breadth, draw (with 1 Stanhope to the Hon. Wellesley Pole, Secretary to the Admiralty, January 13, 1808.

CHAP, stores, guns, c.) 13 J feet of water, and be rigged with four masts x- instead of three.

To guard against such a report as that of 1808 the inventor begged the Commissioners to give a scientific reason for their opinions. When the report appeared, three Commissioners favoured the Weatherer's construction and three opposed it. The critics were the three naval officers, while the champions were those to whom the description ' properly qualified persons ' might be applied. The excellent qualities of his method of shipbuilding received confirmation in the year of his death in the expedition of Captain Tuckey to explore the river Congo in a small vessel built for the purpose. ' In sailing from the Nore to the Downs she beat every vessel that sailed with her, she scarcely felt her sails, was perfectly safe at sea, and in the worst weather was always dry and comfortable. It is worthy of notice adds Tuckey, ' that the principle on which she was built was very similar to that for which the late Lord Stanhope so strongly contended, as being the most proper for ships of war, uniting, in one body, strength, stability, storage, accommodation for the people and a light draught of water; but his ideas were rejected by a committee of naval officers as crude and visionary." l This vessel (called the Congo) was built by Seppings on the principles advocated by Stanhope, which have since been universally adopted in the Government merchant service, and for which Seppings has received the entire credit. In science not less than in politics he was condemned to the disappointments which befall men who are before their age.

In addition to his naval inventions Stanhope devoted much thought to the problems of inland navigation, and elaborate plans preserved at Chevening attest his interest. In 1793 he projected a canal designed to connect the Bristol and English Channels, starting from Bude Haven and passing Holsworthy, of which he was lord of the manor. The difference of levels was over 500 feet and water was scarce. The paper in which he sketched his ideas fell under the eye of Fulton, who traced l Narrative of an Expedition to explore the River Zaire (or Congo in 1816, by Captain Tuckey, p. xxvii; and article in the Quarterly Review, 1818, p. 339, written by Sir John Barrow, third Secretary of the Admiralty, who had seen Stanhope's model, c., in 1813. See Royal Institution MSS., July 24, 1813.

thereto the awakening of his own interest in canal construction. 1 CHAP. While staying at Torquay the young American wrote, enclosing x-a scheme for obviating the necessity of locks and minimising the loss of water by a preponderating cistern to draw the canal boat up an inclined plane from one level to another. Stanhope at once replied from Holsworthy that the idea of the inclined plane had been anticipated about sixteen years before. Though less original than he had believed, Fulton pursued his task. Canal construction was at that time in fashion, for large profits were being made and the public were hungry for shares. He proposed to dispense with locks, especially where water was scarce, and substitute either inclined planes along which the boats might be drawn in rails, or else vertical lifts or hoists. He took out a patent in 1794, and kept Stanhope informed of his work. On January 6, 1796, he announced the invention of a digging-machine. ' If such a machine he concludes," or any other can be made to answer, it will set me independent in great measure of canal-diggers. As I am convinced a machine may be made which may be very useful, your Lordship may be so good as to throw some hints into the scale." The machine was the first attempt at mechanical excavation; but it was impracticable, and he quickly realised it.

Stanhope, for his part, was glad to discuss the problems of the Devonshire canal with Fulton. To overcome the difficulty of the hilly country and the scarcity of water he invented what he called the ' pendanter ' in 1796. ' I am making drawings, sections, models and estimates of the pendanter for the Bude Canal he wrote to a friend in May. It consisted of two boat-carriers, about 50 feet apart, connected so as to balance by a set of chains passing over pulleys. Unless a steep cliff were at hand, two pits would have to be sunk. A letter of enormous length from Fulton, dated April, 1796, thanks Stanhope for his three last letters, and confesses that the idea of the pendanter was new to him. After a number of technical criticisms of the plan, which he pronounced inferior to the inclined plane, he concludes, ' I hope ere this your Lordship's eyes are perfectly well, and return my thanks for the high opinion you are pleased to entertain of my conduct and exertions." Stanhope promptly replied in a long letter, defending the pendanter as economising water, and proposing to obtain estimates of the cost of raising a given freight by the rival methods. Letters followed in rapid 1 Treatise on Canal Navigation, p. xiii. My account of Stanhope's cooperation and correspondence with Fulton is drawn from chapters iii. and iv, of Dickinson's admirable biography of Fulton.

CHAP, succession, each inventor stoutly maintaining his standpoint. x- But the controversy was thoroughly amicable, and the ' Treatise on Canals ' was hailed with delight. ' Your book he wrote, ' has set me on fire; particularly about America and your note about the enormous expense of horses. So I hope that at last I shall burn to some purpose; provided you keep on blowing the fire, as you have done Fulton had hoped for employment, or at any rate for the adoption of his schemes, in the Bude canal; but Stanhope naturally preferred his own methods. The canal, thirty-four miles long, was not actually constructed till both men were in the grave, and the differences of level were after all surmounted by inclined planes. Though still in existence, only a portion of it is now in use.

Fulton had always been in straits for money, and he had already borrowed from Robert Owen. At the close of the year 1796, in which so many letters had passed, he turned to Stanhope not as a man of science, but as a friend in need. ' Penury frequently presses hard on the projector, and this, my Lord, is so much my case at this moment that I am now sitting reduced to half a crown without knowing where to obtain a shilling for some months. This is an awkward sensation to a feeling mind, which would devote every minute to increase the comforts of mankind. Thus circumstanced, would it be an intrusion on your goodness and philanthropy to request the loan of twenty guineas, which I will return as soon as possible? P. S.â I have pondered much on the liberty of requesting a favour, which really gives me pain; but men of fortune can have no idea of the cries of necessity, and I must rely on your Lordship's goodness There can be little doubt that Stanhope readily came to the rescue of the struggling inventor, whose talents he esteemed so highly. In the following summer Fulton left England for Paris, where he found a home in the family of his fellow-countryman, Joel Barlow, the warm-hearted poet and diplomatist. The paths of the two inventors were to cross again before many years were over.

BACK IN PARLIAMENT, 1800-1811

AFTER five years' absence Stanhope returned to the House of CHAP. Lords on February 20, 1800. The Great War was still raging. XI-His last words had been to demand peace with France, and his first words were directed to the same goal. 1 ' Not having for several years troubled your Lordships with my sentiments on public affairs," he began, ' I consider it my duty, in the present alarming situation of the country, to suggest why you ought and how you might put an end to the war. I have to regret, more than I can express, that the honest and judicious advice I gave early in the war did not meet your approbation." Without attempting to discuss the justice of the struggle he now based his case on the ground of finance. Our resources, he declared, were wasting faster than those of the French. Our debt was a burden from which France was free, and our population was outnumbered several times over. Quoting from a pamphlet by George Rose, the Secretary of the Treasury, he reminded his audience that in taxes and tithes the Englishman paid Â 6 ios., while the Frenchman paid less than ten shillings. ' Yet we are told that this country is the best governed in the world and that France is oppressed by its rulers, distracted in its councils, ruined in its finances and incapable of defending itself." In the next place, the land of France was far better cultivated than our own. ' I have been in several districts in Devonshire, and I find, in that one coanty, more waste than all the land of Middlesex. In France, since hunting has been so much diminished, that is, since the Revolution and the overthrow of the feudal system, it has been remarkably well cultivated. I assert that 1 Parl. Hist., xxxiv. 1505-13. The speech'was published as a pamphlet.

CHAP, inevitable ruin awaits the country if you go on with the war. XI. I am come down to this House to implore your Lordships most earnestly, and upon my knees, to put an end to the calamities of this cruel war, to preserve the country and to save the people." He then invited the clerk to read his protest of 1793, and added that what he had prophesied had come to pass. He concluded by moving an Address to the King to open negotiations for peace without delay.

Five years had made equally little difference in the opinions of the House of Lords, and no one took the trouble to reply. The Lord Chancellor curtly remarked that the reading of his Protest was an irregular proceeding which he should have stopped had it been any other Peer. He had not felt it necessary to interrupt (what their Lordships had heard, sometimes with good humour, sometimes with gravity, but throughout with great patience) the visitation of God which their Lordships had that night witnessed. In the division the mover was supported by Lord Camelford alone. Resuming his former practice he entered a protest on the journals.

' Dissentient, i. Because I have uniformly considered the war against the French Republic as both unnecessary and unjust.

' 2. Because I feel revolted at the idea that the blood of my fellow-men is still to be spilt in order to endeavour to re-establish the ancient despotism and to restore the Bourbon family, the hereditary princes of which race have for so many centuries disturbed the peace of Europe and threatened the liberties of this country.

' 3. Because the war has already operated in a very dreadful manner to increase the scarcity in Great Britain."

It was in reference to this debate that young William Lamb, afterwards Lord Melbourne, aged twenty-one, wrote to his mother: ' Does any one pay any regard to Lord Stanhope? What has made Lord Camelford wheel about? He is a noble accession to the Opposition Lords, and I think he, Stanhope, King and Holland may challenge Europe to produce equal oddities." 1 Hardy, Secretary of the Corresponding Society, was more appreciative.

' Citizen,â I have read the speech which you delivered in the House of Lords introductory to your motion for peace with the French Republic. It pleased me muchâ you have added another manly testimony to your others against the injustice, impolicy and inhumanity of carrying on the war against the 1 Lord Melbourne's Papers, ed. Lloyd Sanders, pp. 24-5.

Republic of France for the avowed purpose of restoring that CHAP, profligate family to the supreme rule over such a great and XI. virtuous nation. I will further say that you have not ceased to deserve well of your country.

' THOS. HARDY.

' London: March 9, 1800." 1

Another old comrade, Major Cartwright, anxious to promote county meetings for the discussion of reform, consulted Stanhope and received the following letter:â ' Chevening: February 1801.

' Dear and excellent Citizen,â You have known me too long not to be sure of the approbation which my heart must bestow on every truly honest and enlightened plan for promoting a reform. I have again and again considered all the means, the legal and laudable means, which you suggest, and others of a similar description. I have weighed the whole in the scales of probability; I am willing to follow London if London acts right, I am willing to follow Yorkshire if Yorkshire acts right. I was (not am) willing to do more; namely, for the minority of one to propose a meeting of men of property and enlightened men. I have spoken to some, thought much, and I repeat it, I have weighed the whole in the scales of probability, and my inference is that success is not likely to attend your laudable plans to effectuate a reform, nor mine at present. I have a firmer, more cheering, and a better trust, namely, in a kind Providence; and many of the best men in the nation are growing of this opinion. But come what will to our dear and threatened country and perfect constitution, be assured, my dear friend, that you will ever find me unaltered, unalterable, and immoveable in the storms of fate.

' Ever your faithful ' STANHOPE." 2

In the House of Lords Stanhope was a political Ishmael, and party men looked askance at him. ' I read Young One's speech in the Courier," wrote Fox to Fitzpatrick on February 19, 1800, ' and thought it very good in many parts. It is impossible to judge what he ought to do with Stanhope unless one knew his particular measure. I own I thought it formerly injudicious in Bedford and Lauderdale to seem so afraid of being with him as they did; but Holland's situation is so different that a different conduct may be proper in his case from that which I should have 1 Add. MSS. t 27818. 2 Chevening MSS.

CHAP, advised in theirs. I agree with you that Stanhope is what XI. Drake called super-imperial in these qualities you mention; but yet, if his proposition is right in itself, I do not think it ought to be opposed or even be without support." 1 At this early period of their acquaintance Holland himself had not learned fully to trust the man who was to become his chief political ally. Lord Holland wrote his wife in her diary on June I, 1800, ' told me a piece of slyness of the Jacobinical party towards him. It seems Burdett and Stanhope grew jealous of his popularity among their friends. Lord Stanhope told him that he had many friends among the most valuable part of the community 2 The remark appears innocent enough, and there is nothing in Stanhope's career to suggest that he was ever jealous of the few men who shared his opinions or supported his efforts.

For the first year or two after his return he intervened rarely in debate. When Grenville moved to consider the treaty of peace on May 13, 1802, he cleared the House before the discussion began. ' We understand," wrote the reporter, ' that the subject of the noble Earl's communication was the improved construction of a diving-boat in France, which was described to be navigated under water with so much skill and certainty as to make it easy for them to blow up a first-rate man-of-war with only 15 Ib. of powder." 3 The reference was to hjs old comrade Fulton, who, on leaving England in 1797, had completely identified himself with the interests of France. In the same year he conceived the idea of a submarine which, he assured the Directory, would annihilate the British navy. An expert Commission approved the scheme; but the Government refused to move. After Brumaire the Nautilus was built at Paris and tested in the open sea off Havre. Fulton had an interview with the first Consul, who gave him a small grant and promised to reward him for the destruction of British ships in proportion to their size. But on further inquiry Napoleon convinced himself that the Nautilus would be of no service, and quietly dropped the inventor. 4 ' The Government and he," wrote Joshua Gilpin, an American friend of Fulton, to Stanhope in 1798, ' are amusing each other (I think, however, to little purpose) on his new invention of the submarine boat. I fear this will keep him from more useful pursuits." 5 But the Englishman took a more serious view 1 Memorials and Correspondence of Fox, iii. 294. ' Young One' was Fox's name for his beloved nephew, Lord Holland.

3 Lady Holland's Journal, ii. 101-2. 3 Parl. Hist., xxxvi. 687-8.

4 See Dickinson's Fulton, chaps, v. and vi. 5 Ibid., p. 91.

of the matter, and felt it his duty to warn the Government. 1 CHAP. ' On May 13," wrote Joel Barlow to Fulton, ' the galleries being XI. uncommonly full to hear the great discussion on the treaty of peace, Lord Stanhope rose and stated that he had a matter of such importance to communicate to the House in secret as would admit of no delay, and he demanded that the galleries should be cleared. The sovereign people then withdrew. In a few minutes the doors were again opened. The Morning Chronicle understands that it was relative to submarine navigation, which to his certain knowledge was brought to that perfection by a person in France as to render the destruction of ships absolutely sure, and that that person could at any time blow up a first-rate ship of war with 15 Ib. of powder. Grant thinks it was a plan concerted between Stanhope and St. Vincent, that the former should give the facts to the House as preparatory to the latter's taking some measures with the author of the invention. My conjecture is a little different. Stanhope disdains any communication with the ministers. He was possessed of the fact, and not wishing to impart it to the ministers alone, he probably made use of his right as a Peer to lay it before the only body with which he has official intercourse." 2

The communication produced the effect which he anticipated. Addington dispatched an agent abroad, and after some negotiation Fulton was persuaded to return to London. When Pitt regained power in 1804 he took him into the service of the Government, and one or two small ships were blown up by his torpedoes. The Whig Ministry, however, of 1806 disapproved this method of warfare, and he returned to the United States. 3 In 1807 Stanhope took out a patent to ' counteract or diminish the danger of that most mischievous invention for destroying ships by submarine explosions '; but Fulton was not impressed by his friend's invention. ' The torpedoes are now so far improved," he wrote to his friend and rival in 1811, ' that any plan I have yet seen cannot defend a ship against a vigorous attack with them." 4

The Treaty of Amiens was a peace, to adopt the words made famous by Sheridan, of which everybody was glad and nobody was proud; and it was welcomed by the man who had unceasingly denounced the war. Though a strong supporter of Catholic claims Stanhope had welcomed the resignation of Pitt and the 1 His apprehensions were shared by the inventor, Cartwright. See Edmund Cartwright: A Memoir, pp. 158-9.

2 Todd, Life of Joel Barlow, pp. 186-7.

3 Dickinson's Fulton, chaps, vii. and viii. 4 Ibid., pp. 208 and 247.

CHAP, accession to power of Addington; and for the remainder of his XI- life he entertained the most friendly feelings for the Tory Minister who had suspended hostilities, if only for a single year. His domestic policy, again, was less oppressive than that of his predecessor. ' It is right to acknowledge declares Lord Holland, a hostile critic, ' that the moderation of Lord Sidmouth had a very beneficial effect on the country, and assuaged, if it did not heal, the wounds which the anti-revolutionary and jealous spirit of Mr. Pitt's Government had inflicted." 1

The renewal of the war was a keen disappointment, but the speech delivered on May 23, 1803, was couched in more measured language than he usually employed. He pronounced the question of Malta important, though less so than the pretension of France to dictate our laws and limit our freedom of discussion. He would cheerfully sacrifice his fortune and life, and die in the greatest tortures that human cruelty and ingenuity ever devised, rather than suffer the rights of man to be trampled on or even invaded in this free country. This, however, he did not believe to be the object of the French Government. He had been one of the most strenuous advocates for the Treaty of Amiens, but for what reason? Because Ministers had already ratified it, and the good faith of the nation was pledged. He supported it because he saw no help for it and felt that peace, even on those terms, might be advantageous. But had he been in the situation of the Ministers, he never would have consented to sign the preliminaries which endangered our Eastern possessions by the cession of Malta. He ridiculed the offer to surrender the island after ten years and the refusal to accept its permanent occupation in return for compensation to France. They could not decide the matter in reference to the individual at the head of the French Government. ' In ten years Bonaparte may be dead. Every one knows that he is an extraordinary, dashing, enterprising man, one who would not hesitate to undertake anything grand, however dangerous; a man that nobody can tell to-day what he may do to-morrow; and added his Lordship emphatically, ' I like him the better for it This singular expression, remarks the reporter, was received with a universal peal of laughter. This country, though burdened with a debt of five hundred millions, loaded with taxes to an enormous amount, was still able, if necessary, to set him and all his power at defiance. But however great our resources, it did not follow that we should not keep ourselves at peace if that was practicable.

1 Memoirs, ii. 213-14.

Were he made a mediator between the two countries, he CHAP, thought he could easily bring them to accommodation. He would XI. say to each of them, ' What is it you wish for? ' If they both affected the same object, accommodation would be difficult; if not, it would be easy, for each party would take what he wanted. England wished for Malta, and the French were willing to let them retain it for an equivalent. France had complained of the speeches made in Parliament, and the liberties taken with the supreme Magistrate of the Republic by the English press. The freedom of the press was an advantage which this country must ever retain while it had any regard for liberty. But it could not be denied that atrocious libels had been published against all the leading persons in the French Government, which could not be expected to pass without remonstrance and complaint. Protection should be afforded to the characters of foreigners, particularly those in amity with us. This was all that justice and the law of nations required; never should a foreign power be allowed to dictate the laws by which we were to be governed. The First Consul was accused of demanding the expulsion of emigrant Princes, some Bishops and others obnoxious to his Government. He did not expect our Government would send away the Bishops, but it could not be concealed that the application was not unreasonable. Those fellows, the Bishops and others (a shout of laughter), were certainly guilty of spreading seditious publications through the maritime provinces of France, which must give annoyance to the Government. The means of doing so were found in the proximity of the Channel Islands, which were no use to us and which France would probably accept as the equivalent for leaving us in permanent occupation of Malta. It would be a fair exchange. We had done wrong to order Lord Whitworth to leave Paris. France had diminished, not increased, in power since the Peace of Amiens, for she had lost ground in the New World. She had lost infinitely in the war for liberty without obtaining that object, and she was now as far from it as ever. He did not know by whose advice this system of war had been adopted by the Cabinet. Certain he was that Mr. Addington, whom he considered as one of the most honest, humane and upright men that ever administered the affairs of this country," must have been desirous of maintaining peace. But when he was called on to give his vote on so important a question, he could not decide in favour of war. 1 1 From The British Press, May 24, 1803, preserved by the speaker.

CHAP. Though Stanhope had spoken with unusual moderation on XI. the war, the old fires still burned fiercely within him. On June 28, 1804, Wilberforce and some other members of the Lower House brought up the Bill for the Abolition of the Slave Trade in a limited time. Lord Hawkesbury opposed it and announced that he would move its rejection on the second reading. Stanhope followed with a warm eulogy of a measure for the abolition of 'that horrid and impious traffic, especially subversive of the duties of religion and the rights of men." 1 He saw no reason why it should not be passed this session. Hawkesbury had invited persons interested in the system to appear at the bar and present petitions; but he declared that, even if he stood alone, he would resist the acceptance of such evidence. Hawkesbury then moved that the Bill should be read a second time that day three weeks. The Duke of Norfolk agreed that it was too late in the session to proceed, and added that it was not a Government Bill. Stanhope at once rose to urge the House to an immediate decision. 2 He would not allow men to come to the bar and ask to be permitted to continue in the commission of crime. Would they allow forgers to petition against prohibition or to claim indemnity? The slave trade was worse, as murder was more heinous than robbery. Owing to information received since he came down to the House he would not divide; but he trusted that the supporters of the Bill would work hard during the recess and finally succeed in abolishing a traffic, the real object of which was ' to enable the slave merchants of Liverpool and other places to gormandise more turtle, to swallow more venison, and to drink more claret." His zeal and courage had always been gratefully acknowledged by Wilberforce; but the author of the Bill was more cautious than its champion, and cried aloud to be saved from his friends. ' Lord Stanhope made a wild speech," he notes in his diary. ' With horror I heard that he was about to divide the House," he wrote to Lord Muncaster. ' Many of our friends were necessarily absent, and we should have been sadly beat. He gave it up, however, very kindly on my remonstrance; but his speech contained some most mischievous passages, threatening the Lords that by means of his stereotype press he would circulate millions of papers among the people and deluge the country with accounts of the cruelties of the Slave Trade and of the barbarous treatment of the slaves 1 Parl. Debates, ii. 872-3. 2 Ibid., 927.

in the West Indies." 1 The word compromise found no place CHAP, in his rich vocabulary. XI.

During the closing weeks of the same session Stanhope intervened several times to oppose a Corn Trade Bill, which slightly modified the measure of 1773, and which he described as a measure to raise the price of corn and bread. 2 He was a friend to the farmer and was against imposing new burdens on his shoulders. If the grower could not sell his corn at a fair profit in a year of plenty, he would accept the Bill. But the framer of the measure spoke of a plentiful season as a curse, and as a remedy they proposed to raise the price by artificial means. This was to excite the people to discontent, to depress the sale of our manufactures abroad, and to increase the expenses of government. Their pretext was the enormous importation of corn and the enormous price we had paid for it. We must therefore, it was maintained, encourage our own farmers by a bounty on export when the price was low. The reason why we had bought so much was that we could buy it cheaper than we could grow it, owing to the price of labour. A bounty was only necessary because labour was so dear. The price of the labour was the evil to be remedied; yet the bill would increase it by increasing the price of corn. We should therefore have to import more than ever. The real remedy was to copy the example of Geneva, which had granaries stocked for seven or eight years' consumption. Carefully dried grain kept for many years, and he had eaten excellent bread made of corn a century old. Let the State buy wholesale when it was cheap and store it for years of scarcity. Farmers would thus have a motive to grow for the average consumption, since they would always have a market and a fair profit. Unless we adopted this policy we might be starved in time of scarcity, for Bonaparte could buy up all the corn on the Continent. ' The people are taxed for the light, for their shoes, for every necessary, and to do what? To provide corn for a time of scarcity? No! to pay a premium for sending it out of the country, for â increasing its price and incurring the hazard of scarcity." Two objections had been raised against granariesâ their liability to be burned and the expense of building. He had invented a means of preventing destruction by fire, and the Government could recover the outlay by selling at a small profit.

Hawkesbury, replying for the Government to this ' very extraordinary speech," admitted that granaries might be useful in a small State like Geneva, but pronounced them unsuitable 1 Life of Wtlberforce, iii. 183. 2 Parl. Debates, ii. 1023-4, i43-7-

CHAP, to a large country. The object of the Bill was to steady the price XI. by a bounty on export when it was unreasonably low and by prohibiting export when unreasonably high. When it again came up for discussion on July 27 1 Stanhope formulated his alternative policy in a series of resolutions. He recognised the necessity of encouraging a larger production of corn; but the bill would increase the burden on the poor, already too heavily laden, in order to recompense the farmer. The increase in the price of corn would raise the price of every necessity of life and therefore the price of labour. The poor-rate would thus become enormous, and even the farmer would in the long run be no better off. His own plan would encourage production by decreasing the price, and farmers and the poor alike would benefit. His first resolution urged the establishment of public granaries, the second the removal of all legal impediments to the free warehousing of grain. These, however, would be useless without a third. He reminded the House that the Government had from time to time embarked on wars and accumulated an enormous debt, which involved crushing taxation of the poor. To these wars, this debt, these taxes were to be attributed the rise in the price of all necessaries, particularly bread. He therefore pleaded for the exemption for ever of farmers from all direct taxes, tithes, parish and county rates, as they were not fit subjects for taxation. This would do more to encourage the growth of corn and decrease its price than any Bill. Such a resolution, he felt sure, would poll a hundred to one on a plebiscite. He did not wish to force the House immediately to accept or reject them, though rejection would answer his purpose best, since half a million hand-bills would soon be issued. He had always been successful in mechanics and unsuccessful in politics. In mechanics, when he had a nail to drive into a piece of oak, he drove it in at one blow. He would act in the very same way in politics. The resolutions were his sledge-hammer, and he was confident they would drive the nail to the head. No member would dare oppose the principle, or at the next election out he must go.

This challenging, almost threatening, utterance provoked lively protests. The Duke of Montrose pointed out that to untax the farmer was to heap the whole burden on the consumer. Hawkesbury rebuked the inflammatory language of the speech, which, like many others that he had been permitted to utter in that House, was calculated to encourage disaffection and thus i Parl Debates, ii. 1134-44.

serve the enemy. He was, however, happy to find that popular CHAP, opinion had now changed. It was a proof at once of the X L security of the Government and of the attachment of the people that the noble Earl was still suffered to propagate these doctrines. He ridiculed the idea that untaxing the farmer would cheapen provisions, and declared that there was never a surplus of corn capable of being stored. The real cause of high prices was the great wealth of the country. The Lord Chancellor shrewdly added that if a tax was taken off the farmer, the landlord would immediately raise his rent. Lord Mulgrave thanked God that very few persons now shared the opinions of the noble Earl. As usual he found no support, and his motion for the rejection of the Bill was negatived without a division. His efforts, however, appear to have met with some support in the country. In answer to a letter from a certain Mr. Clegg of Stockport, he wrote on November 21, 1804:â ' You do right to petition the House of Commons for its repeal. But the simple repeal of that measure will do but little good. It is the whole defective system of Corn Laws which requires to be repealed. I cordially wish you success, and am, Sir, your faithful fellow-citizen, ' STANHOPE

A month later he wrote again, in reply to a further letter.

' Sir,â I am very glad to find that my plan about the Corn Laws is, in your opinion, beyond comparison the best. If your worthy friends and the public at large shall, when they come to understand the scheme thoroughly, be of that same opinion; a new system of laws upon that most important subject may be introduced, by means of which this sinking country may yet be saved. Strike in your petitions at the root of the evil, or petition not at all. Half-measures will never satisfy me.

' Your faithful fellow-citizen, ' STANHOPE." 1

In the session of 1805 a similar sermon was preached from a different text on Lord King's demand for a Committee to consider the recent measures relating to national defence. 2 Stanhope employed the occasion to attack the Act of June, 1804, which inflicted a charge on parishes where there was a deficiency in the numbers raised. These fines would fall upon the farmers, who would indemnify themselves by raising prices.

1 Chevening MSS. Park Debates, iii. 799-802.

CHAP. This led straight to the starvation of the poor, and was as bad XI as the Corn Law which he had recently opposed. It was a mistake to tax the farmers at all, for any burdens placed on them would raise the price of grain, which in turn would increase the cost of labour. As to the military system, he wished to see the country well armed, and indeed desired the arming to be more general. Passing from the Act to its author he violently attacked Pitt, who had returned to power in I804. 1 The present Minister, he remarked, was perhaps a man of more brilliant talents but not of more good sense than his predecessor. Addington had indeed more good sense in his little finger than Pitt in his whole body, though that was not much.

Since the return of Pitt there were moments when Stanhope felt that all effort was useless. During the recess Cartwright approached Fox, Grey, Norfolk, Bedford, and other Whig leaders with a view to calling a meeting of the county of Middlesex. Most of them replied that the time was unfavourable, and Stanhope reluctantly agreed. ' I must confess," he wrote, f I have seen too much not to be thoroughly sick of the old dull road of meetings of freeholders convened by the aristocracy. If the people be true to themselves, they will inquire of the candidates for high offices what it is they will solemnly pledge themselves to do for the people in case they should come into place. Everything short of this is firing at sparrows."

Stanhope was not among those who regretted the death of Pitt either on public or private grounds; but he could feel no great enthusiasm for a ministry with his old enemiesj Grenville and Fox, at its head. The abolition of the slave trade, however, was a source of the keenest satisfaction. He took part in the debate on June 24, 1806, on the resolution which prepared the way for the Bill of the following year. Following Sidmouth he denounced him and other speakers who confessed that the traffic was inhuman and unjust but were not willing to abolish it. The interest of the planters was often mentioned, but the people of Africa ought not to be forgotten. Lord Westmoreland had asked what would be the practical effect of abolition. He replied that it would stop the infamous practices that took place 1 Gillray wrongly includes Stanhope among the followers of Pitt and Fox in the attack on Addington, entitled ' Storming Heaven."â Wright's Gillray, p. 310.

on the mainland, abolish the horrors of the sea passage, save CHAP. thousands of our fellow-creatures from the miseries of slavery, XI. and oblige the planters to grant better treatment to those who were already in that unnatural state. He knew of no event which would be attended by so many blessings. Turning to the plea of the opponents of the resolution that the rising in St. Domingo sprang from the ideas of the French Revolution, he explained it by the breach of faith of the French legislature, which had promised the abolition not only of the slave trade but of slavery itself. ' It held forth the rights of man to the whole human race, and then it most infamously abandoned every article, so that it became the scorn of all the enlightened and virtuous part of mankind 1 The resolute defence of Catholic claims which led to the fall of the Grenville ministry commanded his respect; but he stood so entirely aloof from party that he watched their disappearance without much regret, and a caricature of Gillray which included him among the satellites of Grenville revealed nothing but the ignorance of the critic. 2 Till near the end of the session of 1807 Stanhope maintained an unaccustomed reserve. But on August 13 he moved to recognise the principles of equality and reciprocity towards countries with which we were at peace. 3 The resolution envisaged our relations not only with America but with all States. He felt it his imperious duty to deprecate a rupture with America. If any man wished to forward the views of Bonaparte, he would find in such a conflict a source of joy. In times of scarcity our relief came primarily from Poland, next from America. As Poland was now shut against us, should we close the ports of America by our own folly? Whence should we derive materials for our naval arsenals? Where was the security and greatness of England when our navy, the source of our pride, our strength and our wealth, was gone? As all individuals, whether high or low, poor or rich, were the same in the eye of God, so nations, whether powerful or weak, opulent or poor, should be the same in the law of nations. The motion was considered too abstract and withdrawn; but the speech is of interest as one of the first warnings against the struggle with America which was soon to follow. A somewhat similar problem was raised by Sid mouth in the following year when Danish ships were detained in British ports in time of peace. Stanhope quoted Magna Charta as to the hospitality to be exercised towards strangers trading on 1 Clarkson, History of the Abolition of the Slave Trade, ii. 554-7. The report in the Parliamentary Debates is very meagre (vii. 809).

2 Wright's Gillray, p. 354. Â Parl. Debates, ix. 1183-4.

CHAP, our coasts and the inducements to the Danes to regard our good XI. faith as secure. How, then, could seizing as lawful prizes the vessels detained in time of peace be regarded as anything short of rascality? The protest, he declared, did great honour to Sidmouth, and must raise him still higher in the opinion of the country and every honest man. 1

The session of 1808 witnessed a sustained attack on one of the first measures of the new Tory Government. ' A Bill," writes Lord Holland, ' enabling the judges to hold a man to bail on the bare accusation of a misdemeanour was brought in by the Attorney-General and passed the Commons without observation. Little attention was at that time paid to any questions affecting the liberty of the subject and the freedom of the press. Lord Stanhope and myself opposed every stage of the Bill in the Lords, but we met with little support." 2 Stanhope opened the campaign on May 19, describing the measure as one of the most important and one of the most mischievous that ever came before the House, since it almost annihilated Trial by Jury in criminal cases. It contradicted every principle of the Common Law that a man prosecuted for any offence should be compelled to give bail or go to prison. Ought he to be imprisoned before he was proved guilty of any offence? Such a law would be cruel to the poor, who could seldom find bail, which the rich could always procure. The House ought to watch carefully over the rights and liberties of the poor and give them all the advantages of the law. His motion for rejection was supported by Lord Holland and Erskine. After a plea from the Lord Chancellor for discussion by a committee and a hint of an indemnity, he delivered a second speech. 3 He ridiculed the notion that because Judges and Attorney-Generals were honest men they should be vested with extraordinary powers. The second reading, however, was carried in a small house. A week later he returned to the charge. When Erskine opposed the commitment, Stanhope denounced the Lower House for sending up such a wicked Bill. The protesters were beaten, and in committee he proposed amendments which were negatived. 4 His opposition to the third reading was equally fruitless. Ellenborough, Chief Justice of the King's Bench, complained that he had been grossly calumniated by Stanhope, who had compared him to Scroggs and Jeffreys; but he would treat the calumny and the calumniator with contempt. Stanhope at once disavowed any intention to impute misconduct; but 1 May 17, 1808. Parl. Debates, xi. 314-15.

2 Memoirs of the Whig Party, ii. 254.

3 Parl. Debates, xi. 416-22. Ibid., 542-4.

Ellenborough's ready application to himself of the attacks CHAP, on wicked Judges convinced him that the power proposed in XI. the Bill ought not to be given to such a man. 1

Stanhope's opinions on national defence were as original as on most other subjects. The old posse comitatus of King Alfred, he declared, was a better means of defending the country against invasion than standing armies. Austria, Prussia, Italy, and all the old governments had fallen like ninepins before the French attack. 2 His views were shared by Cartwright, who having drafted two Bills, one for arming the people, the other for Parliamentary Reform, was anxious to have them discussed. He believed that his friend Burdett would bring them forward; but he allowed the session to pass without taking any steps, convinced doubtless that they would receive but little support. The Major, who had devoted six months to framing the measures, wrote in the greatest excitement to Stanhope on May 2Q. 3 ' Not being acquainted with Lord Folkestone, I have submitted to Cobbett whether he should mention the subject to his lordship; but time is flying, the session draws near its conclusion. Before another it is probable the King of Sweden may cease to reign, Spain may be completely French, and Napoleon in readiness to direct to the destruction of this country all his immensity of means. Stand in the gap, my good Lord, whether anything can or cannot be done in the Commons. Fashion the Bills to your own liking; make a stand in the House of Lords, and let us call to this great object the public attention. Cobbett's paper has a circulation and authority which nothing of the kind ever had. Suspend your shipbuilding for a few days, and prevent the vessel of State from sinking." Stanhope was unable to champion his Bills, but he presented a petition from the Major declaring the Local Militia Bill then before the House a defective system of defence and inconsistent with the Constitution. On June 20 he reported as follows:â ' My dear Sir,â On Saturday I had the pleasure to present your petition to the Lords; and in order to shew them my approbation, I read the whole very loudly and distinctly myself. They wished not to receive it, because it was not addressed to the Lords spiritual and temporal; but I got it received, notwithstanding.

' I am, dear Sir, most sincerely yours, ' STANHOPE." 4 1 Parl. Debates, xi; 710-12. 2 Ibid., 958-9.

3 Cartwright's Life, i. 355-6. Ibid., 367.

CHAP. In the session of 1810 he submitted a motion relating to the XI- navy. He had some years ago called their attention to the subject on which he should now speak plainly as a man of science and not like those who bamboozled people with mysteries. He would make every noble Peer understand him. He then recalled the experiments tried some years ago off the French coast and since then in America by Fulton to discover means of destroying vessels at sea. He was invited over here, and Stanhope had seen an engagement between him and Pitt and Melville, agreeing to give him large sums in certain circumstances. After the failure of a trial at Boulogne he had received Â 15,000. Since then he had made experiments in America before Jefferson and Madison, and been voted Â 1000. He raised the question now, as he had received a pamphlet from America describing the invention. 1 ' He then proceeds the reporter, ' entered into a very scientific discussion and exposition of the theory of fluids and the principles on which the machine acted, and pointed out the means of counter-acting its dreadful effects." He asked for an account of the measures taken by Government to counteract the effect of submarine attacks; but no one rose to continue the debate.

When Grey moved an address 2 in June on the state of the nation and the shortcomings of the Ministry, Stanhope scornfully congratulated Liverpool on the brilliant condition of the country under the present blessed administration. With respect to Reform he quoted the opinion of Sir George Savile, ' one of the wisest and most honest men of his day that while the present system of representation continued, general elections could only be regarded as so many septennial fairs or markets. He related the story of a borough-owner who demanded an important place. On being informed that it was already promised he twice replied in significant tones," There are seven of us and obtained the post. He spoke of Catholic claims, the danger of invasion, and the depreciation of the paper currency. He then chaffed both the Government and the Opposition. ' The best service the two parties could render their King and country he concluded jocularly, ' would be to hang together

A few days later 3 Lord Holland opposed the appropriation of Â 100,000 to Queen Anne's Bounty for the poorer clergy, which was defended by Lord Harrowby. Stanhope declared that if he had made such observations, he would be denounced as the libeller of the Church, the enemy of our religious interests and 1 Parl. Debates, xvii. 305-6. 2 Ibid., 585-8. 3 Ibid., 768-70.

the plague knew what. Harrowby had said that the Church CHAP, could only contend with its foes by votes of public money. Such XI. a policy would increase instead of diminishing the number of Dissenters. ' These Dissenters will continue to increase when they find that the advocates of the Establishment conceive that the best means of security is to be continually applying for public money. I venture to predict that whether you vote six or sixty millions, whether you build churches or not, their numbers will increase as long as they see the Church of England made the engine of State policy, and the prelates preferred not for their religious merits but for their slavish support of the Minister of the day. When I see the Bishops voting against wars and supporting the liberties of the people, then I shall pronounce that the Church has no reason to fear."

In the session of 1811 Stanhope's minute knowledge of the Statute-book proved of unexpected assistance to the Whigs. At the end of 1810 the King's mind gave way under the shock of Princess Amelia's death. With the renewal of the Regency the question of restrictions, discussed but not settled in 1788, was revived. Perceval, following the example of Pitt, proposed restrictions, which were once more opposed by the Whigs. In the Upper House Grenville supported Perceval, while Lansdowne and Holland led the Opposition. His Majesty, declared Stanhope, ought not to be placed in the hands of his worst enemies, the present Ministers. 1 The voting was close, and on report the Ministerialists called for proxies, in the hope of restoring words struck out in Committee, where no proxies were allowed. The Opposition determined to resist their use, and Lauderdale, their teller, refused to mark them. The division was accordingly postponed, and the propriety of receiving proxies was discussed. The Opposition insisted that none had been called for in 1788, but Lord Holland confesses that there was little else to allege in favour of the doctrine. At this moment Stanhope came to the rescue. ' He drew a very ingenious inference from the form of a proxy, which is grounded on– the permission of our Lord the King, that Session obtained," or some such words. He contended the privilege could not be exerted in a case where it was manifest from the matter in hand that such permission could never have been given. The argument, whether plausible or really sound, was sufficient to satisfy what Lord Stanhope called the Whig majority of Peers. Those present deserved that appellation, and proved that " les absents ont tort " by voting 1 Parl. Debates, xvii. 1084.

CHAP, that the proxies which would have placed them in a minority XI. were inadmissible. The resolution was, I think, tenable and perhaps constitutional, but it was voted by persons who probably did not require that recommendation to make it go down. Lord Stanhope, delighted with the uproar and the success, embraced me with his long arms as we went downstairs, and whispered in my ear, "This, my dear Citizen, is rare fun. If I could often have such nights as these, I would live in the House of Lords; it is such high fun." ' 1

Shortly after this exciting incident, on the renewal of the Mutiny Bill, Stanhope moved to insert a clause that Catholics and Dissenters might attend any place of worship they liked. 2 Nearly half the army and navy was composed of Dissenters from the Established Church, and they must be treated fairly. How would the Peers like being forced to hear Mass? The Government replied that in effect no such compulsion was exerted, and that it was needless to amend the law. Rejoining that he exulted in proposing a clause the principle of which no one dared to question, he carried it to a division which was lost. On the third reading he produced details of cases where compulsion had been exercised, and again vainly urged its prohibition. 3 The religious liberty of another class was endangered by Sidmouth's proposal to drive dissenting ministers into the Militia. Presenting a large number of petitions against the Bill, 4 Stanhope declared that he had never felt more pleasure in his whole Parliamentary life than in surveying the immense heap strewn on the floor and piled on the table. He rejoiced to find the public alive, active and energetic. He had read as many statutes on the subject of religion not only as the lawyers but as the Bishops. He had gone through them with a professional man by his side and had abstracted 300 laws. He assured them that they would make them disgusted with the Statute-book and ashamed of their ancestors. What need had religion of Acts of Parliament? Was it not capable of standing by itself? Was not America religious? Yet there was no established religion and no tithes.

A spirited account of this brief and victorious conflict was written some years later by his comrade Lord Holland. 5 ' Lord Sidmouth, to ingratiate himself with the Church, had introduced a Bill to deprive dissenting ministers of their exemption from serving in the Militia, unless they could procure a certificate from respectable householders belonging to their congregation.

1 Further Memoirs, pp. 78-80. 2 Parl, Debates, xix. 368-71.

3 Ibid., 383-7. 4 Ibid., xx. 233-50.

5 Further Memoirs, pp. 101-2.

On the first notice I sounded the alarm on the hazard of meddling CHAP, with the Toleration Act. The appeal was heard, and the Bill, XI. which was held in abhorrence by the Methodists, served only to display the numbers and improve the organisation of that powerful sect. For some days no places were to be had in the stage-coaches; all were occupied with petitions to Parliament against the measure. On the day fixed for the debate such innumerable petitions were presented by Lord Grey, Lord Erskine, Lord Stanhope, myself and others, that not only the table but the House was filled with parchment. The Peers could hardly get to the doors, the avenues were so crowded with men of grave deportment and puritanical aspect. Lord Sid-mouth, with a bad grace, was obliged to yield. In the result, religious liberty was a gainer. To pacify the alarms raised and the passions excited, several important concessions were successively granted in subsequent sessions to the various Protestant Dissenters." During the years of the Great War British liberty made little progress; but without the unceasing efforts of men like Lord Holland and Lord Stanhope it would have made none at all.

THE LAST BATTLES, 1811-1816

CHAP. AMONG the domestic problems created by the Great War there XII was none more grave nor more difficult than that of the currency. The suspension of cash payments by the Bank in 1797 had produced its inevitable results. Gold almost ceased to circulate, and there was an over-issue of notes. After a decade the depreciation could no longer be hidden. The alarm was raised by Ricardo, and in February 1810 Homer moved for returns as to the quantity of bullion and the issue of bank-notes. A committee was appointed to investigate the causes of the high price of gold and the state of the circulating medium. The committee, presided over by Horner, reported that paper issues were always liable to depreciate unless at any moment convertible into gold. The paper currency had in fact depreciated, and the only remedy was to provide for the resumption of cash payments after two years. Horner's principles, sound though they were, aroused sharp opposition. ' Such was the repugnance felt at that time to doctrines now universally approved," wrote Lord Holland some years later, ' that I was assured by Lord Lansdowne that the borough of Calne would hardly have chosen the Chairman of the Bullion Committee for their representative even if supported by his recommendation." 1 On May n Horner moved sixteen resolutions, embodying the findings of the committee, in a celebrated speech. The Bank and the Government were hostile and he was defeated. The report, however, influenced public opinion, and prepared the way for the resumption of cash payments after the close of the war.

In June 1811 Stanhope expressed his opinions in a letter 1 Further Memoirs, p. 104.

to the Lord Chancellor, which he read in the House of Lords. CHAP. Bank-notes, he maintained, ought not to be made legal tender, XI1-since no one knew if a particular note was forged. He therefore proposed that the Bank of England should have branches all over the country. Possessors of bank-notes, on depositing them, should be credited with the amount, and could transfer the whole or part of it to any other person. Such a transfer might be legal tender, as the danger of forgery would be avoided. The rapidity of such transfers without any danger of loss from the mail being robbed or from insurrections or invasion was an additional recommendation. The plan was that which he had proposed to Condorcet twenty years before.

At this moment the problem was rendered urgent by the action of a Peer. Lord King, now remembered only as the biographer of Locke, determined to enforce the strict letter of his leases and to call for the payment of rent in the lawful coin of the kingdom. He sent a circular to his tenants while Parliament was still in session. ' Lord Stanhope writes Lord Holland, ' by some accident obtained very early intelligence of this proceeding." The nature of this ' accident' is revealed by the Chevening archives. Two days after his speech in the House of Lords Stanhope received the following letter:â ' Kingston: June 26, 1811.

' My Lord,â Will you excuse the address of a private citizen to a peer of the realm? Yes! my Lord. I know the freeness of your heart is such that you can and will, more particularly when it is a public subject. Why I address you is that I see you mentioned the subject of money in last night's debate. My Lord King, who is a great landholder in this county, has served all his tenants with notice that he will have guineas for his rent or otherwise take paper after the rate of i6- in the pound, and if they do not approve of it they may quit. It does, my Lord, strike me, that something said in the House before the prorogation might be very useful in this matter.

' Your Lordship's most humble servant and one of your best wishers, 'JOHN LEACH

Stanhope acted with his usual promptitude. On the following day (June 27) he introduced a Bill to give effect to his plan. 1 The matter, he remarked, was rendered urgent by a Peer ordering his tenants to pay their rents in gold; and he was reported 1 Parl. Debates, xx. 762-70.

CHAP, to have said that if he took bank-notes it must be at the rate of sixteen shillings in the pound. Such a proceeding was a gross injustice. Why should a tenant owing Â 400 pay Â 500 in notes? His scheme would obviate all such difficulties. The remedy was as simple as the evil was alarming. They had merely to render it illegal for any man to pay more than 2is. for a guinea, or to receive less for a bank-note than its face value. The farmers were a most oppressed class, and would suffer most if his plan was not adopted. Liverpool and the Chancellor praised the speaker's motives and described his remedy as most efficacious; but they felt sure that the evil example of a single landowner would not be followed, and the matter could therefore wait. Stanhope rejoined that the mischief arose from considering gold the proper or only circulating medium, and that he wished there were no gold in the country. Among his audience on this occasion there was at least one very critical listener. ' I happened to be waiting at the bar of the House of Lords yesterday wrote Horner to Grenville on June 28, ' when Lord Stanhope presented a Bill for maintaining and enforcing the value of Bank of England paper. The manner in which his extraordinary proposal was received by Lord Liverpool and the Chancellor convinces me that the Ministers are prepared to make bank-notes legal tender. As there will be no recovery after bank-notes are made legal tender, the discussions which precede such a measure are evidently of the last importance. If your Lordship can make it convenient to take part, the expression of your sentiments might deter the Ministers from that course into which their own infatuation and the ignorance of their commercial advisers seem driving them." I

On July 22 Stanhope moved the second reading of his Bill. It was not, he explained, a measure to make bank-notes legal tender; yet it was impossible to pay large sums in gold. He again explained his proposals, and congratulated himself on its welcome by men who seldom approved any motion of his. The only argument against action was that Lord King's example would not be followed; but he had received information that others had already demanded payment in gold. He was followed by Lord King himself, whose elaborate speech defended not only the legality but the equity of his conduct. In view of the great depreciation of bank-notes he had no alternative but to recover the real amount stipulated in the contract, neither less nor more.

1 Horner's Memoirs and Correspondence, ii. 92-3.
2 Parl. Debates, xx. 784-90.

Lord Holland supported him, and regarded his action as a CHAP. salutary warning to the Government. The only remedy was for the Bank to resume its payment in specie. He never listened to the speeches of his noble friend without instruction; but his latest proposal would involve the country in calamity. Though the Bill did not make bank-notes legal tender, we should soon be unable to get anything else. It was legal tender in disguise, and would banish all money from circulation while increasing the issue of paper. Bank-notes would become like assignats, and would ultimately be valueless. If specie payments could not be resumed at once, let a period be fixed. Grenville recalled the fact that Pitt had suspended cash payments as a purely temporary measure, and confessed that he himself now regarded it as a mistake. He opposed the Bill as leading away from the goal of resumption.

After a prolonged debate Stanhope replied that he was very little given to views of self-interest. 1 He had always thought that the man who was in possession of a large property, not gained by his own talents and industry but derived from the mere accident of birth, was in fact but a trustee for the public, and should return some part of that estate for its benefit. He had never received a shilling from the public, and had expended thousands and thousands for its advantage. After many years' application and at much expense and with the assistance of the ablest artists, he had invented an effectual mode of preventing the forgery of bank-notes. He had also discovered how to strike off a million plates, all of them proofs; and when he had it complete he would give the invention to the Bank. ' On the second reading of this foolish and mischievous Bill records Romilly in his Diary, 2 ' the Ministers had not determined what course they should take; but after consultations between Perceval, Liverpool and other Ministers while the debate was going on, the " resolved to support it." When the second reading was carried, Grenville, Grey, Holland and other members of the minority entered a protest in the journals. On moving to go into Committee Stanhope once more pointed out that it compelled no one to accept a bank-note. Something required to be done, since gold was not to be obtained. The evil did not arise from the Bank of England but from the issue of notes by small country banks. Rebuking Lord King's action he remarked that with great landlords a few pounds ought to be no object. He once more urged his scheme for making legal tender the sums 1 Parl. Debates, xx. 830-1. 2 Romilly's Life, ii. 410-11.

CHAP, entered in the books of the Bank of England. On the third XII. reading he denied the depreciation of the paper currency, and declared that it never need take place if book entries were introduced. 1 The rumble of ancient controversies was heard when he suggested that British Ministers had encouraged the forging of assignats and the deluging of France with them. Grenville immediately rose and indignantly repudiated the charge on behalf of himself and his colleagues, living and dead.

After the passage of the Bill through the Upper House, Stanhope renewed his efforts to secure the system of transfer in the books of the Bank. 2 The measure, he declared, was only a palliative, a plaster for the wound calculated to keep the wasps and flies off till next session. He proceeded to move resolutions embodying his plan. Lauderdale complained that he failed to recognise that the precious metals were the best circulating medium. Stanhope sharply rejoined 3 that some men, like parrots and magpies, could say nothing but gold, gold, gold. To believe gold necessary to a circulating medium was an idea only fit for Hottentots. Gold was difficult to get and difficult to keep, and a far better circulating medium would be bank entries. When the Lords considered the Commons' amendments on July 22, he declared that he meant his Bill as a hint to Lord King and to all who should act like him. His example had been little followed, because people did not wish to expose themselves to the execration of the country. The amendments were accepted, and the Bill became law in July, though its operation was limited to the end of March, 1812.

For once Stanhope had won a conspicuous victory. Lord King's tenants had been delivered from the oppressor, and the impending repetition of the offence had been averted. But the theoretical foundations of his argument were extremely insecure. ' Though technically it was not making the note legal tender," declares Professor Smart, ' the practical difference was perilously thin." 4 Lauderdale, an expert economist, wrote that the Bill would not achieve the objects its author intended. William Frend, the Unitarian scholar who had been expelled from Cambridge for his support of the Revolution, declared that, as they agreed so much on political and philosophical subjects, he was particularly anxious to sift his own conclusions to the utmost when they differed. To him and to other correspondents 1 Parl. Debates, xx. 863-6. Â Ibid., 908-14, 3 In an adjourned debate of July 16; ibid., 980-5.

4 Smart, Economic Annals of the Nineteenth Century, pp. 299-304,

Stanhope replied at length, explaining and defending his position. 1 CHAP. Among his most severe critics was Lord Holland, whose ' Memoirs' XII. once more add the personal touch which brings the eccentric Peer vividly before us. 2 'He was a zealous promoter of the paper system, though with views very different from those of its other advocates. He was the first to call the attention of Parliament to the consequences of Lord King's demand. The Bill he presented, without actually declaring bank-notes legal tender, deprived the creditor to whom they were offered in payment of all legal remedy; and the Bill, though entirely altered in form, received the sanction of Parliament. Lord Chesterfield, a man of very large landed property, was on the point of issuing a similar demand on his peasantry, when Lord King's operations brought the subject before the public. Lord Stanhope, who had panegyrised the system of assignats in France, very consistently approved the bank-notes in England. When I told him that he expected them to have the same effect in England he whispered with a suppressed chuckle in my ear, "And if they take property from the drones and give it to the bees, where, my dear Citoyen, is the great harm of that? " He had invented an ingenious device for preventing forgeries; and the hopes of that experiment being adopted very possibly inflamed his zeal in support of a paper currency."

The later part of the session of 1812 was largely occupied with the familiar problem of religious liberty. In discussing Wellesley's motion on the Catholics, Stanhope declared that he could turn all the Bishops out of the House by a statute of Charles II. 3 He intended to bring this Act before the House when the Bill came on. He should have no occasion for it if the Bishops behaved like good boys, as he hoped they would; otherwise he should certainly turn them all out neck and shoulders. Two days later he moved the second reading of a Bill for the relief of Dissenters. 4 He gloried in being a Protestant, for Protestantism contended for the unlimited right of private judgment. He pointed out that there was not room for everybody. Moreover, there were now far more dissenting places of worship than churches, which proved that the majority of the people were Nonconformists. Taking into account the Scottish 1 These and other letters on the subject are preserved at Chevening.

2 Further Memoirs, pp. 104-5.
8 Parl. Debates, xxiii. 868, July I. 4 Ibid., 887-91.

CHAP. Presbyterians and the Irish Catholics, Anglicans were in a very XII. decided minority. This disposed of the common argument that the majority must bind the minority in matters of religion. He quoted the provisions and penalties of many obsolete statutes, and declared that laws not fit to be enforced ought to be repealed; but the Bill was thrown out without further debate. His efforts were attacked by William Smith, a rival legislator, in a letter to the papers which drew from him a spirited reply.

' In consequence of a strange letter, signed " W. Smith " and dated " Park Street, Westminster, July 4, 1812," which has appeared in the Morning Chronicle of the 6th instant, I deem it necessary to interrogate that gentleman before the public. As a warm, zealous and sincere friend of religious liberty it is my duty towards those millions of clients, whose just and sacred cause I have voluntarily espoused, to expose to their particular notice every attempt either to maintain the foul and execrable cause of intolerance, or to support the no less despicable system of mere toleration. Liberty duly recognised in matters of religion breaks the people's chains; but toleration (which always necessarily implies a right to be intolerant) tends to rivet them."

A rejoinder from Smith provoked a longer and more militant letter, the closing sentences of which once again expressed Stanhope's deepest convictions. 1 ' If he thinks proper to stoop in order to pick up from the kennel the rotting carcase of toleration, I tell him openly and distinctly that I will not condescend to follow his example. The inalienable right to perfect liberty in matters of religion has been given to all the human race by the Deity Himself. Who therefore, upon earth, ought to presume to limit or curtail it? But the vile idea of toleration originated in the darkest ages in the lawless usurpation of infallible dominion over conscience, and is worthy of hell itself."

When Lord Liverpool introduced a Toleration Bill a few days later Stanhope complained that it did not fully recognise the right of religious freedom; but while criticising its provisions he gave it a general support. 2 His efforts were gratefully recognised by Nonconformists throughout the country. The resolutions with his replies lie folded in neat little packets endorsed in his own hand. The Protestant Society for the Protection of Religious Liberty met at the New London Tavern on July 29 and 1 These letters are preserved in newspaper cuttings at Clievening. 8 Parl. Debates, xxiii. 1192, July 23.

drew up a grateful resolution. ' After our repeated intrusions CHAP, on your valuable time," runs the covering letter from the Secretary, ' we now address you with peculiar satisfaction. To the discharge of our official duty we must add our personal acknowledgments for the polite and liberal attention we individually received." Stanhope's reply expressed his hope ' finally to annihilate the hydra of persecution and to gain that glorious victory over intolerance which will ensure all men the maintenance of their sacred and inalienable rights, in spite of false friends, lukewarm supporters and open enemies."

A resolution of the Methodists gave Stanhope so much satisfaction that he sent it to the press, with the following reply:â ' Gentlemen,â It is highly gratifying to me to find that my exertions in behalf of religious liberty have met with your full approbation, and with that of the General Committee of the Societies founded by the late Rev. John Wesley. May I beg the favour of you to return my cordial acknowledgments to your worthy colleagues for their obliging expressions and great friendship towards me, and for their concurrence in those principles respecting the sacred right of private judgment in matters of religion which I have never ceased to maintain, and which were most emphatically and unequivocally declared in the Bill which I introduced last session to the House of Lords? The already tottering tower of intolerance could not any longer stand in opposition to the power of argument, aided by the force of ridicule. That rotten and despicable system has at last given way; and it is only necessary to attack it properly and with united efforts, directed by the light of principle, to cause it totally to disappear like an empty dream.

' Your ever faithful servant, ' STANHOPE."

To the Society for the Extension of Religious Knowledge in Suffolk he wrote on November 30: 'I beg to return you my most cordial thanks for the kind notice of my sincere and zealous endeavours to support the sacred cause of religious liberty, and the inalienable rights of private judgment. There is not anything which, in my opinion, can exceed the unprincipled wickedness and the folly of attempts to coerce conscience and to inflict punishment upon individuals for exercising their natural rights. These just and correct principles were instilled into me at an early age by the best of fathers; and these principles of liberty and social harmony I shall never change."

CHAP. Stanhope's services were always in demand. His old friend XII. Major Cartwright wrote to solicit his patronage for the Hampden and Union Societies, and received a characteristic reply x:â ' Dear Sir,â I have uniformly disclaimed the false and unprincipled proposition that the people's right to representation was co-extensive with direct taxation. Suppose some Chancellor of the Exchequer were to contrive to raise the whole revenue by indirect taxation, would that in any degree invalidate the sacred right of people to be represented? I will not allow my name to be made use of. I have correct principles which you will never change. But, as I have already told you, I have too indifferent an opinion of men to consent to form an union with any men for any purpose, good, bad or indifferent. I stand alone and shall probably continue to do so; but if it please my God that I shall live but a short time longer, I trust that I shall leave to my fellow-men a rich legacy of utility."

In the following year the Major was seized, kept in custody for several hours and grossly insulted. When he asked for protection and redress, Stanhope vigorously supported the plea of his old and honoured friend, and complained that justice was too expensive for the poor man.

He was equally ready to direct attention to other miscarriages of justice and to assist the humblest citizen in time of need. He drew up a form for debtors to fill in, giving their debts, disputed claims, assets and creditors; and one such form, filled up by a Newgate prisoner, is among his papers at Chevening. The following correspondence shows with what self-sacrificing zeal he championed the cause of the unfortunate. Early in October he received a letter from William Parr, a prisoner in Maidstone gaol, asking in what manner he could communicate certain inventions. Stanhope promptly dispatched a servant to fetch the plans, inquired why he was in prison, and wrote to his friend Sidmouth, the Home Secretary:â ' My dear Lord,â As my thoughts are constantly directed to the welfare of my country, I have to request your Lordship's special attention to the subject of this letter. Please see him yourself. As a man of science I know the practicability of many things which men of less scientific information may not 1 Cartwright's Life, ii. 43, deem to be possible. If not, please let him write to me without CHAP, his letters being opened. This man is to me a perfect stranger; XII. but he has written to me twice."

Sidmouth's brother replied that the plan had already been fully investigated and was useless. It was therefore needless to see Parr; but orders would be sent to allow the prisoner to communicate directly with him. Stanhope was by no means satisfied. ' I have examined the papers and drawings of Mr. Parr, and it is quite clear that the subject is of much greater importance than your Lordship is aware of. His principal project has not yet been communicated to Government ' There is good reason to believe rejoined the Home Secretary, ' that Parr's sole object is to delay the execution of his sentence in order to avail himself of the means he has devised to escape." Stanhope reiterated that the scheme had not been shown to the Government. ' I am sure the plans are the reverse of impracticable. I therefore refer you to my previous letter, which I do with every feeling of personal respect, which I have ever felt." He had done his best; but the Government was obdurate.

Parr's case was followed by others, and Stanhope determined to seek legislative remedy for the sufferings of debtors. On April 6, I8I4, 1 he presented four petitions relating to civil liberty, which, he declared, not even the enemies of political and religious liberty dared to attack. Magna Chart a enjoined that justice should not be sold, denied or delayed. ' My Lords, it is notorious that justice is sold in this country. I do not mean that it is sold by the judges; but such are the fees and expenses that it is impossible for certain classes of the community." The cases were of men imprisoned on a charge of debt before being found guilty, and one of them proved an illegal arrest for an unjust demand. A month later he again directed attention to the subject. 2 He held in his hand a petition from a prisoner in the Fleet who could only avoid starvation by paying illegal fees to the gaoler. While felons were by law allowed bedding, fuel, and food, unfortunate debtors were refused common sustenance. Could the House any longer acquiesce in such gross injustice and cruelty? Cases of greater oppression had never been witnessed in any nation. The humanity of the House and the country had at length succeeded in abolishing the African Slave Trade, a glorious act; but imprisonment for debt was aptly described as the English Slave Trade. The wisest and most humane had . Debates, xxvii. 418-23. 2 Ibid., 607-19.

CHAP, long and unanswerably demanded its abolition. The speaker XII. reverted to the cases he had mentioned in the previous debate, and moved for a return of the fees demanded or paid in the prisons for the last three years. Was it consistent with our constitution that upon the mere asseveration of an individual any British subject should be condemned to imprisonment without a trial? Not every man could find bail, and a creditor could gratify his spite by sending his victim to prison. He trusted that the Peers would commence a work of reform in this, the most improved nation of Europe. They had seen elsewhere the consequence of a reformation beginning with the tail, how it had led first to anarchy, then to military despotism. He therefore presented two Bills, the one abolishing committal till the jury had declared the existence of a debt, the other enacting that no one should be imprisoned for any sum under Â 15. ' If these Bills pass he concluded, ' I have no doubt all the swindlers and rogues will meet and hang up the effigy of your humble servant." The Bills were thereupon read a first time.

In moving the second reading of his Bill 1 to abolish mesne process, he declared that lawyers could do more good and more mischief than any other class. He lamented that Magna Charta was no longer respected. He quoted the case of a naval officer who returned home after a long absence, was mistaken for another man, was arrested on the quay and would have gone to gaol but that the admiral became bail. He then gave illustrations of the exorbitant charges of the attorneys, whom he denounced as harpies. Lord Holland warmly supported his friend; but Ellenborough opposed the Bill, which was rejected by 43 to 10. The second reading of the Poor Debtors' Bill was then moved and negatived without a division. Undeterred by these rebuffs Stanhope presented a petition from a prisoner for debt complaining of gross oppression in Gloucester gaol by being refused permission to consult his solicitor in reference to an appeal to the House of Lords. 2 By what authority did the gaoler refuse? Moreover he was confined during the day in a solitary cell, without writing materials, and at night was herded with criminals. The Chancellor defended the prison authorities of Gloucester, and the petition was ordered to lie on the table. On June 20 3 the King of Prussia, attended by his two sons and Blucher, visited the House, which quickly became crowded on the news of their arrival. Stanhope promptly seized the oppor-

Parl. Debates, xxvii. 955-9. 2 Ibid., 93-4, June 15.

3 Ibid., 102-3.

tunity and rose. As there were many persons in the House, CHAP, he remarked, some good persons too, he would call their attention XII Â to a subject of great public importance, namely, the abuses in Gloucester gaol; and as the subject was new to many present he asked the clerk to read the prisoner's petition. As the clerk was proceeding to obey, Lord Kenyon moved the exclusion of strangers, who accordingly withdrew. Stanhope then moved for a Committee of the House of Lords to inquire into the case of the Gloucester petitioner. 1 Liverpool replied that it should first be examined in the office of the Secretary of State. The Chancellor admitted the illegality of detaining the prisoner's letters and debarring him from legal advice, but opposed a Parliamentary inquiry.

Stanhope's fearless championship of prisoners led to the receipt of numerous petitions, which he presented at frequent intervals. 2 One was from a woman whose husband had been arrested on mesne process while dangerously ill and carried off to Newgate, where he lost his reason and died. The Coroner had declared that his death was accelerated by his removal to prison. Another was from two prisoners in Bristol gaol, complaining of the same treatment as the Gloucester petitioner. 3 A third was from a petitioner who had been made bankrupt nine years ago, but had never learned on what grounds, and had spent considerable sums in attempting to procure justice. 4 A fourth came from prisoners confined ' in this extraordinary gaol of Gloucester." 5 Despite the order of the Home Secretary, letters were still examined and access was denied to legal advisers. One prisoner had been put in irons for attempting to petition the House of Lords. It looked as if they had been crazy, to bid such open defiance to the law. He had never in his life been more indignant. He accordingly moved that Mr. Mogg, a Gloucester attorney,, be called to the bar and examined on his fruitless efforts to obtain access to his clients. After hearing the witness he left it to the House to decide whether a committee should be appointed to consider the case or whether, as he would prefer, the Attorney-General should prosecute the gaoler. Sidmouth replied that he had sent his letter not to the gaoler but to the Chairman of Quarter Sessions, and added that he would not object to the appointment of a committee. The magistrates, however, informed him that access had never been denied to legal advisers. Stanhope rejoined that their evidence 1 Parl. Debates, xxviii. 116-21. 2 Ibid., 297-8., 3 Ibid., 746-7. 4 Ibid., 79.7-8. 5 Ibid.,, 825-6.

CHAP, weighed nothing in comparison with that to which they had just XII. listened. The abolition of imprisonment for debt was in some degree due to his persistent efforts to bring the sad plight of prisoners before the public conscience.

After the renewal of war in 1803 Stanhope had rarely spoken on foreign affairs. He had, however, raised a warning voice against the policy which seemed likely to produce a conflict with America, and he watched its approach with the strongest disapproval. As usual he was for more energetic measures than his political friends were willing to adopt.

' Chevening House: February 27, 1812.

' To Lord Holland.

' My dear friend,â You may assure both Lord Lansdowne and Lord Erskine that no man in England is more decidedly against war with America and against every measure which has led towards it than myself. Having answered your question I will now add that our friends in Opposition appear to me not to have yet gone as far as justice and principle require. Whatever be the law between sovereign and independent nations at peace with each other, one principle appears to me to be quite clear, and that is that they ought to be considered as upon a footing of equality as to their rights; and that upon the honest, though simple principle, of "not doing to others that which we will not admit should be done to ourselves." When you were abroad I moved the House to that effect, as you will see by the journals. Had you been there, perhaps one

" conscientious man" (as you truly and correctly call yourself) would have supported me; but that principle, such as I have stated it, was not countenanced by a single individual!!! I make it a rule never to impute want of principle to any man who does not go along with me in any opinion; but I may say that a principle of inequality between independent nations is one that I do not profess to understand. Give my best compliments both to Lord Lansdowne and to Lord Erskine, and be so good as to shew them this letter. I wish Lord Lansdowne success in every motion about America which does not shock the fundamental principle which I have mentioned. I hope to be in town in less than three weeks.

' I am, my dear Lord, ever sincerely yours, ' STANHOPE," l i Holland House Af 55,

When war had broken out he directed attention to the short- CHAP, comings of naval administration. 1 He was educated under a man whom he could never mention without feelings of the greatest venerationâ his father, who was one of the best mathematicians of the country. He had quickly discovered the bad construction of ships; but the Board of Admiralty had with unaccountable obstinacy persevered in the old methods. If his advice had been followed, the French coast would have been vulnerable at every point; and if the French adopted the true methods, they could seriously damage our country and trade. There was another matter, he proceeded. By a decree of the Rolls Court it was forbidden to cut down what was called ornamental timber, which was the fittest for naval purposes. He was glad, however, that the Lord Chancellor appeared to be of a different opinion. According to a recent report nearly half our large ships were either rotting or rotten, and were serviceable for not more than eight or nine years. This was wholly due to faults of construction. Finally he had warned the Admiralty to prepare against Fulton's torpedoes; but nothing had been done, and he feared that the Americans might use them in the war. When the war was over Wellesley moved for papers on the peace negotiations, and discussed the causes and issues of the struggle. 2 In approving the motion, Stanhope reminded his hearers that before the outbreak of hostilities he had pleaded for reciprocity of rights among all maritime nations, but had met with no support. Again, when Liverpool moved an address approving the peace, 3 Stanhope contested his assertion that we had claimed no maritime rights which did not belong to other nations. The right of search, on the contrary, belonged only to belligerents, not to the nations at peace. If Denmark declared war against Sweden she might, according to this pretended right of search, claim to examine our ships for Danish subjects. Would this be endured? Yet America, when at peace with the world, was condemned to have her shipping subjected to the most vexatious search by British cruisers because we were at war with France. Even if the right was well founded, it was liable to so much abuse that it should be abolished.

While Stanhope unreservedly condemned the American War, the later stages of the long struggle with France received his approval. The conflict was no longer with the Revolution but with its destroyer. Accordingly when, after the abdication of 1 Parl. Debates, xxvi. 187-90. May 14, 1813. 8 Ibid., xxx. 607. 3 Ibid., 651.

CHAP. Napoleon in 1814, a national grant to Wellington was proposed, he warmly supported the motion. 1 It was a matter of exultation, he declared, that they had not only annihilated the conquests but destroyed the power of one of the vilest tyrants that ever existed, who made war merely for the pleasure of carrying it on. The Duke richly deserved his grant; but the best expression of national gratitude was neither land nor houses. His soldiers in conjunction with his talents had gained his victories, and their future situation and comforts should be secured. Among them were many Catholics who, now the danger was over, should not be suffered to remain the objects of exclusion or oppression. Great numbers had been paid off, and it was the duty of their House to protect the soldiers and sailors who had fought their battles from those worst of human beings, pettifogging attorneys, which their Lordships could do by supporting his Bills. The same practical note was struck on the occasion of a vote of thanks to the army and navy. 2 He suggested that the brave tars might be employed in our coast fisheries, which were capable of immense development.

Though he rejoiced over the downfall of the Emperor in 1814, he had no desire to aid the Bourbons to expel him when he returned from Elba. On April 6, 1815, 3 Liverpool presented the Prince Regent's message announcing the augmentation of the land and sea forces. After Grey had expressed a hope that hostilities would be avoided, Stanhope passionately protested against their renewal. He challenged the extraordinary pro position that England ought to assist the King of France or any other Government if attacked. Why should we not likewise go to the aid of King Ferdinand of Spain? He would rather die in the most horrid torture than agree to a declaration of war on such principles. On this occasion, however, the Government was wiser than its critic, and the battle of Waterloo was not only to destroy the tyrant but to inaugurate a generation of European peace.

With the return of peace England entered on the period of high agricultural protection which lasted till 1846, the ' Waterloo Corn Law' allowing importation only when the price reached 80s. a quarter. The Whig party was divided. ' Lauderdale 1 Parl. Debates, xxvii. 817. May n. 2 Ibid., xxviii. 536-7.

3 Ibid., xxx. 347-8.

writes Lord Holland, 1 ' had been the secret instigator and was CHAP, the open champion of the restrictive Corn Law. Grey's real XII. opinion, fortified and perhaps inoculated by Lauderdale, leant towards any measure that kept up the price of that article and prevented any sudden reduction of rents. Lord Grenville and Mr. Horner were decidedly friends to a free trade." Stanhope sided with the latter. In June, 1814,2 he presented a number of petitions against the measure, which he described as absurd and injurious. By raising the price of food and labour it would injure manufactures and commerce. ' Take away the taxes from the poor," he concluded, ' take away the taxes from provisions, the taxes which affect the price of bread and beer, candles, soap, salt and all those which fall on the poor and industrious bees of the community." A month later 3 he moved a reasoned resolution urging that food taxes bearing heavily on the growers of corn or the labouring classes should be repealed on the return of peace. He next 4 proposed a resolution adducing evidence of the rise of wages in harmony with prices. Corn-growers asked for relief of taxation, not for the increase of the price of corn. The duty of the Government was to unburden the growers, to diminish the taxes on the farmer or the labourer or both. Could the tax on horses be justified? or candles, or sugar, or leather? He had often been in small minorities in attempts which in the end succeeded, and he therefore did not despair of the success of this resolution. Lord Hardwicke protested against the name of famine-mongers as a vulgar term which he had never heard before. He must remind the noble Earl that there were also mischief-mongers. The question should, however, be debated next session.

In a debate next session on a petition from Kentish landowners to take into consideration the state of the Corn Laws, Stanhope renewed his opposition to the proposed law, the effect of which, he asserted, would be to starve the poor. 5 Lauderdale, as usual, followed in criticism of his old comrade. Next day 6 he presented three petitions, numerously and respectably signed against the proposed regulations. One, from Spital-fields, bore 6000 names. A day or two later 7 he presented ten more petitions against the alteration of the Corn Laws, two signed by 10,000 people, a third by 8000. Could that House, he demanded, refuse to attend to the wishes of the people of 1 Further Memoirs, p. 215. 2 Parl. Debates, xxvii. 1066-8.

3 Ibid., xxviii. 537. Ibid., 830-5, 6 Ibid., xxix. 1167-71. March 2, 1815. 6 Ibid., 1204.

7 Ibid., xxx. 1-2.

CHAP. England so generally expressed? Shortly after, 1 he brought forward his familiar motion for lightening the burden of taxation on agriculture. He appealed for support to friends as well as foes of the new Corn Bill. Liverpool's reply denounced him for deluding people by hopes of relief which could not be realised; since the burden of taxation resulted rather from the extent of the taxes than from their distribution. Grey complained that he had not pointed the way to any definite reform. The mover demanded a division, even if he had only a single vote on his side. The House accordingly divided, and the motion was lost by 30 to i. He continued to present petitions against the Bill, till the number of signatures amounted to about half a million. On the third reading he moved its rejection, but the measure passed by 128 to 21. So ended a conflict into which he had thrown himself with passionate intensity, but, as usual, without success.

The closing months of Stanhope's life were mainly devoted to urging different aspects of legal reform. In February, 1815, 2 he presented a Bill for allowing trial by jury in civil cases in Scotland. The Scotch were on the whole more enlightened than the English, and at least equally well qualified to judge points of law. As the Chancellor had introduced a measure admitting the jury where it was so directed, he reluctantly withdrew his more ambitious proposal. On the second reading of the Chancellor's Bill he complained of the option given to the Court whether to order a jury or not, whereas in questions of damages it ought to rest with the plantiff or defendant. 3 Again the jury was only to decide in questions of fact, not on the whole issue as in England. It was an insult to the people of Scotland to say that they were not prepared for trial by jury in the English manner. In Committee he declared that he had received communications from Scotland against the limitations of the Bill; but he was in some degree mollified by the Chancellor omitting the words which confined the duty of the jury to a decision in matters of fact.

Writing some time after to Lord Holland he lamented that he found so little assistance in the defence of popular rights and in the attack on evil measures. 4 1 Parl.

Debates, xxx. 206-8. March 16. 2 Ibid., xxix, 720-1. 3 Ibid., 1000-1003. February 23. 4 Holland House MSS.

' Chevening House: August 24, 1815. CHAP.

1 My dear Lord,â Many thanks to you for your two letters. xn-I have always been of opinion that ignorance has been the great root of all evil. Without it the "Divine Right" would never have prevailed; nor would military despotism, either from high or from adventurous extraction, ever have existed. I rejoice to find that my sentiments upon that subject are rapidly gaining ground. If the Opposition, as they are called, instead of taking up mere party questions, were, with the spirit that prevails in your breast and mine, to exert themselves to spread intellectual light to all, to amend our laws, to benefit the poor, to enable them to obtain justice, which is their right as between man and man, but from which they are by unconstitutional expense debarred; and if such objects should be made to appear to be their object, we need not despair of doing good, in spite of those who may, at first, resist us with success. Witness what passed last session. After I had at the end of the preceding session given notice to bring in a Bill, as last session, to extend the trial by jury in Scotland in civil causes, the Lord Chancellor preceded me by bringing in a Bill purporting to be for the same purpose, which Bill had been drawn by a Scotch Junto. I opposed his Bill most violently; he withdrew it instantly, and presented the House of Lords a second Bill almost as bad. I opposed that also in like manner. I had not one supporter in the whole House. Erskine called at my house to endeavour to make me drop my opposition. I persevered notwithstanding. The Lord Chancellor in Committee gave way from one end of the Bill to the other, and adopted my ideas throughout. The House of Commons spoilt the Bill afterwards; but I prevailed with the Lord Chancellor and the House of Lords to rectify that which the Commons had attempted. Thus Trial by Jury is, in civil causes, in existence in Scotland, which without the unconnected individual who now addresses you would not have been the case; but a measure worse than none at all would have taken its place by the strange acquiescence of all parties. What might men not do who act in unison, if they act with right good intentions!

' Ever cordially and truly yours, 1 STANHOPE."

Though determined that every accused person should have the benefit of trial by jury, he was not opposed to the infliction of severe sentences in cases where heinous guilt was established. An ardent humanitarian in his efforts for the abolition of the

CHAP. Slave Trade and the better treatment of prisoners, he claims XII. no place in the ranks of those who were labouring for a milder criminal code. ' Lord Stanhope, whom I saw to-day in the House of Lords," wrote Romilly in his diary of March 26, isig, 1 ' told me he was against both my Bills. His arguments against the Freehold Estates Bill are not worth repeating; but of the Shoplifting Bill he said " it was a Bill to screen the greatest villains on the face of the earth, men who were much worse than murderers." I stared with astonishment, as well I might, and my astonishment was not much diminished when he proceeded to explain his meaning. There are, he says, a great number of young children who are thieves by trade. They are educated to this trade by men who are the greatest of villains. Shoplifting is frequently committed by these boys, and when they are capitally convicted the men who put them on are accessories before the fact, and might be capitally convicted too; and by this means we might bring to the gallows these worse than murderers."

Patient study of the Statute-book had made Stanhope aware of its countless anomalies, and the experience of recent years had brought home to him the extent of the hardships involved by many of its antiquated provisions. On May 3 2 he made one of his longest and most important speeches on the revision of the statutes. Lord Grenville had obtained the codification of all Acts imposing the punishment of death in revenue cases, and he himself had secured the unification of the measures imposing the punishment of the pillory. Even in the latter case the Judges, who had prepared the Bill, had overlooked two of the statutes. It conveyed some idea of the condition of the law when even the Judges could not accurately state what it was. In like manner, when the Commons had ordered a return of the laws on transportation, inquiry was made after a long time why it was not ready; and the answer was that it was so extensive as to require another year. ' The glorious uncertainty of the law ' was a proverbial expression. Glorious it might be to attorneys, conveyancers, special pleaders, barristers and so forth; but it was most inglorious to the public. He suggested that forms of leases should be attached as Schedules to Acts of Parliament, so that parties could copy them and fill them in. They would thus in nine cases out of ten require no assistance from lawyers. The more their Lordships looked at the Statute-book, the more clearly they would see it was i Romilly's Diary, iii. 237-8. 2 Parl. Debates, xxxiv. 173-82.

like the Augean stable and required a similar remedy. There (CHAP, were 977 statutes on wool, 964 on fisheries, 440 on the poor, X H-and others in proportion. Moreover, 1455 Acts had been repealed in the reign of George III; so that they had been passing Bills by waggon-loads and repealing them by cart-loads. There were, however, plenty of curious provisions still unrepealed. He also complained of the phraseology of modern Acts, so unlike the brief, clear language of the older statutes. ' Look at Magna Charta and then at the modern Statute-book, and see what an oppressive, dark, ill-arranged, disgusting farrago of unintelligible nonsense it is." Then there was the excessive cost of actions. It was quite a common thing to have a verdict for Â 3 and Â 28 costs. A poor man could not recover a sum without absolute ruin. He proposed to appoint an assessor, who, with twenty or thirty clerks, should arrange the statutes under their proper heads. Wilberforce had lately informed him that he had once contemplated a similar plan. It could be accomplished without much expense and its utility would be incalculable. A committee of the House should draw up a plan of classification, and the statutes under each head could be summarised in a single Act. As an honest man was the noblest work of God, a well-arranged Statute-book was certainly the noblest work of man. 1

The Chancellor professed himself willing to refer the matter to a committee for consideration; but he had no hope that it could be carried out as completely as the mover had suggested. Lord Holland, as usual, was pressed into the service by his eager friend. 2 ' 49 Berners Street: May n, 1816.

' My dear Lord,â If you come to the House on Tuesday next, pray have the goodness to be there before 5, in order to attend the Conference with the House of Commons respecting the statute-book.

' I am, my dear Lord, ever cordially and ' Most sincerely yours, ' STANHOPE 1 The whole speech breathes the practical spirit of Bentham. So far as I know the only document connecting the two men is a letter preserved in Bentham's Correspondence in the British Museum (Addit. MSS. 33541, f. 320. March 19, 1792). 'Earl Stanhope presents his compliments to Mr. Bentham, and returns him a great many thanks for his obliging present of the Panopticon. Earl Stanhope returns herewith the French Memoire that Mr. Dumont lent him. Lord Stanhope has received great pleasure from the perusal of it." 2 Holland House MSS.

CHAP. After a good deal of deliberation Parliament passed resolutions XII. approving the plan. The Lords declared it highly expedient that the Statute-book be arranged under distinct and proper heads, and a person learned in the law, assisted by twenty clerks, be appointed for supervising such arrangement. The Houses then presented a joint address to the Prince Regent begging him to take ' effectual measures to arrange the laws under heads." In a packet of papers at Chevening endorsed by Stanhope ' About the Statute-book' these declarations are accompanied by an elaborate memorandum on the ' Duty of the Assessor," in which he gives directions how the work should be carried out. The first duty, he declared, was to make a list of the laws which had been wholly or in part repealed. Some preliminary meetings of legal reformers in both Houses were held; but before the great project was effectively launched its author was dead.

Stanhope was anxious to bring order into another part of the national machinery. On May 7 he spoke on the second reading of a Weights and Measures Bill. Though it aimed at uniformity, it was not calculated to produce the desired effect. He read a letter from Dr. Hutton," that very able mathematician," condemning the retention of old names for new quantities. If the people really wanted new weights and measures, continued Hutton, let them follow the example of France and adopt the decimal standard. In this opinion Stanhope concurred. He had letters from many mathematicians and several very sensible tradesmen on the subject, and they all pointed in the same direction. Men of science should be fully consulted. Let them be sent to him, and he would examine them. He moved the rejection of the Bill, which was thrown out without a division. A fortnight later he reverted to the subject, and proposed that it should be submitted to a commission of experts. 2 A proper scientific standard might be introduced without any great inconvenience, a standard worthy of the country of Newton, Hutton, Simpson, Napier and Maclaurin. The question was urgent, for there was an office in Westminster where weights were stamped without being weighed. A commission of scientists should be appointed, with such men as Dr. Hutton, one of the first mathematicians of Europe, and Dr. Playfair of Edinburgh. They should consider the subject by themselves, unharassed by questions of Lords or Commons. The ideal was a common standard for the principal nations of Europe, which would be of prodigious commercial advantage to ourselves. But this was 1 Pavl. Debates, xxxiv. 306-9. z Ibid., 771-5 only possible if we adopted a standard founded on nature. For CHAP, once a motion by Stanhope was carried unanimously. XI1-

Some of Stanhope's last words in the House of Lords were devoted to the Irish question. When Buckingham moved for a committee to inquire into the state of Ireland, 1 he declared that if concessions to Catholics were contemplated, they should be given

fully and frankly, and without that odious and mischievous accompaniment, the Veto."
2 To refuse their claims was injustice; to grant them with a veto on the appointment of their spiritual leaders would be an insult. He then reverted to the sufferings of the peasantry from the exaction of the middleman. There was also another bitter grievance, namely, the insults of Orangemen to their fellow-countrymen. He had been told by Catholic priests and gentlemen that of two evils they would prefer the getting rid of the Orange system to emancipation. It was not merely for their own outrages that the Orangemen were answerable, but for the illegal associations which they in their turn engendered. The Ribbonmen followed their example, and both went on from one lawless outrage to another till the country was hardly worth living in. A further grievance was tithes. He would not call on the Catholic and dissenting population of Ireland, who were in the ratio of ten to one, to contribute to the maintenance of a Church in which they never set their foot. He would adopt a much easier and safer mode of supporting the Church, that of the late Lord Melville, who declared that the best way of securing the permanence of the Church Establishment was by founding it on the rock of poverty. He also strongly advocated the extension of education. The speech was a remarkable contribution to Irish statesmanship. His last utterance, delivered on June 21, was made on the cognate subject of Catholic disabilities, of which he had been the life-long enemy. 3

No movement during the later years of Stanhope's life gave him greater satisfaction than the foundation of elementary schools for the children of the working classes. He was one of the most generous supporters of Lancaster, who acknowledged a contribution in the following letter. 4 ' ist month, 6th, 1809. Royal Free School,
Borough Road.
My very kind sic, â I am honoured and obliged for thy letter and enclosure, and shall take care it is only applied to the 1 Parl. Debates, xxxiv. 819-21.
See Bernard Ward, The Eve of Catholic Emancipation, vol. i.
3 Parl. Debates, xxxiv. 1252. 4 Chevening MSS.
CHAP, purpose for which it is intended. I have long considered all XII. m y inventions and improvements as public property of which the bounteous author of all good has made me steward. ' I remain thy obliged and respectful friend, ' Jos. LANCASTER
His sympathy and support continued to the end. In 1814 he greeted his friend Fletcher with the words, ' Well, friend, take a chair, I have some good news to tell you. I have long had it in contemplation to assist the public schools, now forming on the Lancastrian plan, for the education of the children of the labouring poor, who, by our cruel system of taxation, are reduced to such a state of extreme poverty as to be incapable of bearing the expense themselves. I intend to subscribe Â 400, on condition of my plan of these mills small metal mills for grinding corn invented by Fletcher being adopted. I, being a subscriber and member, can appoint you to act for me on the Committee. I shall attend their next meeting and inform them of my resolution." 1 As usual he gave his time as well as his money. A few months before his death we find him signing the report of a sub-committee of the West London Lancastrian Association appointed to discuss the invitation of the British and Foreign School Society to become an auxiliary body. 2

The knowledge of Stanhope's latest political sentiments derived from his speeches and correspondence is supplemented by the notes of his conversation published three years after his death by the same forgotten writer. ' Having in the spring of 1814 invented a machine to assist certain operations of manual labour," writes Fletcher, ' and hearing that Lord Stanhope was esteemed a scientific and able judge of mechanism, I called. In ten minutes he entered, and taking a small rule from his pocket, began to measure and inspect it." Fletcher then produced a small metal mill which had been in use twelve years, and was capable of grinding wheat. Stanhope was delighted, expressed a wish that every labourer had one, and promised to obtain a metal cast. At the next visit the conversation turned on politics. Fletcher: ' I often hear it said there are not half a dozen men of common integrity to conduct a public undertaking calculated to produce any real good to the people. I hear the Government 1 The late Earl Stanhope's Political Opinions of Public Affairs, Foreign and Domestic, and of the Real Causes and Consequences of the Increase of Crimes and Miseries of the People,.., London. 2S.

2 Chevening MSS.

begins to view this project of education with an evil eye, and CHAP, that one of their spies has crept into the committee in the garb of X H-a patriot, and is carrying on a systematic plan for its destruction." Stanhope: ' Very possible. The very foundation on which the present system is raised is depravity of principle. One of the worst of the bad practices of the Government is the employment of spies and informers. The political character of the Government has changed, and through that change the vital character and the condition of the people cease to be what they were." Fletcher then expressed his desire for a civil code, and produced a petition for it which his host perused. Stanhope: ' Very good. You are aiming a well-directed blow at the tap-root of that stem whose branches bear the bitter fruits of all our woes. The unwritten laws of our forefathers are known to very few, though they are talked about by every one, and are totally disregarded by those who have to administer them in all cases where the interest of the Crown or of the party in power is concerned. And as to written or statute laws, we have more than a man could read in the course of a long life."

Fletcher then raised the question of the war. Stanhope: ' Had Pitt not been in power and had Burke been left without a pension, we should have found them both as vehement opposers of these abominable crusades as they were advocates for them. Pitt was politically and morally wrong, and no one knew it better than himself. Having, however, once committed himself and struck into a wrong course, he was too proud to own his error. Mr. Fox, when in office, finding he was not allowed to do several good things which he intended, neglected many which he might have done, and did also that which he ought not to have done, and thereby brought disgrace on a party and its cause. The present system acted upon by the party called the Opposition never was calculated to produce any great good. At present there is nobody in either House. In the Upper House I stand alone. If I attempt to move on any point which would tend to lighten the burden of taxation or extortion or the oppressions of perverted or defective laws and rapacious lawyers, they all start back as if scared by a ghost. Sir Francis Burdett is a good public speaker and a true friend to the people, and in every way most respectable and independent; but he is not at present a man of business. As to Mr. Whitbread and all the party-coloured birds of that feather, they will never be distinguished from the Treasury and borough-dealing tribes but by their unmeaning clamour. There is Mr. Homer, the clearest headed man I ever met with, and Mr. Brougham, a great candidate CHAP, for popularity. They might do great good in exposing and correcting the abuses of our civil code; but the system has become so contagious as to contaminate the principles or paralyse the moral faculties of every man who approaches it."

The last topic was codification, of which Fletcher was a zealous champion. ' The more I think of it declared Stanhope, ' the more it appears an object of incalculable importance. I have such cases of daily enormities brought forward by persons oppressed and ruined as would employ half my time to read and attend to them; and after all I have the extreme mortification to find that, except in one or two instances, my endeavours are all in vain to obtain redress of wrong. Against the poor suitor the doors of justice are carefully closed." Fletcher then showed him the resolutions framed at a meeting at the Thatched House Tavern, urging that all should assist ' that enlightened and human Senator, Earl Stanhope to obtain a printed Civil Code. The same meeting had also drawn up a petition to the Commons. Stanhope promised his support, and reported at the next interview that he had spoken to some members who were likely to lend a helping hand. ' But if I fail to form anything like a party or committee, you must not be discouraged or surprised. We cannot make silk purses out of sows' ears." He had been labouring at that ungrateful task for forty years, and, like other reformers, he died without witnessing the realisation of more than a fraction of his beneficent projects.

THE loneliness of Stanhope's later political career was paralleled CHAP, by the distressing circumstances of his domestic life. The death XIII. of his first wife was a tragedy, for neither his second wife nor his children inspired him with deep affection. Finding his happiness in political activity and scientific research, he came to depend less and less on human sympathy, and the softer lines in his character faded away.

The friendship with Pitt, which had been the inspiration and delight of his early years in Parliament, was shattered on the rocks of the French Revolution. The Minister's neutral attitude for the first two years, midway between the furious pessimism of Burke and the sanguine hopes of his brother-in-law, was that of the majority of his countrymen; and though Stanhope was disappointed at his coolness, there was no ground of active complaint. A letter from the Duke of Buckingham, then Viceroy of Ireland, to his brother in February 1790 shows that their relations were at that time still relatively friendly. ' Hobart has prevailed on Coote to stand for Queen's County, and I am earnestly pressed to endeavour to get for him Lord Stanhope's interest. I should think Pitt might manage it; but it is clear that I cannot ask any favour from his Lordship, as we hardly exchange bows." It was not till 1792 that an open and final split occurred. By that time France had declared war on Austria and Prussia, the King was virtually a prisoner, and the Revolution was heading rapidly towards violent courses. Pitt's first decisive challenge to the Revolution was the Proclamation against Seditious Writings in May 1792, accompanied 1 Buckingham to W. W. Grenville, February 24, 1790. Thirteenth Report of Hist. MSS. Comm., part iii. 504.

by his declaration against Grey's Reform Bill. On the outbreak of hostilities Stanhope entered on the course of passionate opposition which lasted without a truce till Pitt's death in 1806. The following letter, written by the Prime Minister to his mother in the summer of 1793, shows that they carefully avoided meeting even on the neutral ground of Burton Pynsent. ' Lord Stanhope's notification of his visit certainly comes at a singular time; but so many miles from the House of Lords he will be very humble and well-behaved, and I cannot help rejoicing on account of the companions of his journey. I think I may be at liberty in about a fortnight; but I should wish to regulate my motions a little by the Eliots and Lord Stanhope, though not in the same way by each of them." 1

The political quarrels of Pitt and Stanhope in no way interrupted the cordial relations of their families, and the correspondence of the Dowager Lady Chatham and the Dowager Lady Stanhope continued unabated. To this invaluable source we owe our knowledge of the family life at Chevening and of the early years and training of the children. The letters enable us to test and correct the picture painted by Lady Hester a generation later and reproduced by the Boswellian Meryon. The unreliable character of this famous book has long been known; and the Chevening Papers prove that no single anecdote relating to her youth can be accepted unless confirmed by contemporary evidence. On the appearance of the volumes in 1845 the fourth Earl wrote to The Times 2 denying that he dined in company with Fox when Pitt was on his death-bed, and added that he neither dined with him nor knew him. ' There are several other misrepresentations and misstatements concerning myself he continued, ' which I forbear to mention, as they relate to private and family affairs." The misstatements were not confined to the fourth Earl. Assuming that Meryon wrote down the general substance if not the actual words of his interminable conversations with his employer, it must be remembered that she was dealing with occurrences thirty years old and that she was an embittered woman of violent personal prejudices. The racy reminiscences are rather a revelation of her own storm-tossed spirit than a serious contribution to history. 3 1 July 18, 1793. Chatham Papers, Record Office. z July 9.

3 Stratford Canning's statement in 1827 that Lady Hester's father had set her to tend turkeys on a common (Lane-Poole, Life of Stratford Canning, i. 121), and the assertion of the Comtesse de Boigne that Stanhope's first wife was driven into her grave by the eccentricities of her husband (Memoirs, i. 137), are typical of the growth of legend.

With these words of caution let us recall Lady Hester's references to her father and to the life at Chevening under his regime. The best-known passages suggest an atmosphere of Spartan severity, only tempered by the diplomatic interventions of a favourite daughter. She rejoiced in her superiority to the purely feminine accomplishments of her sisters. ' My father would say to Lucy, "Now papa is going to study, so you may go to your room." Then when the door was shut he would turn to me, "Now we must talk a little philosophy," and then, with his legs stuck upon the sides of the grate, he would begin. " Well, well," he would cry after I had talked a little, " that is not bad reasoning, but the basis is bad." ' 1 Sometimes, however, the youthful logician succeeded in converting her father. ' My sister Lucy was prettier than I, and Griselda more clever; but I had from childhood a cheerfulness and sense of feeling that always made me a favourite with my father." She exemplified this by an anecdote of her step-mother, when her father, in one of his republican fits, put down his carriage and horses. ' Poor Lady Stanhope she said, ' was quite unhappy about it; but when the whole family was looking glum and sulky, I thought of a way to set all right again. I got myself a pair of stilts and out I stumped down a dirty lane, where my father, who was always spying about through his glass, could see me. So, when I came home, he said to me, "Why, little girl, what have you been about? " " Oh! papa, I thought, as you had laid down your horses, I would take a walk through the mud on stilts; for I don't mind mud or anything. 'Tis poor Lady Stanhope who feels these things; for she has always been accustomed to her carriage, and her health is not very good." After a pause, he said, "Well, little girl, what would you say if I bought a carriage again for Lady Stanhope? " " Why, papa, I would say it was very kind of you." " Weil, well, we will see; but damn it! no armorial bearings." So, some time afterwards, down came a new carriage and new horses from London, and thus, by a little innocent frolic, I made all parties happy again."

' My father," she added, ' always checked any propensity to finery in dress. If any of us happened to look better than usual in a particular hat or frock, he was sure to have it put away the next day and to have something coarse substituted in its place." ' Nobody," she remarked on another occasion, ' ever saw much of me till Lord Romney's review. I was obliged to play a trick on my father to get there. I pretended the day before that I 1 Meryon, ii. n.

CHAP, wanted to pay a visit to some friends, and then went on from XIII. their house. Though all the gentry from Kent were there, my father never knew, or was supposed not to have known, that I was there. The King took great notice of me, and, I believe, always after liked me personally. When he was going away and the Queen had got into her carriage, he said to her, "My dear, Lady Hester is going to ride bodkin between us; I am going to take her away from Democracy Hall." But the old Queen observed, in rather a prim manner, that I had not got my maid with me, and that it would be inconvenient to go at short notice; and so I remained." 1

There is, however, evidence in Lady Hester's own recollections that life at Chevening was not so drab as she sometimes painted it. Sitting in her bare and lonely room on the rock at Djoun on the last night of the year 1837, she looked back with fond regret to the joyous scenes and good cheer at her old home. To-night in my father's house there used to be a hundred tenants and servants sitting down to a good dinner, and dancing and making merry. I see their happy faces now before my eyes, and when I think of that and how I am surrounded here, it is too much for me She fondly recalled the stately etiquette and the quantity of food consumed by the household, how an ox was killed every week and a sheep every day.

When the master of Chevening entertained his friends, there was nothing grudging or penurious in his hospitality. ' Just before the French Revolution," records his daughter, ' the French ambassador was the Comte d'Adhemar. I was but seven or eight when I saw him. When he came by invitation to pay a visit to my papa, there was such a fuss with the fine footmen, with feathers in their hats." 2 Mrs. Stapleton attended several banquets and described her experiences to the Dowager Lady Chatham. ' I dined at Lord Stanhope's yesterday; we had a most magnificent dinner; perfectly well served in all respects, eight livery and four at least out; a fine and very convenient house but sad situation. Lord and Lady Chatham, Lord and Lady Harrington, Lord Fortescue, Mr. Neville, Mrs. G., Mrs. S. Lady Stanhope dressed better and don't look ill, but much out of beauty, and is in the folly of living I think upon air and water. They have had an open window every night this cold winter. He is handsome to what we remember, cheerful and good-humoured." B On the other hand we learn from the same correspondent that 1 Meryon, ii. 24-6. " Ibid., 12.

3 April 27, 1789. Pitt Papers, Record Office.

Stanhope rarely accompanied his wife when she dined out. After CHAP, an evening at Mrs. Grenville's, Mrs. Stapleton wrote to Lady XIII. Chatham: ' Lord Stanhope as usual has too many engagements to meet us." x James Grenville adds that he ' disliked the hurry and frolic of any parties abroad."

Political dinner-parties were now becoming rather embarrassing. ' I dined at Lord Stanhope's," wrote the Duke of Leeds on April 16, 1791; ' a mixed company, Lord Chatham and Lord Grenville both there. The Duchess was much struck with Lord Grenville appearing extremely out of spirits and scarcely speaking the whole time." 2 As Stanhope became more and more prominently identified with the championship of French ideas, he felt it his duty to discard the emblems of his rank. He rolled up the magnificent tapestry which the first King of Prussia had presented to the first Earl. ' Even the coronets over the iron gates at Chevening," adds the Duchess of Cleveland, ' were taken down, and he was styled Citizen Stanhope. Later in life, I believe, his opinions were modified; he dropped the citizenship and replaced the coronets." 3 Stanhope did nothing by halves, and he was ready to sacrifice his own comfort as well as that of his household to the exigencies of political principle.

The voluminous correspondence of their grandmother renders it clear, nevertheless, that the girls enjoyed every privilege and pleasure suitable to their station and age. However stern to his sons, to his daughters Stanhope was an affectionate and even indulgent father. On the least symptom of illness, doctors, dentists and oculists were sent for, and his anxieties are mirrored in the bulletins of his mother. When the three little girls were sent to the seaside and Hester was recommended bathing, her father hurried down to test the baths. The legend that Chevening was a sunless prison in which the children were immured by a selfish tyrant cannot survive the following typical extracts from the letters of Grisel, who, from her quiet retreat at Ovenden in a corner of the great park, watched with loving interest the fortunes of the family.

November 29, 1790.â ' The Three Graces have just left me. They drank tea with me, and we were a very happy parti carre."

February 24, 1791.â ' The three and Mahon dined with me a few days ago on Lucy's birthday. I must say they are very thankful for any little advice I am capable of giving, and return 1 April 28, 1791. Pitt Papers, Record Office.

2 Political Memoranda of Francis, fifth Duke of Leeds, p. 167. Life of Lady Hester Stanhope.

CHAP, me thanks with a kiss. Such good heads and hearts make me XIII. hope that they will conduct themselves well and creditably throughout life. God bless them, sweet dears."

July 28, 1791.â ' The three and the governess dined with me yesterday, very happy and very busy, finishing a trimming they have worked to present to Lady Stanhope on her birthday, and I hear were out in the garden by five o'clock in the morning and erected a small theatre of hurdles and boughs, in which they acted a play composed by Griselda for her, Lucy and brothers to act. Hester, too tall to match, was chief engineer."

October 4, 1791.â ' Hester is much better. I believe that the greatest attention is paid to their health at all times, and what is thought right to preserve or restore it is never neglected."

The children entered into some, at any rate, of their father's interests. That they shared his detestation of the Slave Trade was shown in a practical manner.

December 4, 1791.â ' The present passion among the flock is leaving off sugar; their motive so commendable (that of humanity) that all one can say is to put it in every light for and against. You cannot imagine their eagerness, and they are a little displeased at not having yet persuaded the elder ones of the family to do the same, who are not less humane in our way of thinking, though at present we make use of sugar as usual." 1

January 8, 1792.â ' Our young ones have, I hear, been well amused at home, dancing, acting, c."

September 17, 1792.â ' I wish they had more settled health, but that may come. That every attention is paid to them in everything is a great satisfaction to me. The rest we must leave to Providence."

November 8, 1792.â ' Hester rides vastly well, and is a fine figure on horseback."

November 5, 1793.â ' Hester looks jolly and well and is in very good spirits. I wish I could say as much of my son's looks; but he says he is well, so I hope with a little rest he will plump up, for at present he is very lanthorn-faced."

November 25, 1793.â ' Yesterday our three girls dined with me. They are very well in health and looks, and very merry and happy. Hester made me admire her brown gown, which colour becomes her very much. She has a very good taste for dress; but one of her jokes is to overdo the fashion in something or other when she comes to me, to amuse me or make me laugh.

1 Cp Clarkson, History of the Abolition of the Slave Trade, ii. 349-50,

Young people must be in the fashion, but I try to laugh them out CHAP, of extremes. I like their innocent mad pranks, as they behave XIII. so well in company; the two eldest were at a ball a few days ago and much admired for the propriety of their behaviour, so much so that a lady there, who has some female children, said to Lady Stanhope that she must consult her about their education, as ours did her so much credit."

December 26, 1793.â ' I fancy you hear from some of the girls, whose talents, I agree with you in thinking, are equal to everything. They ride, they drive with neighbours, and go to balls and amuse themselves."

March 19, 1794.â ' This day at last a letter from Hester, who says, "My dress, a pink train, drapery done round with gold fringe and a white spangled petticoat, cap, little more than four feathers, with a quire of white satin tied up and gold tassels, very much frightened. I think it very dull and formal; at Gloucester House not much better.

I have been at a ball, not a good one, but expect a better soon." I hear from another quarter that she made a good appearance."

March, 26, 1794.â ' I have just been informed that a lady met Hester at a great Rout at Lady Amherst's, and was much pleased at her appearance. I have also heard from another that she goes everywhere where Lady Stanhope goes and that she looks incomparably well."

August 13, 1794.â ' Hester has had a friend with her for about three weeks. Every amusement that riding, visiting, c. can produce, they have had without interruption and which the uncommon strength of Hester bears most amazingly, for none can keep up with her. Yesterday they wished to go to a ball at Tunbridge Wells on the Prince of Wales' birthday."

January 2, 1795.â ' Our three lasses have passed a very merry Christmas, and this night are going to the great annual ball in our neighbourhood,â that is, used to be so, but gentlemen are in general pretty scarce at balls, as I am told."

April 17, 1795.â ' About a week ago my four females were at a great ball and supper, and they took the two eldest boys with them. After supper the ladies retired and the two little boys remained, and thought themselves, no doubt, persons of importance. The gentlemen said to M ahon, Come, you shall be toast-master; and he accepted with the greatest gravity. The first toast he gave was " To the immortal memory of Lord Chatham." I do love him for it, more than I can tell you, 'tis a sweet dear and a sensible, for it came from his heart and head, both good as you see. Tis said that old people

CHAP, are twice children, perhaps 'tis so, for I cannot write this with XIII. dry eyes."

December 28, 1795.â ' The three dancing away; every week of late at one or two balls, I hope to their hearts' content."

January 12, 1796.â ' As to the three damsels they are this night gone to a ball, of which there has been one every evening for some time, and after them suppers. I hear they looked well, and caps elegant and becoming. They return never before five, often seven o'clock. One of the old attends, sometimes both, but papa the oftenest, as late hours don't suit others. The three are much obliged to him, as it don't suit him much either."

Not the most exemplary father could do more than take three daughters some sixteen miles over the heavy Kent roads, wait patiently at a ball, and return at seven in the morning.

December 29, 1796.â ' Balls begin as usual next week."

August 19, 1797.â ' I heard yesterday from Hester from Tunbridge Wells. Lady Stanhope, Griselda and her are there; Hester had not been quite well, and it was thought the waters would be of service. Hester says that Griselda goes to all the balls, but, as she is prudent, she has not yet been. But fair or foul I don't believe they miss riding. Hester to be sure shews to great advantage on horseback, and peaks herself on her horsemanship, and very vain that her opinion is often asked, as being knowing in jockeyship."

The picture painted by the fond and gentle Grisel shows that the boys and girls enjoyed a normal and happy childhood. But as they grew up difficulties arose, and Stanhope was at last left alone in the great house which had echoed with the prattle and laughter of half a dozen children. The daughters were older than the sons, and with them the trouble began. Lucy, the youngest, had fallen in love with Taylor, the family doctor, and in 1796, when only a little over sixteen, married him. Stanhope's democratic principles did not cover such a case, and the match was treated as a mesalliance, though Taylor was a man of excellent character. The ministerial caricaturists naturally made the most of the incident. His old enemy Gillray drew a picture of the ceremony, entitled the ' Union of the Coronet and the Clysterpipe," in which Fox, the officiating clergyman, read the service from Paine's ' Rights of Man," and Stanhope looked on with approval. Since my last wrote Grisel on October 6, 1796, to Lady Chatham, ' I received a present of game from those who for some time have taken up much of my thoughts. I took a hint and wrote desiring they would dine here to take a share of it, which they did yesterday, with papa, CHAP. Griselda and the elder brother. All went as if nothing had ever XIII. happened, and all seemed pleased with me. I think now the ice has been broken and melted, I need not write anything more and that you will now be easy on this subject." But peace was only outwardly restored, and Lucy ceased to form part of the family circle. Pitt, however, came to the rescue of his niece, and gave Taylor a place in the Customs which at once improved the position of the newly married couple and removed them from the thundery atmosphere of Chevening. 1

Not very long afterwards Griselda left home for unknown reasons, presumably because she was not happy. ' She took refuge records her niece the Duchess of Cleveland," in a cottage at Walmer, lent her by Pitt, and four years after she became the wife of John Tekell, an officer in the army. My grandfather she adds, ' offered no opposition to his daughters' departures, though when Lady Griselda left he was heard to compare himself to Lear Only Hester, the eldest, was now left, and she was before long to follow her sisters' example. Before doing so, however, she was to play a leading part in the escape of her brother, the heir to the title and estates.

Lord Mahon frequently appears in Grisel's correspondence as a gentle and attractive child. Stanhope had merely tasted Eton, and he saw no need to send his sons to school or college. The boys were therefore educated at home, their first tutor being their father's secretary, Jeremiah Joyce. The Duchess of Cleveland naturally takes her father's side, and shares his indignation at the treatment to which he was subjected. ' He kept strict watch and ward over his eldest son she writes, ' all the stricter as he approached his majority. He was kept immured at home, in a situation (to quote his own words) of all others the most odious and oppressive. He bitterly deplored the loss of the wasted years passing away unheeded over his head that should have been employed in fitting him to take his place in the world. At length in 1801 he determined to attempt to shake off the yoke, having just entered his twentieth year. He asked to be sent to college, and made proposals regarding the entail which

Their son was later entrusted with the task of editing the Chatham Correspondence. Their grandchild, Miss Pitt Taylor, was feted at the recent Pittsburg celebration as the lineal descendant of the Pitt family.

CHAP, had been drawn up for him by Pitt; but they were unacceptable, XIII. and he found to his dismay that his father's object was to obtain the power of disposing of the estate. This would have meant his ruin. In his distress he opened his heart to Lady Hester, who vowed she would extricate him from his cruel position. She alone contrived and effected his escape from his father."

' Money, you know wrote Lady Hester shortly after to Lord Glastonbury, ' was a very essential article; that has been liberally supplied by Sir Francis Burdett, though he chose to be ignorant of the plan and gave it into the hands of a third person. Mr. Jackson got Mahon's letters of credit made out and provided him with a passport. He is gone abroad to be placed at a foreign university at Erlangen, and he will enjoy the best society of that place. Mr. Jackson's advice and assistance in the most minute things was particularly fortunate, as Mahon was so perfectly ignorant of the world; but with Mr. Jackson's directions he has got on wonderfully well. He has a man with him whose fidelity I can rely on. This man, with directions from me, accomplished Mahon's escape from Chevening most astonishingly; for, though he was pursued in a few hours, no tidings could be had, and till this moment they have never been able to trace him one step. As soon as I knew he was safe out of the country I wrote to my father's lawyer to desire that he would inform the female members of Mahon's family that he had gone abroad and was in good hands. His astonishment, his happiness and gratitude to his friends is quite delightful. Charming, incomparable Mahon!"

That the coup was a success, not only in its execution but in its results, we learn from a series of letters from Lady Hester to Francis Jackson, who was appointed Minister to Berlin in isoi. 1 ' Grandmama is quite delighted with the account Mahon gives of himself and his happiness," she writes from Burton Pynsent. She received a long letter from the Margravine of Bayreuth, blessing her for saving the young plant from ' the infernal principles of Jacobinism." Of far greater importance was it that ' Mr. Pitt speaks in the highest terms of approbation of all that has been done, and gives me every assurance that he will do everything in his power for dear Mahon." Many eyes looked with friendly interest on the fortunes of the young man. The Marquis of Buckingham told Lady Hester that Mahon would always find a home under his roof, and that he did not offer to be a mediator only because he knew reasoning was in 1 Printed in the Duchess of Cleveland's book.

vain. In 1802 Lady Hester joined her brother abroad, and CHAP, they visited Italy together. But the young man, however XIII. grateful for her help at a critical moment of his life, rebelled against her tutelage, and their relations were soon strained to breaking-point.

Mahon's flight naturally created the greatest excitement at Chevening, and Lady Hester was anxious to screen the younger brothers who remained at home from suspicion and vengeance. ' If some precautions are not taken," she wrote excitedly, ' they will be flogged to death to make them confess what they are really ignorant of." Her father's wrath was, however, reserved for herself. 'The Logician her nickname for him has often said that from the hour I was born I had been a stranger to fear. What could Mahon have done better? Reasoning was in vain. How distressing it is for each branch of his family in turn to take up arms against him in its own defence. How much it will become the topic of conversation in the world, and what disgrace it will for ever reflect upon him! Besides, by his own mode of proceeding he is entirely depriving himself of all domestic comfort. Lord Lansdowne, his great friend, has taken decided part against him."

Chevening had already virtually ceased to be Lady Hester's home at the time of her brother's flight. In 1800 she went to her grandmother at Burton Pynsent, where she spent most of her time till she joined Mahon abroad in 1802. On her return in the autumn Lady Chatham was dead, and she had no mind to revisit her old home. She had inherited her father's imperious temper and inflexible will, and there could be no peace with two such autocratic spirits under one roof. Moreover Hester's political principles were opposed to those of her father. I am an aristocrat," she remarked to Meryon, ' and I make a boast of it. I hate a pack of dirty Jacobins that only want to get people out of a good place to get into it themselves." She had, however, been happy enough till the friction between her father and the other children rendered the house uncomfortable. Long afterwards she gave Meryon a picture of her feelings and motives at this time. ' Bouverie used to say to me when I lived at Chevening, "I know you like this kind of life; it seems to suit you." And so it did; but why did I quit home? Because of my brothers and sisters and for my father's sake. I foresaw that my sisters would be reduced to poverty if I did not assist them. As for my father he thought that in joining those democrats he always kept aloof from treason. But he did not know how many desperate characters there were who were

CHAP, always plotting mischief. I thought therefore it was better to XIII. be where I should have Mr. Pitt by my side should he get into great difficulty. This was one of the reasons why I went to live with Mr. Pitt." Lady Hester's memory was on this occasion even more treacherous than usual. There is no ground for supposing that she ever gave her father's safety a thought. Moreover, when she went to her uncle, Addington was Prime Minister and Pitt a private member. On the death of his mother Pitt, with some trepidation, offered his high-spirited niece a home; and his unselfish act was rewarded by the happiness of both. The clever, unconventional woman brought sunlight into the bachelor chambers of Walmer and Downing Street, and four years later the dying Minister was to pay her the greatest compliment she ever received in the words, ' Dear soul, I know she loves me."

After the flight of Mahon the two younger boys, Charles and James, remained alone with their parents. ' Charles," wrote Hester to her friend Jackson in 1801, ' is my favourite, though he has the least ability of the three, but a degree of openness and good nature which wins every heart and an air of nobility his quizzical education cannot destroy; for in the blacksmith's forge he looks like a gentleman." Stanhope, himself a first-rate mechanician, desired his younger sons to learn some manual trade; but there is no reason to conclude with the Duchess of Cleveland that he destined them to the careers of blacksmith and shoemaker. Soon after the flight of Mahon a new tutor was installed at Chevening. George Burnett, after studying at Balliol and Edinburgh, had become a friend of Coleridge and Southey and had shared in their dazzling visions of pantisocracy. A man of literary tastes and one of Lamb's ragged regiment, he lacked energy and application, and found the problem of earning a livelihood by no means easy. At the end of 1801 he was appointed tutor to the younger sons through the influence of friends. f l am much pleased wrote Rickman to Southey on January 5, 1802, ' that Burnett is well placed. I think he will do well for instilling the languages into the young nobles. Lord Stanhope is an acute man, and will instil other things himself, and Burnett will have leisure enough." 1 In less than a month, however, his pupils followed the example of their elder brother by leaving home. Stanhope refused to punish the tutor for their misdemeanours, and invited him to remain as private secretary. ' Did I tell you," wrote 1 Orlo Williams, Life and Letters of John Rickman, p. 71.

Southey to Rickman on February 17, ' how Burnett's tutorship CHAP, is like my secretaryship, a happy sinecure? His pupils have XIII. both eloped, and he receives his salary for eating and drinking with Lord Stanhope, and talking late after supper. The Lord, who is not only a good man but a very clever one, has many mechanical inventions to bring forward, of which I suppose some one will fall to the share of Burnett, and so make him lazy for life by a valuable patent. He is as happy as the Great Mogul 1 When he left in the autumn Stanhope paid him a full year's salary of Â 200. Burnett at once resumed his vagabondage and took to opium. ' Does he see you idle wrote Rickman to Southey, ' or me? Lord Stanhope gave him so fair a chance in giving him Â 200, and that he has thrown away so completely that I deem the moonstruck man a hopeless case." 2 Hopeless it was, for in 1811 he died in a workhouse at the age of thirty-five.

Lady Hester claimed in later life to have been the agent in the elopement of her younger brothers as well as of Mahon. She wished to remove them, records Meryon, in order that they might be under her own guidance, fearing that her father's politics might injure their prospects. Accordingly Mr. Rice, a trusty person, brought them furtively to town in a post-chaise, and they remained under Mr. Pitt's protection. 3 ' To both these brothers, shut out from a father's care," wrote their nephew, the fifth Earl, ' Pitt extended a most constant and generous kindness." 4 ' When Charles and James left Chevening," declared Lady Hester to Meryon, ' Pitt said to Mahon he was glad to have the young men at his house and table; but for their military equipment, c. he had not the means. You, therefore, Mahon, said he, must do that for them, and if you have not money, you can always let their bills be charged to you with interest." Mahon took his advice, James entered the navy and Charles obtained a commission in the army at Gibraltar. ' They have made a dreadful fuss at Chevening wrote Hester to a friend, ' but fear has prevented their stirring Their father never wholly forgave them, but he did not cherish the feelings of settled hostility which he was before long to entertain for his eldest son.

On his return from abroad Mahon attempted to persuade his father to give him some money; but Stanhope, after some delay, declined. It is to this that Pitt's letter to Mahon of 1 Orlo Williams, Life and Letters of John Rickman, p. 75, 2 Ibid., 82-5. 3 Meryon; ii. 86. 4 Stanhope's Life of Pitt, iv. 40.

CHAP. March 10, 1803, refers. ' I am very much grieved and rather XIII. surprised (after what has passed) at the strange letter from Lord Stanhope. It certainly puts an end to all reasonable ground of hope from that quarter, and is in the manner of it very provoking. But as no good can arise from any answer you can return to it, I think it best for you to take no notice of it." 1 Soon after this rebuff he became engaged to a daughter of Pitt's friend, the first Lord Carrington. The happy event appeared to afford an opportunity of resuming friendly relations with his father. 2 ' 52 Manchester Street: June 10, 1803.

' My dear Father,â I cannot help indulging a hope that notwithstanding our unfortunate separation you still continue to take a lively interest in whatever is conducive to my happiness and welfare. It is under this conviction as well as from a strong sense of duty and filial affection that I now communicate to you the wish that I have formed of marrying Miss Catherine Smith, fourth daughter of Lord Carrington. I am most anxious, my dear father, to learn that such a step would meet your approbation. Your own acquaintance with Lord and Lady Carrington, as well as their general character in the world, will, I trust, incline you to think favourably of such a connection, and I flatter myself that if I should ever be fortunate enough to be allowed the pleasure of presenting to you the person in question, such an opinion would be strongly confirmed. In a point of so much importance and so intimately connected with my happiness you will easily believe how desirous I am of obtaining your sanction. I should indeed feel doubly happy if that event were to procure me an opportunity of being restored to your paternal regards, of which it has always been matter of the deepest regret to me that my circumstances should have deprived me and which it is the earnest wish of my heart to regain. I shall ever continue, my dear father, your very dutiful and affectionate son, ' MAHON."

To this letter Stanhope replied on the same day.

' June 10, 1803.

' My dear son,â Your happiness and real welfare have ever been real objects too near to my heart for me not to feel a lively interest in the approaching event. I most cordially wish that it may in every respect contribute, as I hope it will, to your felicity.

i Stanhope Miscellanies, ii. 67. 2 Chevening MSS,

I have had the pleasure of knowing Lord Carrington. Few CHAP, persons, at one time, agreed better in opinion than he and I did; XIII. and I believe that we have still many feelings and sentiments in common. As for Lady Carrington I really believe that there does not exist in Europe any woman more excellent, more amiable or more truly respectable. May her daughter be exactly like the mother, and I am convinced you will be happy; and I hope and trust that you will ever act as you ought to do to such a partner for life. That you may ever respectively promote each other's happiness is my sincere prayer to that infinite Being, on Whom all events depend. I thank you kindly for your affectionate letter. You know me; and you must be certain that my views are and ever have been uniformly directed towards the happiness of my fellow-men. I will be frank. Your close connection with Mr. Pitt and certain other persons of his description will certainly prevent our being reconciled. But be assured that I shall never cease to have towards you the love and affectionate feelings of an affectionate parent. Your dear mother sends her kind love to you; she takes the most lively interest in this event and sincerely wishes you joy. I shall inform my mother of the contents of your letter, and I am sure that she will cordially partake of the same sentiments.

' Believe me ever, my dear son, ' Your most affectionate father, ' STANHOPE."

Mahon next wrote to the Dowager Lady Stanhope, informing her of the good news and of his father's approval.

' I have just received from him a very affectionate letter in which he gives his consent in the kindest manner, with many nattering expressions of respect and esteem towards Lady Carrington. It is impossible for me to say, my dear grandmama, how happy his approbation of this measure has rendered me, nor how grateful I am for the kindness with which he has expressed himself. I cannot conclude without expressing my sense of the affectionate interest which you have always taken in my welfare.

' Your very dutiful and affectionate grandson, ' MAHON ' My ever beloved Mahon she replied," will easily imagine the pleasure it gives me to receive a letter from you in which you inform me of your father's approbation of your wished for marriage. Words cannot express how much I hope this event

CHAP, may produce all the happiness I wish you. What you say in XIII. regard to me has affected me deeply. I thank you. Be assured of the tender affection of your old Granma, who can never forget you.

Pitt, as usual, actively interested himself in his nephew's fortunes. f On our way home he wrote to Mahon on October 24, ' Lord Carrington and I have been comparing Lord Stanhope's answer with the preceding proposals; and Lord Carrington has written to Harrison to make the inquiry which strikes us as essential under the 24th article." x While Stanhope never saw his daughter-in-law nor his grandchildren, he made no attempt to prevent his wife visiting her son. ' Lady Stanhope wrote Hester to a friend in November, 1802, ' is allowed to see Mahon, and you will be surprised to hear she has got so completely hold of him that I believe few persons have more influence with him 2

The death of Pitt was the end of Lady Hester's greatest happiness. He had expressed a wish that, if his services were to be publicly recognised, provision should be made for his nieces. His prayer was heard, and Lady Hester took a house in Montagu Square, of which her brothers were invited to make use. But the experiment proved a failure, and was soon given up. Her brothers' friends seemed flat and unprofitable after the brilliant company she had known, and her income was too small to indulge her passion for riding. But a new interest before long entered her life. She became deeply attached, if not actually engaged, to Sir John Moore, to whom her brother Charles was aide-de-camp, and they corresponded during his absence in Spain in 1808. His death and that of Charles at Corunna was a staggering blow. Her other brother, James, was with the hero to the end, and it was to him that he remarked, ' Stanhope, remember me to your sister She treasured some sleeve-links which contained his hair, and a blood-stained glove. A year later she left England, never to return. 3

Stanhope's quarrels with his children were already well known in society; but they were now to be dragged into the full light of day, and he was to taste the bitterness of filial retaliation.

1 Stanhope Miscellanies, ii. 70.

2 Life by the Duchess of Cleveland, 3 In addition to Meryon's volumes no less than four biographies of Lady Hester have appeared in recent years. By far the best is that by her niece, the Duchess of Cleveland.

As the bulk of the estates were entailed, he possessed no more CHAP, than a life interest. When his heir came of age he applied to his XIII. father's agent to know what was being done with the property, but was refused information. When he married and was himself the father of a son, the question of his inheritance became still more urgent. Moreover he now heard stories of the sale of land and the felling of trees which rilled him with apprehension. After consultation with friends and legal advisers he resolved to set the machinery of the law in motion against his formidable parent. The following letter to Lord Holland, his closest political and personal friend, gives the first indication of Stanhope's emotions on hearing of his son's design.

Stratford Place: January 27, 1806.

' My very dear Lord,â The Rev. M. T. you allude to is the brother of that very man, my son-in-law, who has been placed in the Customs by Mr. Pitt, and who (in order, if he could, to provoke me) did, some years ago, so scandalously insult me in my own house by taking forcible possession of my own room, which he repeatedly refused to leave, that I was at last obliged to send my steward for a Justice of the Peace. You see it is impossible for me to serve you in that question; but I intend to write this day to an old friend of mine. In addition to all the persecutions I have experienced, my eldest son is now excited to drag me into the Court of Chancery!!! Do what they will, they shall never make me change.

' Ever most cordially yours, ' STANHOPE." 1

The lawsuit, Mahon v. Stanhope, was reached in the Court of Chancery on March 7, i8o8. 2 Mahon charged his father with felling and selling the timber on certain estates in Kent and disposing thereof to the prejudice of the plaintiff. He called on the defendant to account for Â 21,000, the price of an estate sold in 1782, and prayed for an injunction to stay the sum of Â 70,000 from being paid by the purchaser of an estate in Derbyshire, of which the defendant had lately disposed. The answer put in by Stanhope categorically denied the allegations, stating that the timber he felled at Chevening was for the purpose of beautifying the estate by opening up prospects from the house, and asserting that he had planted 140,000 new trees in lieu of 1 Holland House MSS.

z Bell's Weekly Messenger and the Conner, March 12, 1808. The newspaper reports are preserved at Chevening,

CHAP, those cut down at an expense of over Â 30,000. He also mentioned XIII. a variety of other improvements effected by him, which he was not compelled to undertake. As to the Â 76,000 due for the estate at Sutton, he intended to apply it in discharge of some mortgages and in purchase of additional property. He had, moreover, invented a method of saving trees from decay, which he had applied to those he had planted. He had also discovered a means of preventing houses, even when built of wood, from taking fire, and this he had applied to the woodwork of one of the wings at Chevening. By all these improvements he had greatly enhanced the value of the family estates.

Three counsel, among them Romilly, opened for the plaintiff. After recapitulating the indictment, they declared that there was no evidence that the money derived from the sale of the Derbyshire property was to be employed in a new purchase. Their client, they added, had now instructed them not to insist on the charge of waste by the felling of timber, but asked only that Earl Stanhope should be restrained from cutting down any more. The counsel for the defendant denied that he had committed waste or dilapidation of any kind. On the contrary, by his skill and attention he had improved and beautified the estates. It was impossible to maintain that he could not sell one estate without having fixed on the purchase of another. As for the proceeds of land sold in 1782, that was an act of his father for which he was not responsible. A foul and scandalous charge had been originally introduced into the Bill, insinuating that he had dilapidated the estate by Â 80,000; but that had now been struck out. By such charges he had sustained an injury for which he was entitled to redress.

On the following day Stanhope himself addressed the Court. He began by saying that his son had struck at his reputation. If it were a cause in which his property alone was concerned, he would not have appeared; but his moral character was attacked, and he must defend it. He then read a letter written to his solicitor on December 26, 1806, in which he asserted that he had taken the greatest pains to instil the best of principles, the strictest integrity and the strongest sentiments of philanthropy into his son, whom he had treated with the affection of a brother rather than the austerity of a parent. He reviewed the charges in the Bill, which included that of threatening to pull down or otherwise injure the house at Chevening and various other farmhouses and buildings. The plaintiff and his advisers had been alarmed by the strength and clearness of his answers, and had begun to make proposals. He had, however, refused all compromise, and was determined that such groundless CHAP, charges should be expunged from the records of the Court. In XIII. January 1801, some time before he came of age, Lord Mahon had written to ask that he should immediately settle Â 400 or Â 500 a year on him for life, and that he should be allowed to live where and with whom he liked. He knew, however, too well the duties of a father and a legal guardian to consent. Soon afterwards, without his father's knowledge, he left home and went abroad. He did not return till he was of age, when he filed the present Bill in Chancery. He was perhaps one of the most persecuted men alive, and he grieved to think that his son should have been advised to exhibit himself publicly as the parricide of his father's character. Such insulting treatment ought to be experienced by no honest man; and little did he expect to be so rewarded while he was daily labouring to serve his country â and mankind in making philosophical discoveries and advancing the arts and sciences.

After reading this letter the defendant informed the Court that he had threatened to file a cross Bill against his son, to compel him to swear to the allegations in the original Bill; but this he was not permitted to do. Was there no redress, he asked, when he was charged in a Court of Equity with robbing the family estate of Â 80,000? His friends would never believe such charges; but they were circulated through the country among people who were ignorant of his character. He read extracts from different volumes of Law Reports to show that persons holding a life interest in landed property had been allowed to cut down trees as they thought proper. He had a large personal estate, the disposition of which would prove an awful lesson for young minds. His son should not have a shilling of it, and he would thus learn that honesty was the best policy.

On the following day the Master of the Rolls gave judgment. The entire proceeds of the sale of property, he found, had not been employed in the purchase of other lands. The sum of Â 21,400 obtained in 1782 had been laid out and still continued in mortgage. In regard to timber no waste had been proved, and if the charge was persisted in, an inquiry would have to take place as to the nature of the fellings. Passing to the sale of lands, it was wrong, he declared, to sell simply because a good price could be obtained and without having another estate in view. The Master must therefore inquire whether the Â 21,400 formed part of the trust and was properly laid out. As to the Derbyshire estate, there was no power to sell without the approbation of the trustee. No specific purchase had been mentioned,

CHAP, nor was there any proposal as to the application of the proceeds XIII. except paying off a mortgage of Â 5000 and the purchase of a small property near Chevening. Finally the existing trustee had been incapable of performing his duties, and should be superseded. Two months later the case was brought again before the Master of the Rolls on a petition from Stanhope to vary the minutes and the Judge's decree. 1 In reply to a long tirade the Master of the Rolls coldly rejoined that the only question before him was whether the minutes expressed the decree as pronounced. 2 It was the bitterest humiliation of his life, and he smarted under its memory till his dying day. Whatever sparks of affection between father and son still existed before the trial were for ever extinguished by the prolonged battle in which the one fought for his reputation, the other for his expectations.

When all the children had left home Stanhope was confined to the company of his wife. The marriage sprang less from affection than from esteem, and Louisa Grenville has left the reputation of a somewhat formal woman, devoted rather to the busy idleness of society than to the cultivation of her mind or the welfare of her family. Lady Hester's recollections depict her as absorbed in her social engagements and a complete stranger to her little step-daughters. ' They never became fond of her," adds the Duchess of Cleveland, ' and she never seems to have gained any influence over them, least of all over Lady Hester. She was a worthy and well-meaning woman; but, as I remember her, stiff and frigid, with a chilling, conventional manner." This unattractive picture, however, is not altogether confirmed by the Chevening papers, which suggest that she had deeper feelings and more serious interests. A number of small, neatly written notebooks, inscribed ' Louisa Grenville' and headed ' Books I read' show that her mind was already well stored before her marriage. Her list includes Hume and Robertson, Plutarch and Chesterfield, Richardson and Gray, De Retz and Le Sage. In most cases a brief appreciation or criticism of the work is appended. Two or three of the little volumes are devoted to religious topics, and show considerable knowledge of the French as well as the English literature of devotion. The following extracts from her letters to Lady Chatham during the early years of her married life show that she was not wholly without interest in her step-children.

March 13, 1786. (On the death of the second Earl.)â ' J 1 Bell's Weekly Messenger, May 8, 1808. 2 Ibid., May 21, 1808.

cannot sufficiently lament the loss of a person whose affectionate CHAP, behaviour and great kindness towards me have left too deep an XIII. impression on my mind ever to be effaced. My lord, who is very much afflicted on this melancholy occasion, desires to be affectionately remembered. P. S.â The dear little children are quite well. Hester's eyes are perfectly recovered, but dear little Griselda seems to have a tendency towards Hester's complaint."

May 14, 1791.â ' I know so well your affectionate feelings towards our little girls or rather great girls. We all long to see you, old as well as young, and Burton and its dear inhabitants are often present to our minds."

October 16, 1791.â ' All our young folks are well. My lord is extremely busy about his famous boat, which is to go against wind and tide. He desires his most affectionate love to you."

However reserved in her relations to her step-daughters, Louisa was at any rate devoted to her eldest son. During his frequent travels abroad he wrote long and affectionate letters, some of them in French, to his mother. None of her letters to him before the death of her husband have been preserved; but those which followed his accession to the title and estates dispel the notion that she was incapable of love. In the early months of her widowhood she wrote: ' I sincerely hope you may never experience those bitter days of adversity which have clouded some of my days, although, thank God, others have been happy. God bless you, my dearest, dearest son. I am in your debt for all the kindness and affection you have always shewn me, for which I assure you I am most truly grateful." In 1822 she wrote: ' Many thanks to you for the very affectionate manner in which you express your wish of my being at Chevening whenever it can be agreeable to me. You already know how happy I am to be able to enjoy your society; and although Chevening recalls to my mind many very painful recollections, yet they are more than counterbalanced by the delight of being under the same roof with mon bien aime fits."

Charles and Louisa never seem to have had much in common, the former being devoted to politics and science, the latter to society and to painting. The flight of her sons must have been a source both of sorrow and indignation to their mother, who found herself alone in a great mansion with an unloved husband. ' We, his descendants," wrote the Duchess of Cleveland of her grandfather, ' are justly and I may say exceedingly proud of his genius and achievements, and yet humbly thankful that we were not called upon to live under his roof; for, ardently as he
CHAP, advocated liberty and enfranchisement abroad, he was the XIII. sternest of autocrats at home. His rule was absolute, his word law, and he enforced the most implicit and unquestioning obedience. Lady Hester, who did not know what fear meant, was perhaps the only one of his children not afraid of him. The others all stood more or less in awe and dread of him, and, as they grew up, one and all escaped from their unhappy home. In the end even my much enduring grandmother found her position untenable The Duchess does not mention the cause of her departure; but the breaking-point was probably reached when a rival was installed at Chevening. The earliest reference to the person who exerted a baneful influence during the closing years of his life is to be found in a paragraph of his will, dated November 22,1805. ' Whereas, some years ago, my wife Louisa did, with my consent, engage Mrs. Walburgh Lackner to give up giving lessons in music, and to agree not to play at concerts for money; and whereas that was a great sacrifice on the part of the said Mrs. Lackner, I give her the sum of Â 5000 of lawful money of Great Britain, and also all my music-books, organs and other musical instruments whatever." These words provide the clue to the relationship. ' He possessed a taste for music records the writer of the notice in the ' Annual Biography and Obituary' for I8l7, 1 ' was a frequent attendant at concerts, and knew most of the best performers, both in England and on the Continent He also invented a new science of tuning, which he explained at length in a highly technical pamphlet printed by his own press in i8o6. 2 Mrs. Lackner,

a foreigner of whose origin and early history nothing is known, had attracted the attention of the Chevening circle by her brilliant pianoforte playing. That the first and by far the largest legacy in the will was to her shows that their relations were intimate as early as 1805. It is impossible to say precisely when the Countess left Chevening; but it must have been several years before the Earl's death in 1816. Louisa divided her time between Tunbridge Wells and her house in London, where she died in 1829 at the age of seventy. 3

Though Stanhope had lost the love of wife and children and his home was desolate, he still held the unchallenged position in one gentle and loving heart which he had always possessed. His mother lived on sound in mind and body, and their relations were never disturbed by the political and domestic storms which broke over her son. In his will, dated 1805, the legacy immediately 1 P. 203. 2 See Appendix iii.

3 See Gentleman's Magazine, 1829, i. 283.

following that to Mrs. Lackner is ' Â 1000 to my most excellent CHAP, and truly venerable mother." The last letter of Grisel preserved XIJJ. at Chevening is dated June 26, 1808. ' The Dowager Countess Stanhope presents her compliments to the Rev. Mr. Francis Stone, and is very sorry to desire that he will not be at the trouble to come and see her, as her health is so very indifferent." But the letter, written in her ninetieth year, bears no mark of failing powers. Three years later she wrote to a friend: 'Thank God, I am enjoying better health in my ninety-third year than many younger people are blessed with." 1 But at the end of the same year she was dead. In writing to Lord Holland on January 10, 1812, Stanhope informed him of ' the very melancholy and afflicting event' which would keep him out of town for some days. 2 A brief notice of her death was inserted in the Gentleman's Magazine on December 28. 'A person more remarkable for acuteness of understanding and exquisite sensibility of heart has perhaps never existed. Notwithstanding her very advanced age she retained her faculties entire. She always took the most lively interest in every event that occurred. Religion and the confident expectation of a future and a better state were to her a never-failing source of comfort and exalted happiness. The distressed always found in her a warm-hearted friend; and her judicious and extensive charity relieved many hundreds of the poor in her neighbourhood. She left her son her sole executor."

Her will 3 gave striking expression to her unwavering devotion to her son. Ovenden, February n, 1805.â This is the last will and testament of me Grisel Dowager Countess Stanhope, written with my own hand. After payment of all my lawful debts, I give and bequeath all I am possessed of to my dearly beloved son Charles, Earl Stanhope, from my approbation of his public and private conduct; and I appoint him my sole executor. If I die at Ovenden, I wish to be very privately buried in the family vault at Chevening Church.â G. STANHOPE." A codicil added in 1808 shows that the lawsuit aroused in her feelings of indignation. ' I, Grisel, Countess Stanhope, having written, in my own hand in several books which I have given to my dear son, the words " For Chevening Library," I do hereby will and desire that all such books shall belong to my said son only, as I am much dissatisfied with the conduct of my grandson Philip Henry Lord Mahon, with respect to my most honest, 1 Gentleman's Magazine, 1811, ii. 661.

2 Holland House MSS.

8 Gentleman's Magazine, 1812, i. 673.

CHAP, most worthy and most dearly beloved husband." The reference XIII. was to the article in the charge which complained of the sale of property shortly before the death of the second Earl. A powerful link between mother and son was their common devotion to his memory. Shortly after his mother's death, in acknowledging a resolution of thanks from the Methodists, Stanhope enclosed a copy of ' the incomparable prayer of my late dear and honest father. He was without exception the man of the best principles and greatest virtue I ever met with."

If his mother was the chief confidant of his private life, the closest political friendship of Stanhope's later years was with Lord Holland. His old patron, Lansdowne, to whom he owed his entry into Parliament, died in 1806, and with Lauderdale, who co-operated in active opposition to Pitt's foreign and domestic policy, he never cultivated habits of intimacy. The enlightened benignity of the master of Holland House exerted its usual fascination. When Stanhope returned to the Upper Chamber in 1800 he found that the brilliant young nephew and pupil of Fox, whom he had known since boyhood, had dedicated himself to the cause of reform to which he was to give forty years of loyal and effective service. While the younger man found his main interest outside politics in literature and the elder in science, they were in almost invariable agreement on the practical issues of the day. In the innumerable combats in the House of Lords which filled the last sixteen years of Stanhope's life, they only took opposite sides when he attempted to secure the virtual recognition of paper currency. His will, drawn up in 1805, contained the paragraph ' To my friend, Lord Holland, my picture painted by Mr. Opie." The portrait, which was exhibited in the Academy in 1803, now hangs on the walls of Holland House as a memorial of the friendship of two remarkable men. The same document appointed Lord Holland one of his executors. The following letter, one of the latest that have been preserved, reflects the warm regard entertained for the younger man by the elder.

' No. 49 Berners Street: August ID, 1815.

' My dear Lord,â I cordially rejoice, and I think all good men in this country should rejoice also, at your safe return. It makes me very happy. I am only sorry that having fixed next Saturday for leaving town, and being occupied in the meantime with (Oarl ojtanao e public business of great importance, the shortness of the time CHAP, will prevent my calling on you and Lady Holland at Holland XIII. House. The bearer of this is the Rev. Mr. Tracey, a very respectable and worthy man, and a great friend of yours. He will introduce to you two of the principal Spanish patriots who have been lately persecuted. They stand in need of your advice, which no man will give them with more judgment or with more feeling and interest for their situation than yourself. My best compliments to Lady Holland; and believe me ever, with the highest esteem, my dear Lord, most sincerely yours, ' STANHOPE." l

These affectionate sentiments were not altogether reciprocated; for though Holland paid a generous tribute to his friend's ability and courage, the elaborate portraits in his ' Memoirs ' suggest an unmistakable disapproval of his eccentricities.

With older political friends Stanhope maintained cordial relations till his death. His colleague in the movement for Parliamentary Reform, Christopher Wyvill, was peculiarly dear to his heart. ' I have just read your spirited and judicious pamphlet '

The Defence of Dr. Price ' with particular pleasure," he wrote in April 1792. ' Every act of your life increases the esteem I have for you." In thanking him for allowing the publication of his letters Wyvill speaks with genuine feeling. ' The editor begs leave to acknowledge the constant and affectionate friendship with which during the course of their long connection he has honoured him. The friendship of this truly generous patriot has been experienced in every possible instance, and he feels it with gratitude, though hitherto he has been without the ability and almost without the hope adequately to repay this debt of kindness. But the wish completely to repay it remains and will ever remain fixed in his breast." 2 With such sentiments he naturally accepted Stanhope's invitation to be one of his executors.

With Major Cartwright, another veteran of the age of Wilkes, he also continued in correspondence to the end. The worthy Major provided the text for Hazlitt's delicious essay ' On People with one Idea." ' He has but one subject of discourse, Parliamentary Reform. It is just as if a man were to insist on your hearing him go through the fifth chapter of the Book of Judges every time you meet. Any other topic, grave or gay, is looked upon as an impertinence. Business is an interruption, pleasure 1 Holland House MSS, Wyvill Papers, v. 79.

CHAP, a digression from it." 1 Stanhope, however, respected a man XIII. who, like himself, championed a cause throughout life, and he met him too seldom to be bored by his conversation. His readiness to help his friends was illustrated when the Major was assisting his distinguished brother, whose patents were being pirated. After a series of trials the offenders were brought to justice and punished. Writing to the inventor of the power-loom on July 3, 1799, the Major records that Lord Stanhope had been ' an excellent legal adviser '; and his niece and biographer gratefully adds that he was a very useful witness. 2

In the year before his death Stanhope wrote a letter to his old friend expressing unwavering devotion to the cause which they had both served for forty years.

' Chevening: January 25, 1815.

' Dear Sir,â I wrote yesterday to decline being in the chair at the Marylebone meeting. My idea is distinctly and unalterably this, confirmed by many years of attentive and instructive observation,â First, that the various oppressions under which the poor labour, and even the most useful among the middling classes, arise from not being duly and sufficiently represented in Parliament. Secondly, my idea is that not the merely speculative, but the actual permanent pinching grievances should be constantly connected with their real and true cause. Any question relative to the repeal or discontinuance of any particular tax, being a question, however proper, only for a time, has not that permanency which I consider is wanted. But the property-tax in one of its important relations is precisely of the description above specified,â I mean that part of it which is technically called the tenant's property-tax. For it tends to compel the farmer to raise his corn and grain on the consumer, and has in principle the same kind of objection to it as exists against those most impolitic and more permanent taxes on candles, soap, leather, coarse sugar, beer, salt, c. The price of meat is affected by the tenant's property-tax in like manner, also the price of beer. My reasoning is as follows: Taxes of this description on the necessaries of life, and most especially on the people's bread, are in every respect injurious, and tend to injure the export trade.

The tenant's property-tax is one of them, and tends to oppress the poor and middling classes. The cause of all this is that the householders, c. have not in the 1 Hazlitt's Table-Talk.

2 Cartwright's Life, i. 258-9; and Edmund Cartwright: a Memoir, PP- I73-9- constitution, as deteriorated at present, the right which they CHAP, ought to have." 1 XIII.

A fourth political comrade, who regarded Stanhope as a friend and whom he was always ready to assist, was Thomas Hardy, the zealous artisan who had founded the London Corresponding Society and had been one of the victims and heroes of the State trials of 1794. The shoemaker and the Peer liked and respected each other, and Hardy freely consulted his friend on his private concerns. 2 ' Citizen,â The enclosed was written in an enthusiastic fit the other night, and in that fit I wished it to be sent over on the wings of the wind; but on more mature considerations I resolved to consult you about it. No soul yet but you knows the design. Will you be kind enough to favour me with a few minutes' conversation if you are to be in London in two or three days, and it will add to the many obligations conferred on ' THOMAS HARDY.

'London: October 14, 1801."

The ' enclosed' is lost and there is no clue to its nature. Stanhope appears to have replied at once, for two days later Hardy wrote again.

' Citizen,â I received your kind communication in due course. I thank you for your adviceâ I will attend to it.

' Yours very respectfully, ' THOS. HARDY.

' To Citizen Stanhope,

October 16, 1801."

A month later Hardy wrote for advice on another matter.

' Citizen,â The Society of Independent Livery who met formerly at the Moon Tavern, Doctors Commons, now meet at the Guildhall Coffee House. At their monthly meeting last Tuesday there was some conversation about the General Election which is likely to take place soon, and the propriety of having a declaration ready to present to the candidates for their signature. What think you of it, and what points ought to be introduced into it?

' I am, citizen, yours very respectfully, ' THOS. HARDY.

' November 19, 1801."

1 Life and Correspondence of Major Cartwright, ii. 98-100, 2 The following letters are in Hardy's Correspondence, in the British Museum: Additional MSS., 27818.

CHAP. A few days later he broached a subject of more direct XIII. importance to himself.

' Citizen,â I must beg your pardon for taking such liberty with you and troubling you so much, but really your opinion in the present instance is indispensable. I wish to consult you now upon a business to which I attach some importance. The 2ist of December next is the day on which the Common Council of the City of London is annually chosen by the inhabitants of the different wards. Some of my acquaintance last year wanted me to offer myself as a candidate; but I had no wish for it at that time. I now feel myself desirous of becoming a member of the Common Council, although I believe they are almost as corrupt a body as the Commons House of Parliament but have not the power to do quite as much mischief. I have not taken any step nor spoken on the subject, neither will I proceed further in the business if it is thought it will give general offence to my friends. Now, my particular friend, what do you think of it?

1 Yours most respectfully, ' THOS. HARDY.

' November 28, 1801."

Stanhope's reply is lost and Hardy's ambition was not realised.

The following brief note, though less familiar in tone, shows that he could count on his noble friend for the rendering of little services.

' My Lord,â I hope that you will excuse me for troubling you with this application. I am a little anxious to hear a part of the trial of Lord Melvill, and if it is quite convenient for you to favour me with a ticket of admission it will much oblige, My Lord, ' Yours with the greatest respect, ' THOS. HARDY.

' ii May, 1806."

The last letter preserved in Hardy's correspondence in the British Museum reached Stanhope when he was beginning to suffer from his fatal illness.

' My Lord,â I hope you will be kind enough to excuse me for calling on you yesterday and also for troubling you with this to-day. The enclosed letter will more correctly inform you what my mission was and what Mr. Percy means than if I had been favoured with an interview. I have known Mr. Percy for many years, and I have only to add that, if there be an opening in that department which he mentions, I believe he would be a CHAP. valuable acquisition for promoting that object which you have XIII. persevered in so long and with so much labour and so much benevolence through good report and evil, and at last effected, yea as it were compelled your opponents to agree to your proposition.

' Accept, my Lord, the best respects of ' THOS. HARDY.

' 29 May, 1816.

' Twenty-two years ago this day I had the honour of being sent to the Tower."

When Hardy in old age compiled his ' Memoirs' he laid a final wreath upon the tomb of his friend and comrade, ' the exalted patriot, Lord Stanhope." 1

A few of Stanhope's friends followed the peaceful pursuits of literature and philosophy. Among the latter was George Hardinge, who after some years in the House of Commons became a judge, and occupied his leisure in the composition of essays and poems which have long been forgotten. The following letter suggests pleasant relations between the two men 2: â ' Chevening House: March 15, 1795.

' Citizen,â I enclose you a bank-note for the Etonian in distress; but as I hate ostentation of every kind I shall take it as a favour to have my name omitted from the list of subscribers. But be well assured, whenever any of you aristocrats apply again to me for subscriptions, that I will apply to you for some sansculotte subscription in return; being ever sincerely ' Your faithful fellow-citizen, ' STANHOPE

A far more interesting name in literary history is that of George Dyer, to whom Stanhope left Â 200 and whom he appointed one of his executors. The friend and correspondent of Lamb was a well-known figure in his day. Absent-minded, slovenly, and a poet of the third class, he was none the less described by Hazlitt as ' one of God Almighty's gentlemen." No one could meet him without being interested in his curious and attractive personality. ' Dyer," wrote Rickman to Southey in 1800, ' is a great curiosity." 3 A vivid description is to be found in Crabb Robinson's ' Diary," under the year 1799. ' I became acquainted 1 Memoir of Thomas Hardy, by Himself, p. 37. z Nichols's Illustrations of Literature, iii. 154. 3 Rickman's Life, p. 27.

CHAP, about this time with George Dyer, one of the best creatures XIII. morally that ever breathed." After mentioning his humble origin, his education and his friendships, the diarist adds, ' Every one loved Dyer." He was, however, the last man in the world to entrust with duties of a business or legal character. ' One day Mrs. Barbauld said to me, "Have you heard whom Lord Stanhope has made executor? " "No, your brother? " "No, there would have been nothing in that. The very worst imaginable." " Oh, then, it is Bonaparte." " No, guess again." " George Dyer? " " You are right." ' But the best witness to character was his old school-fellow and lifelong friend, Charles Lamb. ' God never put a kinder heart into flesh of man than George Dyer's." ' A head uniformly wrong and a heart uniformly right." ' The oftener I see him, the more deeply I admire him. He is goodness itself." George was born without original sin." 2 Which of Elia's friends ever received such handsome and repeated testimonials? That he could not tell good poetry from bad was his misfortune, not his fault. Lamb was ever scheming to find money to fill the empty pockets of his friend. ' Of course you have heard that G. Dyer is one of Lord Stanhope's residuaries," he wrote on August 31, 1817, to a friend. I am afraid he has not touched much of the residue yet. He is positively as lean as Cassius." 3 Crabb Robinson records that he rejected the legacy and renounced the executorship, but that the fourth Earl generously insisted on his acceptance of a small annuity. 4 How Stanhope became acquainted with this odd but lovable being and what induced him to make him his executor is not known; but the conjunction of names is an interesting curiosity in literary history.

The name of another executor possesses no significance for the world of to-day; yet ' the Rev. John North, clerk occupied a privileged position in the circle of his friends. For thirty years Stanhope devoted much time and thought to logical speculations. He privately printed portions of a work on ' The Science of Reasoning, clearly explained upon new principles," and invented a Demonstrator for the mechanical performances of logical operations. His voluminous writings on the subject, piled upon the shelves of Chevening, remained unknown till they were examined in 1878 by Robert Harley and described by him to the British Association. 5 In formulating his definitions and in constructing tables of syllogisms, as in every other branch 1 Crabb Robinson's Diary, i. 34-5. 2 Lamb's Letters, passim.

3 Letters, i. 363, ' Everyman' edition.

4 Crabb Robinson's Diary, i. 34-5. 5 See Appendix II.

of his activity, he had the welfare of society directly in view. CHAP. ' One of the first duties of a good citizen is to endeavour to diffuse XIII. the light of reason," run the opening words of the Introduction. His intention was to keep his speculations secret till they were complete; but he died leaving his task unfinished. No branch of his many-sided activity interested him more than the attempt to create a new science of logic; and one of his many titles to fame is that he was the author of the first attempt ever made to solve logical problems by mechanical methods. The correspondence with North preserved at Chevening covers the last five years of his life and throws a pleasant light on his character. Though the clergyman differed widely from the statesman and assailed his assumptions and methods without circumlocution, Stanhope never wearies in expressing his gratitude for the criticisms and suggestions. 'My very dear North," he writes on November 8, 1811, ' I have more thanks to return you for your letter than I have words to express." A year later he gratefully acknowledges ' your kind and friendly scold."

Stanhope's chief interest outside politics was applied science, and he was acquainted with most of the scientific men of his day. He had a high opinion of Hutton, the geologist, and bequeathed to him ' my original picture of the great Sir Isaac Newton." He frequently visited the works of Rennie to learn what was going on. 1 The great drawing-room at Chevening was turned into a laboratory, and an accomplished man of science was installed in a small house close to the mansion. The longest paragraph in his will was as follows: ' To Mr. Samuel Varley, of Chevening, Kent, Â 1000, and all my tools, machines, and instruments, mathematical and astronomical, chemical and mechanical, save and except such only as are bequeathed to Mr. Robert Walker." But in case the said Mr. Robert Varley should not survive me, I give the said before-mentioned Â 1000 and said tools and machinery to Miss L. Varley, eldest daughter of the said Samuel Varley; but in case both of them should not survive, then the said Â 1000, tools and machinery, to go to Jane Varley, the second daughter." Samuel Varley had begun life as a watchmaker, jeweller and constructor of microscopic lenses. He was also a keen student of chemistry, and, after carrying on experiments at home, took a large room for the purpose in Hatton House, where he founded a Chemical and Philosophical Society, which anticipated by a few years the Royal Institution. Stanhope was one of the patrons of the lectures, and learned to admire the 1 Smiles, Lives of the Engineers, ii. 142-3, 'CHAP, inventive gifts of its leading spirit. He invited Varley to join XIII. him in perfecting the stereotype process, and later persuaded him to act as his scientific colleague and assistant. 1 He figures with Davy, Rumford, Banks and other leading men of science in the cartoon ' Scientific Researches," in which Gillray pokes fun at the newly opened Royal Institution. Stanhope holds in his hand a pamphlet entitled ' Hints on the Nature of Air required for the new French Diving-boat." 2

Only second in importance in the field of invention to Stanhope's construction of the steamboat were his services to the art of printing, above all the process of stereotyping. 3 The fragments of a projected book ' On Printing' reveal the spirit in which he worked. ' The art of printing has contributed so eminently to the civilisation of society that men of science ought to do their best to improve it. To every man who is fully sensible of the importance of diffusing knowledge the dearness of books must be a subject of considerable regret. This evil arises in a great measure from the expense and risk to which publishers are liable." If the author printed too many copies it was a loss; if too few, he must incur the expense of a new edition. Printers, again, often employed very worn type, which destroyed the beauty of books and rendered their perusal unpleasant. ' The inaccuracy of printed works is another great objection to the present system. In literary works correctness is desirable; in scientific, important; and in some books, such as tables for navigation, indispensable. A wrong figure in one of those tables may produce a false reckoning, and thereby occasion the wreck of a vessel. The object of this publication is to point out by what means the public may have books at a much cheaper rate, as well as more beautiful and more correct. The arts I have described above are evidently of great importance. The improvement of them is one of the first objects L have had in view for the good of mankind. I shall be truly happy if what is contained in this little treatise contributes efficaciously to the wide diffusion of intellectual light."

Stereotype printing had been invented by several persons 1 Story's James Holmes and John Varley, pp. 222-5. John Varley, the painter, always asserted that his father Richard, who died in 1791, was tutor to the son of Earl Stanhope (ibid., pp. 200-1). This would account for the acquaintance of the Earl with Samuel Varley.

2 Wright's Gillray, p. 289. May 23, 1802.

3 See the admirable description by Horace Hart in the Oxford Historical Society Collectanea, Third Series," Earl Stanhope and the University Press," PP- 363-412.

working independently, and Stanhope warmly acknowledged his CHAP, obligations to his predecessors, while emphasising the superiority XIII. of his own inventions. In a ' Letter to the Authors, Booksellers and Printers of Great Britain issued or at least written in 1803, he announced that his inventions would save 25 per cent, of the cost, while his new printing-ink was only half the usual price. His results, he declared, would be specially valuable for school-books. ' The importance of reducing the price of such books is greatly increased since the ingenious and admirable system of Mr. Lancaster has been carried into execution. It is pleasing to reflect how these inventions might tend to give new vigour to the printing business, and would open many new and valuable branches of foreign commerce if it were not for the tax on paper, which of all taxes in this country is without exception the most injurious and the most impolitic. For it is evident that every impediment thrown in the way of giving the community at large a good education must tend in a high degree to affect the morals of the people." With the repeal of the paper-tax and the introduction of printing with fixed plates, the price of books would fall 50 per cent. In this, as in so many other directions, he was before his time, and the taxes on knowledge were only tardily repealed after his death.

In 1805, after several years of labour, Stanhope offered the Oxford University Press his inventions,â ' the secret process of stereotyping the iron hand-press called the ' Stanhope press and his system of logotypes and logotype cases. He also volunteered to instruct the University printers in the new art. The delegates of the Press decided that stereotype printing should be immediately adopted, and Â 4000 were paid to Andrew Wilson, his printer. Wilson explained the nature of the new processes, and, after some years of struggle and failure, stereotyping on the Stanhope system became part of the general business of the Clarendon Press. The delegates had high hopes of the new process, which, however, cost more than they anticipated. Only when the plaster mould was superseded by papier mdche did it become an assured success. Stanhope's fertile mind had seen the next step but not the final goal. His attempt to introduce logotypes, that is, the casting of common words in a single piece, was tried at Oxford but never generally adopted, as the compositor's case was thereby swollen to unmanageable dimensions.

After his negotiations with the Oxford Press he continued his experiments, both at the office which he had taken in town for Andrew Wilson and at Chevening. He printed on his

CHAP, own press his treatises on tuning and on the paddles of steam-XIII. boats. The following rules were drawn up for the guidance of the office:â 1. Nothing is to be printed against religion.

2. Everything is to be avoided on the subject of politics which is offensive to any party.

3. The characters of individuals are not to be attacked.

4. Every work is to be composed with beautiful types.

5. School books, and all works for the instruction of youth, will be stereotyped at a lower price than any other.

He must have sunk many thousands in his experiments, and his services to printing were considerable. ' Stereotyping," writes Mr. Hart, as he understood it, namely the gypsum or plaster process, has been practically abandoned. The Stanhope iron hand-press was superseded in a few years, and the hand-press printer has been nearly improved off the face of the earth by the power of steam and the cylinder printing-machine. Stanhope type-cases survive only as curiosities, and the Stanhope logotypes have long since been consigned to the melting-pot. But he did solid good to the art of printing when help was sorely needed x His services were fully recognised by the fraternity. Writing from Paternoster Row in 1811 to ask his help in a Bill affecting printers about to come before the House of Lords, Woodfall gave warm expression to his esteem. ' We shall consider ourselves under great additional obligations to your Lordship; as, independent of your known attachment to the liberty of the press, the improvements which your Lordship has introduced into the mechanical part of it are universally acknowledged by the trade and as generally adopted by them 2

Among Stanhope's minor inventions the most useful was the small but powerful lens which bears his name. Writing in 1840 to a correspondent the fourth Earl explains its object. ' I am happy to learn that you have discovered a curious and ingenious application of the lens which was invented by my father. It was designed by him to render visible the insensible perspiration, and may, I conceive, be very useful in cases of fever to ascertain whether any action has been produced upon the skin. I always carry one about me, as I find it a most useful convenient microscope for examining minute objects." 3 A quarter of a century 1 Collectanea. I am informed that the Stanhope Press is still or was recently in use at the Government printing works at Simla, and that until recently it was employed for the second edition of the Times.

2 Chevening MSS.

3 Letter to Dr. W. Arnold. Chevening MS. S later it was still being manufactured. A little pamphlet of seven CHAP. pages entitled, ' The Stanhope Lens: Directions for its Use: XIII. Made and sold by F. L. West, Optician appeared in 1864. 4 The following directions are given for examining all kinds of objects, especially animalcules, insects, fossils, flowers, mosses, sea-weeds, c., by means of this ingenious and useful lens, which may be justly termed the best pocket-microscope extant. At the price of 45. 6d. what has hitherto been considered a costly toy will bring the charm of microscopic studies to the firesides of the people." How rapidly and surely Stanhope's mind worked

in the field of applied science is suggested by a letter from an inventor named Jennings written in 1858 to the fifth Earl. ' In the year 1812 your grandfather much improved a life-bed which I had invented. His Lordship in a few hours so improved the construction (to avoid the cork fibre from shifting) that he almost made it his own." x

Stanhope must have enjoyed excellent health to enable him to live such a life of unremitting activity; but in 1816 he began to exhibit signs of dropsy. His home had been for some years a very temple of discomfort. He had never cared about luxuries, but under the regime of Mrs. Lackner he had barely enough to eat. While continuing to spend very large sums on his beloved experiments, he endeavoured to economise in the kitchen. ' Lord Stanhope has, it is believed wrote Lord Carrington to Mahon, who was then abroad, ' let his housekeeping for a certain sum to a lady, and as she is naturally anxious to make a purse, the servants are as ill-kept as his Lordship." 2 As the summer merged into autumn, the symptoms became so alarming that James Stanhope hastened to Chevening, and at once dispatched a report to his elder brother. ' October 17, 1816. Dear Mahon, I have just returned from Chevening. I had long heard that my father was ill, but it did not seem to be dangerous. The bad accounts we heard yesterday pronounced his illness to be so. I wrote two letters entreating earnestly to see him. He sent me his blessing but declined it. I therefore came away. He has no idea of being in danger and expects soon to be well. His legs are much swelled and now his stomach. I cannot 1 Letter in Chevening MSS., accompanying ' The Life-bed: Description and Testimonials, by the inventor, H. C. Jennings."

2 October n, 1816. Chevsning MSS.

CHAP, but think you should return home immediately. Madame XIII. de L. is still there and has complete ascendancy, keeping from him the old servants of the family. By all accounts she and Varley have secured themselves against all reverses of fortune here." Lady Stanhope added her wishes that Mahon should return at once.

On receipt of the news Lord Mahon, who was then at Vienna, dispatched a sheaf of letters to England. He instructed the agent to see that nothing was removed; and added, I am resolved to support by all legal means my just claims and expectations to the personal property." To his brother-in-law Thomas Taylor he wrote, ' I cannot delay an instant, my dear friend, to thank you for your letter." He would return on the news of his father's death, and expressed a wish that when that event took place the room should be locked up. ' I wrote to my father several weeks ago," he informed his brother James, 'to assure him that if my presence could afford him comfort or be in any way desirable to him I would hasten to obey his call. I have ordered legal proceedings to be at once begun which will secure from the grasp of legatees the personal property in money as well as in goods and clothes." As the news increased in gravity the heir moved homeward; but there was indignation, not sorrow, in his heart. Writing on December 14 from Paris he speaks bitterly of ' the family which, till he became the head of it, was happy and united." On December 17, the day of Stanhope's death, John Brampton, the agent, wrote to Freshfield, Lord Mahon's solicitor. ' I understand all the personal property is in the hands of eight executors, one of whom, Mr. Stone, surgeon at Brasted, attended the late Earl. Colonel Stanhope, who was here yesterday, sent Mrs. Lackner away, Mr. Stone and myself examining what she took with her in the chaise; but she says she will come again to take her other things away, but I am sure she shall never see Chevening House again. All property in the house is sealed up, and now she, Mrs. Lackner, is gone, I am not afraid, for she was a very bad woman as ever lived." ' Lord Holland and Lord Grantley," he wrote a day or two later, ' were here to-day for the funeral. They allowed Mrs. Lackner to come on Thursday and take her things, and we are ordered to behave very civil to her."

On December 31 the new Earl, who had now reached London, wrote at length to Lord Carrington. ' C. E. S. left much smaller assets than I expected, but he appears to have continued his experimental extravagance and to have bought this year or last a musical instrument for Â 1400, and a machine for some printing purpose for a similar sum; exclusive of which he built in the CHAP, house inhabited by Varley, between the mansion and the XIII. kitchen garden, a room for grinding a speculum for the telescope and another for a furnace for melting it. He is supposed also to have given away much money to schemers, though he gave away none in the neighbourhood. He lived most penuriously, but the machinery of his establishment was useless and expensive. B. heard him praise Mrs. L., whom he always called Wally (Walburga), for her good management, as it appears that the average expense of their eating and drinking for two or three years amounted to Â 75. This appears almost incredible, but is strictly true. He lived on soup, on the most meagre diet, on barley water sweetened with sugar, and, as Sir Joseph Banks thinks, starved himself to death. When he came to Chevening about August 10 he looked and in fact was very ill. He asked Brampton " Where is James? " whose attempt to see him before had irritated him extremely. B. answered " He is in the neighbourhood; has your Lordship any message? " The other paused some time and said, "No, it is better as it is." On the same day, the day of his death, he said that he wished and expected to live thirty years. Wonderful to relate he appears to have died without having been conscious at any one moment, even at the last, that he was dying. About nine a servant brought him a draught, which he sipped but seemed unable to swallow. The servant observed, "Your Lordship seems worse. " "No, no," was the answer, " you have no patience. I shall be better in two or three days." Mrs. L. soon afterwards kissed his hands, wept and wished him adieu. He died at eleven without a sigh or a groan." l ' I desire," wrote Stanhope in his will in 1805, ' that my funeral may be conducted without the least ostentation, as if I were to die a very poor man." That his wishes were respected we learn by a notice from a friendly eye-witness in the ' Gentleman's Magazine." 2 'The funeral took place on December 24. The ceremony was conducted with the utmost possible plainness, according to the directions in the Noble Lord's will. There were neither hearse nor mourning coaches, but the body was carried to the grave. The chief mourners were his son, the Hon. Colonel Stanhope, and his son-in-law, Mr. Taylor. It was attended by Lord Holland, Lord Grantley, Mr. Jekyll, Mr. Dyer, the Rev. Dr. Cartwright, Mr. Stone, Mr. Polhill, c. To his 1 Mrs. Lackner left England before long, married and settled at Prague, where she died in 1838.

2 1816, ii. 564.

CHAP, executors, after a few legacies, he leaves all his disposable property.

XIII. On his separation from Mr. Pitt his family preferred the patronage of the Minister to the paternal roof; and he has frequently been heard to say that as they had chosen to be saddled on the public purse, they must take the consequences. He wished them all to devote themselves, as he had done, to some useful calling."

Friend and foe agreed that in the third Earl Stanhope one of the most striking personalities of his time had passed away. Now that the great struggle with France was over, it became less difficult to recognise his anxious and untiring devotion to the public weal. The earliest appreciation came from the ' Gentleman's Magazine." 1 'Though we did not coincide with his political principles, we admired his talents. His death is justly considered as a public loss. He maintained during a long political life those principles of freedom which he had imbibed from his education or inherited from his ancestors without the slightest desire of office, emulation or dignity, yet with an ardour now but seldom excited except by ambition, avarice or pride. His speeches were full of matter, ingenious in argument, perspicuous in arrangement, but they were neither persuasive nor judicious. It was often more difficult to answer than to agree with them. His loss will make a chasm in public life. The great and useful work for which he was peculiarly qualified and to which he had for a long time applied the most earnest attention will, we fear, now fall to the ground. We allude to a digest of all the Statutes, a work of such stupendous labour as well as information that few persons can be expected to set about it with vigour, unless they had acquired a sort of parental fondness for the subject by brooding over it for years. His plain, unaffected and amiable manners conciliated as much affection as his integrity commanded respect. He was a kind landlord, and a liberal benefactor to the poor." The ' Annual Register' 2 remarked that' he pursued with ardour everything he undertook, unchecked by disappointment and regardless of criticism. He appeared to regard perfect independence as more dignified and honourable than high office or court favour." The ' Quarterly Review ' 3 called attention to the distinguished though unpretending service to his country ' rendered by Lord Stanhope, ' with all his peculiarities in watching and revising the Bills which came before the Upper House. Wraxall pronounced his death ' a public misfortune." 4 1 1816, ii. 563-4. " 1816, p. 224.

3 Vol. xxi. 427. 4 Memoirs, iii. 401.

A few traits were added by a friendly hand in the detailed CHAP, appreciation which appeared in ' The Annual Biography and XIII. Obituary' for 1817. ' In person he was tall and lank, with a polished forehead. His countenance of late years was wan and pale and shrivelled, so as to render him much older in appearance than in reality; while his locks were straight, stiff and formal, sacred alike from hair-powder and curling-irons. As an orator his person, manner and action were all against him; for he set the Graces at defiance. Yet so replete with matter and in general so original were his speeches, that he could not be listened to for any considerable time without a certain degree of impression being made even on a reluctant audience. There was a certain quaintness in his manner which added poignancy to his remarks; and we have seen the gravity of more than one Chancellor discomposed by his sallies. On some occasions even the Right Reverend Bench seemed to forget its accustomed gravity. Though he was the grandson of a distinguished general, he detested war, and deprecated his sons engaging in the conflict with France. His son-in-law obtained a place and his girls pensions, which he hated, as he panted for independence. He wished his sons, instead of becoming what he termed a burden to their country, to addict themselves to useful professions, and to earn their bread honestly. His corpse was deposited in the tomb of his ancestors, without pomp or splendour, which appeared despicable in his eyes. He was borne thither in all the simplicity of ancient times, and interred like one of the philosophers of old."

We owe by far the most complete and authoritative portrait to his friend, executor and political colleague, Lord Holland. The sketch in the ' Memoirs of the Whig Party written before 1802 and revised shortly after his death, is too valuable to be abridged. 1 ' Lord Stanhope, who had till very recently been a bitter opponent of the Coalition and of Mr. Fox, and was brother-in-law to Mr. Pitt, was one of the " true old enthusiastic breed." His fanaticism was, indeed, so far adapted to modern times, that it was chiefly confined to political objects, and not founded exclusively on religion. He possessed great command of temper and profound knowledge of science; understood thoroughly the forms of Parliament; and, though not a professional man, had read much law, and was familiar with the practice of our Courts and the rules of our jurisprudence. His constitutional learning was both accurate and extensive. He was not very 1 Memoirs, i. 33-8

CHAP, scrupulous, either in argument or conduct, about the means of XIII. rendering others subservient to his designs; but those designs were never to promote his private advantage. They were, in his judgment, beneficial to his fellow-citizens and useful to mankind. In his ardent pursuit of impracticable schemes, he was actuated neither by ambition nor avarice, nor pride nor resentment, and as little by more amiable affections. If we except his mother, and a certain pious regard for the memory of his father, he seemed to care little for anybody.

' As a speaker, he was full of matter, ingenious and subtle, and very perspicuous both in language and arrangement. Inelegant and coarse, even to buffoonery and scurrility, in his illustrations and invectives, ungraceful and grotesque in his gesticulations and delivery, but yet not deficient in vigour, spirit, and effect. His speeches, however, were neither persuasive nor judicious; he never adapted his views to the opinions of the time, the state of parties, or the temper of his audience. It was more difficult to answer than easy to agree with him. His logic was close, subtle, and scholastic, but neither practical nor convincing, and his conclusions, though to appearance clearly deduced, were often manifestly absurd and to all practical purposes unintelligible. He was in some senses of the word the truest Jacobin I have ever known; he not only deemed monarchy, a clergy, and a nobility, but property, or at least landed property by descent, unlawful abuses. He more than once complimented me by telling me in a whisper that he thought me more mischievous than people imagined, and he sometimes gave me a glimpse of his designs in proposing measures apparently preposterous, by hinting their tendency to subvert the fundamental principles of society, or by laughing immoderately when such was suggested to be the probable effect of them. He inherited through father and mother a strong attachment to freedom. His education at Geneva, his habits, his pursuits, all tended to confirm it; and on every question affecting the principles of popular government, he uniformly and strenuously stood forth the champion of the people and the enemy of power.

' I am afraid that in his private character he was less praiseworthy, and he was certainly less amiable. He was a bad husband, an unkind, perhaps an unjust, father;

yet he exacted nothing from his children that he had not himself been willing to render to his own parents; he was, as his principles required, an easy landlord and an indulgent master, an obedient and affectionate son, and on many occasions an active, friendly, and generous promoter of the arts and sciences; in many of them, especially mechanics, he was himself a great proficient. He was the first, CHAP, or at least among the first, who suggested that wonderful improve- XIII. ment, the application of steam to the purposes of navigation. With his usual perverseness of ingenuity he built a vessel in 1792 for conveying coals from Newcastle to London, which would have consumed its cargo before it could have reached its destination. He showed it me, Admiral Blanket, and Lord Wycombe, at Deptford in that year. By a contradiction still more characteristic of his ingenious but not practical understanding, the steam carriage, which he also invented (and tried between Calais and Boulogne, somewhere about the year '90 or '91), ran uphill with extraordinary rapidity, got along with some difficulty on plain ground, but came to a dead stop at every descent. His inventions in music and musical instruments were also ingenious, but not very generally adopted; but his stereotypes are still in use, and an alteration in the printing press devised by him is considered as the greatest improvement in the art since the discovery of printing. On the whole, if a scrupulous regard to truth prevents me from pronouncing my friend and benefactor, without some qualification, a wise, a good, or an amiable character, none can deny that he was an ingenious, diligent, disinterested, useful, and remarkable man."

In his ' Further Memoirs of the Whig Party," written several years after, Lord Holland added a few words on his friend's death. ' The House of Lords, in spite of his eccentricities, and I, perhaps in consequence of them, regretted his loss, and missed the originality with which he seldom failed to enliven our debates. It fell to my lot as his legatee and executor to compose the inscription on his monument in Chevening, and I have the satisfaction of thinking that I have there recorded the peculiarity for which he would most like be distinguished, without wounding the feelings of his family who had some reason to be hurt at his conduct and his will. The present Lord told me very handsomely that he always read it with pleasure, for there was not a word in it which was not true." 1 The inscription in the Stanhope chapel in Chevening church is as follows:â 'CHARLES, THIRD EARL STANHOPE.

' He was endowed with great powers of mind, which he devoted zealously and disinterestedly to political and general science, to the diffusion of knowledge and to the extension of civil and religious liberty. He requested, by his will, to be 1 Pp. 245-6,

CHAP, buried " as a very poor man ": and in the spirit of that injunction XIII. this plain tablet is inscribed to his memory. His understanding and integrity would have raised him to the notice of his fellow-countrymen even if his lot had been cast in the humblest condition of life." 1

After the detailed narrative of his activities and the sketches of Lord Holland and other contemporaries, there is no need of a further elaborate appreciation of the character and achievement of Charles, third Earl Stanhope. He narrowly missed greatness both in politics and science. If his defects are obvious, they are outweighed by his shining qualities. He was throughout life, as Wilberforce once described him,

' earnestly busy." In the House of Commons, in the House of Lords, in the laboratory his whole strength was devoted to the service of his fellow-men, without a thought of personal interest or advancement. He was perhaps the most unselfish politician of his age. Embracing certain principles in early life, he remained unfalteringly loyal to them throughout a public career of forty years. Co-operating first with the Whigs, then with Pitt, then with the Whigs again, he stood completely outside party politics. His passionate belief in liberty led him to champion the cause of the French Revolution with more zeal than discretion; but he was anything but the Jacobin of Gillray's heated imagination. He pronounced the English Constitution the best in the world, and sturdily resisted every encroachment on what he believed to be its principles either from the Crown or from the Ministry. He deemed it the duty of Parliament to remove from the Statute-book cruel and antiquated laws, to correct administrative abuses, and to defend and extend popular liberties. Humble victims of injustice laid their case before him, confident that he would spare neither time nor trouble to secure redress.

It was in some degree the very loftiness of his aims that rendered him comparatively ineffective as a reformer. Perceiving the goal plainly in front of him, he resolved to march straight towards it, turning neither to the right nor to the left. The compromises which secure far more than they sacrifice were abhorrent to him, and he poured scorn on men who were not ready at any moment and under all circumstances to speak, vote and work for what they believed to be right. He refused to allow the French 1 Further Memoirs, pp. 261-2.

Revolution to call a halt to British progress, and he continued CHAP, to labour with unabated zeal for Parliamentary reform, religious XIII. liberty and the abolition of the slave trade. Such rigidity is magnificent, but it is not politics. It inspires respect, but reaps a scanty harvest. He said himself that he had been successful in science and unsuccessful in politics; and the reason was that in the laboratory he could work alone, while the forum was crowded with human beings whose management required a subtler alchemy than he possessed. Though Lamb was not thinking of him when he wrote his essay on ' My Relations the following sketch may be applied to him without the alteration of a comma. ' My uncontrollable cousin is but imperfectly formed for purposes which demand co-operation. He cannot wait. His amelioration plans must be ripened in a day. His zeal makes him outrun and put out his coadjutors. He thinks of relieving while they think of debating, because the fervour of his humanity toils beyond the formal apprehension and creeping processes of his associates

The same incapacity for the little compromises and adjustments of life was equally the cause of his domestic shipwreck. He was so penetrated with the soundness of his principles and the purity of his intentions that he never stopped to inquire how far they were compatible with the happiness of his children. Instead of mellowing with age he became more and more dictatorial, till his family fled from his roof and his home became a wilderness. He loved humanity far more than the individuals who compose it, and never recognised that self-realisation within rational limits is as sacred a privilege as political and civil liberty. The passion of his life was the service of his fellow-men; but it was his misfortune that while few men have laboured so ardently and so consistently for mankind, few have reaped so little gratitude.

THIS is, c. of me, Charles Earl Stanhope, which I make this 22d day of November, 1805, in manner following:â

I direct my executors hereinafter named to pay all my just debts and funeral expenses, and I desire that my funeral may be conducted without the least ostentation, as if I were to die a very poor man.

Whereas, some years ago, my wife Louisa did, with my consent, engage Mrs. Walburgh Lackner to give up giving lessons in music, and to agree not to play at concerts for money; and whereas that was a great sacrifice on the part of the said Mrs. Lackner, I give her the sum of Â 5,000 of lawful money of Great Britain, and also all my music-books, organs, and other musical instruments whatever.

I also give to my most excellent and truly venerable mother Â 1,000.

To Mr. Samuel Varley, of Chevening, Kent, Â 1,000, and all my tools, machines, machinery, and instruments, mathematical and astronomical, chymical and mechanical, save and except such only as are bequeathed to Mr. Robert Walker. But in case the said Mr. Varley should not survive me, I give the said before-mentioned Â 1,000 and said tools and machinery to Miss L. Varley, eldest daughter of said Samuel Varley; but in case both of them should not survive, then the said Â 1,000 tools and machinery to go to Jane Varley, second daughter of the said Samuel Varley.

To Mr. George Dyer, B. A., Â 200.

To Mr. David Stone, surgeon, of Kent, Â 100.

To my friend Lord Holland, my picture, painted by Mr. Opie.

To my friend Lord Grantley, my picture representing a picture gallery; my picture of Dr. Tronchin, of Geneva, painted by Liotard; and my picture of Madame Tronchin, of Geneva, which was painted by myself.

I give to Mr. Dean Franklin Walker, of Westminster, son of that valuable man Adam Walker, the Lecturer on Philosophy, my picture of Dr. Benjamin Franklin.

I give to Dr. Hutton, F. R. S., my original picture of the Great Sir Isaac Newton.

I give to the Secretary of the Society of Arts, Manufactures, and Commerce, in Westminster, the picture of my most worthy and excellent father, painted by Liotard.

To my steward, 500.

To Robert Walker, of Vine-street, Piccadilly, my printing-press-maker, 200, and likewise all tools and instruments belonging to me which shall at the time of my death be in his possession.

To Mr. A. Murray, of Symond's-inn, Chancery-lane, 100.

To W. Hillier, my under-butler, to W. Morsam, my footman, to Peat, my carpenter, to Matthews, my plasterer, to his son George, and to Martin Tye, my lime-burner, or to such of the before-mentioned six persons as should be employed by me at the time of my decease, 50 each.

I likewise give and devise unto the said Lord Holland, Lord Grantley, Geo. Dyer, the Rev. Christopher Wyvill, of Bedale, in Yorkshire, the Rev. John Robinson, of Halstead, Kent, Joseph Jekyll, Esq., M. P., of Spring-gardens, the Rev. George Gregory, of Bedford-row, the Rev. John North, of Saffron-Walden, Essex, the Rev. David Stone, and Dr. E. Godwin, M. D., of Ashden, Essex, and to their heirs, all my messuages, lands, tenements, hereditaments, and real estate, which I shall be seised or entitled unto, either in law or in equity, and which I have the right to dispose of, subject to the payment of my just debts and funeral expenses, and the legacies aforesaid, in case my personal estate should not be sufficient to pay the same.

And I appoint the said last named 10 worthy persons executors; and I give and bequeath unto my said executors, or unto such of them as shall, within 12 calendar months after my death, prove, at Doctors'-commons, this my will, or act as executors in the execution hereof, all the remainder and residue of my personal estate and property whatsoever; and I hereby revoke and annul, c.

(L. S.) (Signed) STANHOPE.

r THOMAS COUTTS. Witnesses EDMUND ANTROBUS. (. COUTTS TROTTER.

Proved by the Right Hon. Henry Richard Vassall Lord Holland, the Right Hon. William Lord Grantley, George Dyer, Esq., Rev. Christopher Wyvill, clerk, Joseph Jekyll, Esq., the Rev. John North, clerk, David Stone, Esq., and Edmund Godwin, Doctor of Medicine, the surviving Executors.

APPENDIX II

THE STANHOPE DEMONSTRATOR

As some readers may desire further information in reference to the Demonstrator, I append a few extracts from Dr. Harley's exhaustive article.

' Earl Stanhope's Demonstrator is much less powerful as a logical instrument than Professor Jevons' machine, but the former is undoubtedly a distinct anticipation of the latter. It is probably the first attempt ever made to solve logical problems by mechanical methods. Both in his quantification of the predicate and in his solution of problems involving numerically definite propositions, we see the Earl struggling, not unsuccessfully, to escape into some less confined system of logic than that of Aristotle. He shewed little respect for the authority of the ancient logicians. The same reforming zeal which he displayed in politics he exhibited also in the treatment of logic. He brought to the study of the subject a certain independence and originality of thought which led him to examine the foundations of the science for himself. " I intend," he declared, " to exclude entirely that long catalogue of pedantic words which are now used for the purpose of drawing consequences, and which are, generally speaking, both unintelligible to youth and unfit for men of any age, so far at least as relates to convenient and habitual use. My system of logic will, on the contrary, be found to have the striking advantage of uniting simplicity, perspicuity, utility, and perfect correctness. The science requires to be totally reformed."

' The materials do not enable us to give a complete or systematic account of Stanhope's views on logic. Even on the working of his Demonstrator we find in his remains no full or formal statement, but only scattered and fragmentary limits, and a very few simple examples. It is possible, therefore, that in the hands of its noble inventor the instrument possessed a range and power somewhat greater than is apparent to us. He attached to it a practical importance; for us it possesses little more than a theoretic or historic interest. " It exhibits the consequences symbolically," he wrote, " and renders them evident to the mind. By the aid of this instrument the accuracy or inaccuracy of a conclusion is always shewn, and the reason why such consequences must of necessity exist is rendered apparent. As the instrument is so constructed as to assist us in making demonstrations, I have termed it the Demonstrator. It is so peculiarly contrived as likewise to exhibit symbolically those proportions or degrees of probability which it is the object of the Logic of Probability to discover."

' All propositions are reduced by Stanhope to one form, namely, the expression of the identity of two or more things or classes of things. This "method of identification," as he calls it, is illustrated by numerous examples. For instance, "Hardness belongs to diamonds," means that " Some of those things which possess the quality of hardness and all diamonds are identic." " Some printing-presses cannot be worked without great labour," means that " Some printing-presses are identic with some of those instruments which cannot be worked without great labour." In these examples we recognise an anticipation of Mr. George Bentham's four forms of affirmative propositions, forms which were afterwards adopted by Sir William Hamilton.

' Stanhope bases his system on what De Morgan calls the arithmetical view of the proposition; and this view determines the form of his method of mediate inference and leads to an extension of the common doctrine. He proposes a rule " for discovering consequences in logic," which is a remarkable anticipation of that given by De Morgan from the numerically definite syllogism. It is a noteworthy fact that he does not limit the rule to a special form but puts it forth as embodying the fundamental principle of all syllogistic ratiocination.

' The Demonstrator consists of a brass plate 4 inches long and 4 inches wide, affixed to a thin block of mahogany. In the centre there is a depression iÂ inches in area and half an inch deep, called the holon. Across the holon two slides can be pushed; one, set in a slender mahogany frame, is of red transparent glass and works through an aperture on the right. The other is of wood, and is called the gray slider. In working the " Rule for the Logic of Certainty " this slide is passed through an aperture to the left; but in working the " Rule for the Logic of Probability," it is drawn out and inserted in an aperture at the top, when it works at right angles to the red slide. Stanhope devised several other instruments of various sizes and construction; but they are both less simple and less effective. It does not seem possible for the Demonstrator in its present form to solve very complicated questions. It is constructed for problems involving only three logical terms; but additional slides would increase its range and power. To Stanhope belongs the honour, and it is a very high honour, of being the first (probably) to attempt the solution of logical problems by a mechanical method. There may be some difference of opinion as to how far he succeeded, but there can be none as to the ingenuity of the attempt. The contrivances of earlier logicians, especially the circles of Euler, probably prepared the way; but Stanhope did undoubtedly take a very important step in advance when he constructed his Demonstrator. His conversion of all propositions into the form of identities by means of the quantification of the predicate, and the principle of his mechanical method, namely, that the process of mind involved in the ordinary syllogism and that involved in the numerically definite syllogism are essentially the same, must be regarded as distinct contributions to logical science and as remarkable anticipations of recent discoveries."

APPENDIX III
THE SCIENCE OF TUNING
STANHOPE'S ' Science of tuning Instruments with fixed tones," printed at his own press, appeared in 1806, after conversing with ' sixteen or eighteen of the most

eminent musicians in England." In the following year, Dr. J. W. Callcott, organist of Covent Garden and a popular composer, issued a reply. His ' Plain Statement of Earl Stanhope's Temperament' describes the new method as ' incorrect, imperfect, and incomplete '; but after formulating his criticisms, he confesses that he 'has conferred a most invaluable benefit on the science of music by agitating a question which will probably lead to discussions of no small importance."

I append a brief precis and criticism of Stanhope's treatise kindly furnished me by Dr. H. W. Richards, Mus. Doc.

' In order to understand a little of the science of tuning, one must know the meaning of the terms: (i) Wolf (as used by tuners), and (2) musical Temperament.

' In a keyed instrument of seven octaves, such as the pianoforte, let us begin by tuning the lowest C, then let us make all the successive octaves quite perfect. We shall then have seven octaves, which will bring us to the upper C. Then on a second instrument, let us begin by tuning the lowest C, then tune up twelve perfect fifths (quints). We shall then arrive at the upper C. The difference of pitch between the C, derived from the fifths (quints), and the corresponding C, derived from the octaves, is what is technically called by tuners The Wolf. Lord Stanhope, however, shews that there are as many as Five Wolves in his system.

" There are a number of different modes of Temperament, which may be broadly classed as follows, The Equal Temperament, and The Unequal Temperaments. The mode of Temperament in which the Wolf is distributed in an equal proportion amongst all the twelve fifths (quints) of an instrument is that which is called Equal Temperament. Every other mode of Temperament is called Unequal Temperament." One form of Unequal Temperament is that a few keys are perfectly in tune, whilst others are so out of tune and consequently harsh that it is impossible to use them. This restricts modulation to a limited number of keys.

' As music advanced, such a system of tuning was naturally unsatisfactory, and Equal Temperament was found to be the successful method. The question was finally settled by Bach, when he wrote his " Twenty-four Preludes and Fugues in all keys major and minor," adding later a second volume of twenty-four, now known as the " Forty-eight Preludes and Fugues," or " Das Wohl-temperirte Clavier " (Equally tempered keyboard).

' Stanhope continues: " Equal Temperament is a mode of tuning which I very much disapprove; according to that erroneous system there is not a single perfect 3rd, perfect 4th, or perfect 5th in the whole instrument. Perfect chords are pleasing to the ear. They strike to the heart, and they are founded on the very nature of musical sounds. In my new method there are none of these defects. Every key in my Temperament is made pleasing and fit for transposition and modulation, and has also a peculiar character which belongs to it. This fact has been established by regular and repeated experiments, made in presence of many of the best judges. Between sixty and seventy of the very first professional persons, of both sexes and of the ablest connoisseurs in England, have given to this New Temperament their decided approbation. It answers well, both in the major and in the minor keys."

' There is real value in his system of tuning; yet the universal adoption of Equal Temperament proves that this is more adapted to the requirements of modern music.

Stanhope possessed a very sensitive and refined musical ear, and his calculations were most careful and minute. But the weakness of his system is suggested by the statement that the tune " Adeste Fidelis" sounded " comparatively intolerable when played in the key of C, although, according to my Temperament, the key of C is tuned perfect." On an instrument tuned on the Equal Temperament system, it ought to sound equally well in any key. It is, however, impossible to measure the value of the system without having an instrument tuned on his method and testing it in all sorts of ways."

WE, whose Names are hereunto subscribed, CATHOLICS of ENGLAND, do freely, voluntarily, and of our own accord, make the following solemn DECLARATION and PROTESTATION.

Whereas sentiments unfavourable to us, as citizens and subjects, have been entertained by English Protestants, on account of principles which are asserted to be entertained by us and other Catholics, and which principles are dangerous to society, and totally repugnant to political and civil liberty;â it is a duty that we, the English Catholics, owe to our country as well as to ourselves, to protest, in a formal and solemn manner, against doctrines that we condemn, and that constitute no part of our principles, religion, or belief.

We are the more anxious to free ourselves from such imputations, because divers Protestants, who profess themselves to be real friends to liberty of conscience, have, nevertheless, avowed themselves hostile to us, on account of certain opinions which we are supposed to hold. And we do not blame those Protestants for their hostility, if it proceeds (as we hope it does) not from an intolerant spirit in matters of religion, but as to their being misinformed as to matters of fact.

If it were true, that we, the English Catholics, had adopted the maxims that are erroneously imputed to us, we acknowledge that we should merit the reproach of being dangerous enemies to the state; but, we detest those unchristian-like and execrable maxims: and we severally claim, in common with men of all other religions, as a matter of natural justice, that we, the English Catholics, ought not to suffer for or on account of any wicked or erroneous doctrines that may be held by any other Catholics, which doctrines we publicly disclaim, any more than British Protestants ought to be rendered responsible for any dangerous doctrines that may be held by any other Protestants, which doctrines they, the British Protestants, disavow.

First, We have been accused of holding, as a principle of our religion, that princes excommunicated by the Pope and council, or by authority of the see of Rome, may be deposed or murdered by their subjects, or other persons.

But, so far is the above mentioned unchristian-like and abominable position from being a principle that we hold, that we reject, abhor, and detest it, and every part thereof, as execrable and impious; and we do solemnly declare, that neither the Pope, either with or without a general council, nor any prelate, nor any priest, nor any assembly of prelates or priests, nor any ecclesiastical power whatever, can absolve the subjects of this realm, or any of them, from their allegiance to his Majesty King GEORGE THE THIRD, who is, by authority of parliament, the lawful king of this realm, and of all the dominions thereunto belonging.

Second, We have also been accused of holding, as a principle of our religion, that implicit obedience is due from us to the orders and decrees of Popes and general councils; and that therefore if the Pope, or any general council, should, for the good of the church, command us to take up arms against government, or by any means to subvert the laws and liberties of this country, or to exterminate persons of a different persuasion from us, we (it is asserted by our accusers) hold ourselves bound to obey such orders or decrees, on pain of eternal lire:

Whereas, we positively deny that we owe any such obedience to the Pope and general council, or to either of them; and we believe that no act that is in itself immoral or dishonest can ever be justified by or under colour that it is done either for the good of the church, or in obedience to any ecclesiastical power whatever. We acknowledge no infallibility in the Pope; and we neither apprehend nor believe that our disobedience to any such orders or decrees (should any such be given or made) could subject us to any punishment whatever. And we hold and insist, that the Catholic church has no power that can, directly or indirectly, prejudice the rights of Protestants, inasmuch as it is strictly confined to the refusing to them a participation in her sacraments and other religious privileges of her communion, which no church (as we conceive) can be expected to give to those out of her pale, and which no person out of her pale will, we suppose, ever require.

And we do solemnly declare, that no church, nor any prelate, nor any priest, nor any assembly of prelates or priests, nor any ecclesiastical power whatever, hath, have, or ought to have, any jurisdiction or authority whatsoever within this realm, that can, directly or indirectly, affect or interfere with the independence, sovereignty, laws, constitution, or government thereof; or the rights, liberties, persons, or properties of the people of the said realm, or of any of them, save only and except by the authority of parliament; and that any such assumption of power would be an usurpation.

Third, We have likewise been accused of holding, as a principle of our religion, that the Pope, by virtue of his spiritual power, can dispense with the obligations of any compact or oath taken or entered into by a Catholic: that therefore no oath of allegiance, or other oath, can bind us; and, consequently, that we can give no security for our allegiance to any government.

There can be no doubt but that this conclusion would be just, if the original proposition upon which it is founded were true; but, we positively deny that we do hold any such principle. And we do solemnly declare, that neither the Pope, nor any prelate, nor any priest, nor any assembly of prelates or priests, nor any ecclesiastical power whatever, can absolve us, or any of us, from, or dispense with, the obligations of any compact or oath whatever.

Fourth, We have also been accused of holding, as a principle of our religion, that not only the Pope, but even a Catholic priest, has power to pardon the sins of Catholics at his will and pleasure; and therefore, that no Catholic can possibly give any security for his allegiance to any government, inasmuch as the Pope, or a priest, can pardon perjury, rebellion, and high treason.

We acknowledge also the justness of this conclusion, if the proposition upon which it is founded were not totally false. But, we do solemnly declare, that, on the contrary, we believe that no sin whatever can be forgiven at the will of any Pope, or of any priest, or of any person whomsoever; but that a sincere sorrow for past sin, a firm resolution to avoid future guilt, and every possible atonement to God and the injured neighbour, are the previous and indispensable requisites to establish a well-founded expectation of forgiveness.

Fifth, And we have also been accused of holding, as a principle of our religion, that ' no faith is to be kept with heretics'; so that no government which is not Catholic can have any security from us for our allegiance and peaceable behaviour.

This doctrine, that ' faith is not to be kept with heretics," we reject, reprobate, and abhor, as being contrary to religion, morality, and common honesty:â and we do hold and solemnly declare, that no breach of faith with any person whomsoever can ever be justified by reason of or under pretence that such person is an heretic or an infidel.

And we further solemnly declare, that we do make this Declaration and Protestation, and every part thereof, in the plain and ordinary sense of the words of the same, without any evasion, equivocation, or mental reservation whatsoever.

And we appeal to the justice and candour of our fellow citizens, whether we, the English Catholics, who thus solemnly disclaim and from our hearts abhor, the above mentioned abominable and unchristian-like principles, ought to be put upon a level with any other men who may hold and profess those principles?

The above Declaration and Protestation was signed by one thousand seven hundred and forty persons; including several Peers, and two hundred and forty-one Clergymen of the Catholic religion.

ADDINGTON, afterwards Lord Sid-mouth, 191-3, 198, 199, 204-5, 214-15, 217
Auckland, Lord, 69, 72, 73, 97, 126, 139
BANKS, Sir J., 262, 267
Barbauld, Mrs., 260
Barere, 134
Barlow, Joel, 186, 191
Beaufoy, Colonel, 182-3
Bedford, Duke of, 189, 198
Bentham, J., 23, 105 (note), 225 (note)
Bentham, Sir S., 171, 176 Boulton, 168-70, 180 Brougham, 229 Burdett, 190, 229, 240 Burke, 36, 37, 40, 45, 51, 56, 59-60, 86, 89-93, 96, 98-9, 100, 102, 117, 126, 156, 159, 229 Burnett, George, 242-3 Butler, Charles, 77-82

CALONNE, 98-9

Camelford, Lord, 69-70, 188, 198 Carrington, Lord, 244-5, 265 Cartwright, Edmund, 256 Cartwright, Major John, 38, 39, 50, 118, 157-8, 189, 201, 214, 255-6 Charlemont, Lord, 48-9 Chatham, first Earl, 5, 6, 10, 16, 18, 23. 30, 32, 33. 35-6, 237 Chatham, second Earl, 171, 234,

Chauvelin, 116, 125, 126 Chesterfield, Lord, i, 20, 21 Clarkson, 108-9 Cobbett, 201

Coke, Lady Mary, 3, n, 19, 30 Coke, Thomas, of Norfolk, 19, 48,
Coleridge, 143, 242 Condorcet, 19, 107, no-n, 114, 115, 123, 125, 170-1

DAER, Lord, in Deffand, Mme. du, 18 Dumont, 105, 225 (note) Dumouriez, 116, 118, 126 Dundas, afterwards Lord Melville, 22, 50, 126, 154, 202, 258 Dyer, George, 259-60, 267

ELDON, Lord, 150, chs. xi. and xii., passim
Ellenborough, Lord, 200, 216 Erskine, 149, 152, 154, 200, 205, 218, 223

FltZWILLIAM, 105

Fletcher, 228-30

Fox, 9, 12, 20, 39, 48, 50-2, ch. iv., passim, 72, 76, 86, 92, 103â 7, 129, 152-4, 163, 189-90, 198, 229, 232, 238

Fran ais, of Nantes, 96, 112-16 Franklin, Benjamin, 34-5, in, 165 Frend, William, 210 Fulton, 166, 173-5, 184-6, 190-1,

GIlLRAY, 152-5, 199, 238, 262, 272

Gilpin, John, 190 Goldsmith, Lewis, 142 Gower, Lord, 95 Grattan, 49-50

Grenville, Lord, 119,120, 123, 124-5, 126, 133, 135, 154, 190, 198-9, 203, 2O8-IO, 221, 224, 235

Grey, 126, 138, 198, 205, 209, 220, 221

HARDINGE, George, 259

Hardy, Thomas, 132, 147-9, 188-9, 257-9

Hastings, Warren, 71, 101-2 Hawkesbury, Lord, afterwards second Lord Liverpool, chs. xi.

and xii., passim Hazlitt, 255-6, 259 Holland, Lady, 162, 190, 255 Holland, Lord, 152,170,188,189-90, 192, 200, 202-5, 206-7, 209, 211, 216, 218, 221-3, 225, 247, 253, 254-5, 266-72 Horner, 206, 208, 221, 229 Horsley, Bishop, 84 Hutton, Dr., 226, 261

JACKSON, Francis, 240, 242

Jebb, 39, 50

Jefferson, in, 202

Joyce, Jeremiah, 147-50, 239

Jullien, Mme., 116

KENYON, Lord, 70, 104, 217 King, Lord, 197, 207-10 Kippis, Dr., 94 Kosciusko, 142, 152

LACKNER, Mrs., 252-3, 265-7 Lamb, Charles, 259-60, 273 Lamb, William, afterwards Lord

Melbourne, 188 Lameth, 95

Lancaster, Joseph, 227-8, 263 Landor, 142-3

Lansdowne, second Lord, 206, 218 Lauderdale, 103, 125, 126, 129, 130, I 3 I Â I 53 5 I 89, 203, 210, 220-1,

Leard, 172, 176, 177 Leeds, Duke of, 139 (note), 235 Liverpool, Lord, see Hawkesbury Loughborough, Lord, 70, 129, 131, 135. 188

MACKINTOSH, 99, 115

Malmesbury, Lord, 156

Maret, 124

Meryon, Dr., 232, and see Lady

Hester Stanhope Miles, William, 124, 145-6 Milner, Bishop, 80-2 Moore, Dr. John, 12, 16 Moore, Sir John, 12, 246

NAPOLEON, 190, 192-3, 195, 199,

Nelson, 181

Norfolk, Duke of, 153, 194, 198 North, Dr. John, 260-1 North, Lord, 25, 48, 53-8

O'LEARY, 81 Opie, 254

PAINE, Tom, 113, 115, 121, 165, 238

Palmer, 128-9
Perceval, 203, 209
Petion, 116
Petre, Lord, 77-82
Pitt, Governor, i
Pitt, Hester, Lady Mahon, 22, 28, 30-2, 42-3 Pitt, William, 20-1, 34, chs. iii.-v., passim, ch. viii., passim, 143, 147, 149-50, 153-4, 92, 198, 202, 229, 231-2, 239, 242-7
Playfair, Dr. 226 Portland, Duke of, 103, 126 Price, 32, 67, 86-7, 94, 97, 98-9, 106, 137, 165 Priestley, 32, 35, 96, 98, 116, 143, 146, 153, 165 Pringle, Sir J., 32, 34
RENNIE, 165-6, 168-9, 173
Ricardo, 206
Richmond, Duke of, 35-6, 39, 5Â Â
Rickman, 242-3, 259 Robespierre, 134 Robinson, Crabb, 259-60 Rochefoucauld, Due de la, 87, 94, IO8, III-I2
Rolliad," the, 24, 28, 45 Romilly, 55, 209, 224, 248 Rose, George, 63, 187 Rutt, sonnet of, 143
SAVILE, Sir G., 40, 44, 47, 50, 133,
Sawbridge, 25, 50, 62 Sayre, Stephen, 120-1 Selwyn, George, 96 Seppings, 184 Sharp, Granville, 72, 108 Shelburne, Lord, later first Lord
Lansdowne, 32, 38-9, 45, 51. 53.
97, 105-6, 125,126,134, 139, 165, 241,
Sheridan, 39, 50, 51, 74, 94, 126, 149, 153-4. J 9i Smith, Adam, 11 Southey, 242-3, 259 Spencer, Lord, 175, 179, 180 Stanhope, first Earl, i, 68, 235 Stanhope, second Earl, ch. i, passim, 20, 34, 67, 248, 250-1,

Stanhope, third Earl: birth and parentage, i; death of elder brother, 3; removed from Eton to Geneva, 4; Genevese society, 6-9; education and visitors, 10-12; sport, 12-15; Genevese politics, 15-17; the theatre, 17; in Paris, 18-19; return to England, 20; friendship with William Pitt, 21; engaged to Hester Pitt, 22-3; stands for Westminster, 23-30; marriage, 30-1; publishes ' Considerations ' on the Gold Coin," 32; securing of buildings against fire, 32-3; calculating machines, 33-4; ' Principles of Electricity," 34â 5; death of Chatham, 35-6; works with Wyvill and Pitt for Parliamentary Reform, 37-40; Gordon riots, 40-2; death of his wife, 42-3; elected to Parliament, 43-4; marries Louisa Grenville, 46; the fall of North, 48; Home Rule for Ireland, 48-50; introduces Bill for reducing election expenses, 50-1; Wraxall's description, 52; attacks the Coalition, 54-7; declines a place in Pitt's ministry, 57; supports Pitt, 58-60; the Westminster Election, 60-2; suggests reduction of the tax on tea, 62-3; Pitt's Bill for Parliamentary Reform, 64; succeeds his father, 67; criticises Pitt's Sinking Fund, 67-70; introduces Registration Bill, 70-1; the Slave Trade, 72-4; the centenary of 1688, 75â 6; Regency crisis, 76-7; the English Catholics and the Protestation, 77-82; Toleration Bill, 82-5; presides at celebration of the French Revolution, 86-9; the Letter to Burke, 89-93 I speech at the Crown and Anchor, 93-5; Horace Walpole on Stanhope, 96-7; withdraws from the Revolution Society, 97; attacks Calonne, 98-9; the trial of Warren Hastings, 101-2; supports Fox's Libel Bill, 103-7 ' the Slave Trade, 107-9;

advises Condorcet on French finances, no-ii; correspondence with La Rochefoucauld and Frangais, 111â 16; kindness to Jullien, 116; relations with Talleyrand, 117-19; appeal from Bishop Watson, 119-20; letters from Sayre, 120-1; letters to Wyvill on the approach of war, 121-2; appeals to Grenville, 123-4 'Â attacks the expulsion of the French ambassador, 124-6; advocates acknowledgment of the French Republic, 126-8; criticises trials of Scottish Reformers, 128-9; the landing of foreign troops, 1 29-30; condemns interference in internal affairs of France, 130-1; gratitude of the London Corresponding Society, 131-3; relations with French politicians, 134; appeals to Wilberforce to oppose the war, 135-8; the Minority of One, and withdrawal from Parliament, 138-41; homage of Landor and Coleridge, 142-3; attack by William Miles, 145-6; the mob attacks his London house, 146-7; arrest, imprisonment, and acquittal of his secretary Joyce, 147-50; celebrations at Chevening and in London, 150-2; Gillray's violent attacks, 152-5; Kentish petitions for peace, 155-6; manifesto against the Union, 158-62; renewal of political activity, 162-4 'â steam navigation, 166-8; correspondence with Boulton Watt, 168-70; the Navy Board and the Admiralty, 171-3; relations with Fulton, J 73-5Â e Kent, 175-80; ship construction, 181-4 J canals, 184-6; return to Parliament, 187-90; Fulton's submarines, 190-1; the Treaty of Amiens, 191-3; the Slave Trade, 194; corn laws and granaries, 195-8; relations with the United States, 199; national defence, 201-2; the controversy on proxies, 203-4; religious liberty, 204-5; the currency and Lord King, 206-11; toleration versus religious liberty, 211-13; the champion of prisoners, 214-18; war with America, 218-19; the fall of Napoleon, 219-20; the Corn Laws, 220-2; the reform of the

Statute-book, 222-6; Irish policy, 227; Lancaster's schools, 227-8; conversations with Fletcher, 228-30; the breach with Pitt, 231-2; Stanhope and his daughters, 233-9; flight of Mahon, 239-41; departure of Lady Hester, 241-2; flight of the younger sons, 242-3; Mahon's engagement, 244-6; Mahon v. Stanhope, 246â 50; Louisa, Lady Stanhope, 250-2; death of Grisel, 252-4; friendship with Lord Holland, Wyvill, Cartwright, Hardy, 254-9; George Dyer, 259-60; Dr. North, 260; Varley, 261; inventions in printing, 262-4 the Stanhope lens, 264â 5; illness and death, 265-8; sketches by Lord Holland, 268-72; summary, 272-3

Stanhope, fourth Earl, 148, 232, 235-51, 253-4, 260, 264, 265-7, 271

Stanhope, Grisel, Countess of, chs. i. and ii, passim, 42-3, 46, 172, 232, 235-9. 253-4.

Stanhope, Lady Hester, 31, 42-3, 147, 232-43, 251-2

Stanhope, Louisa, Countess of, 46, 233-8, 245-6, 250-2, 266

St. Just, 134

Stone, 123-4

St. Vincent, Lord, 181, 191

TALLEYRAND, 112, 116, 117-19 Taylor, M. A., 153, 155 Thurlow, 57, 73, 76, 84, 99, 103, 129 Tooke, Home, 39, 94, 135, 148-50,

Towers, Dr., 75, 94, 106-7 Tronchin, Dr., 3, 4, 5, 8, u

VARLEY, 261-2, 266-7

WALPOLE, Horace, letters of, 2, 18, 22, 27, 32, 35, 41, 60, 96-7 Watson, Bishop, 107, 119-20 Watt, 165, 168-70, 180 Wellesley, Lord, 211, 219 Whitbread, 229 Whitworth, Lord, 193 Wilberforce, 57, 64, 65, 72, 74, 107-8, 135-8, 194 Wilkes, 2, n, 12,

23-9, 32, 50 Wraxall, Memoirs of, 52, 54, 59, 63, 76, 268 Wyvill, 37-8, 39, 40. 44. 47 65, 70, loo-i, 106, 121-2, 149, 162-4,

PRINTED BY
SPOTTISWOODE AND CO. LTD., COLCHESTER LONDON AND ETON
RECENT HISTORICAL WORKS.

PAGEANT OF THE BIRTH, LIFE, AND DEATH OF RICHARD BEAUCHAMP, EARL OF WARWICK, K. G. (1389-1439). Edited by Viscount DILLON, D. C. L., F. S. A., and W. H. St. JOHN HOPE, Litt. D., D. C. L. Photo engraved from the original Manuscript in the British Museum by EMERY WALKER, F. S. A. Bound in boards with linen back. 410. (n in. by 8 in.). 21 s. net.

EXTRACT FROM INTRODUCTION.

The Warwick Pageant is a Cottonian MS. (Julius E IV) and in a series of fifty-three outline drawings portrays the chief events in the life and death of Richard Beauchamp, Earl of Warwick, the father-in-law of the kingmaker.

This M. S., which it may be presumed from various evidences was done between 1485 and 1490, presents to the armour student and to the artist a most rich series of authorities for the costume of that period. It was rather imperfectly reproduced in Vol. II of Strutt's Horda Angel-cymian in i?75, and again in facsimile in a very limited edition for presentation by the late Earl of Carysfort to the Roxburghe Club. The present work places within reach of students and others at a moderate price a reproduction as accurate as that of the Roxburghe Club, but without the meticulous details as to paper and tone. A short list of the chief events recorded has been added with some explanatory notes to each plate. The MS. consists of 28 leaves of vellum, measuring n inches by 8 inches, and this work is practically on the same scale as the original, being reproduced by photography, so that every detail may be shown in its present state.

A HISTORY OF ENGLAND. From the Defeat of the Armada to the Death of Elizabeth. With an Account of English Institutions during the Later Sixteenth and Early Seventeenth Centuries. By EDWARD P. CHEYNEY, Professor of European History in the University of Pennsylvania. In 2 vols. 8vo. Vol. I. i6s. net.

THE PASSING OF THE GREAT REFORM BILL. By J. R. M. BUTLER, Fellow of Trinity College, Cambridge. With Illustrations. 8vo. izs. 6d. net.

This book narrates the events leading to the passing of the Reform Act of 1832, in the light of original documents published and unpublished. deals particularly-with Lord Grey's difficulties with the King and in the Cabinet, and with the agitation in the country

THE LIFE OF WILLIAM PITT, EARL OF CHATHAM. By BASIL WILLIAMS. With Portraits and Maps. 2 vols. 8vo. 25. net.

THE ECONOMIC ORGANISATION OF ENGLAND. An Outline History. By W. J. ASHLEY, M. A., Ph. D., Professor of Commerce in the University of Birmingham.

THE REIGN OF HENRY VII FROM CONTEMPORARY SOURCES. With an Introduction by A. F. POLLARD, M. A. Three volumes. Crown 8vo. Vol. I., Narrative Extracts, IQJ. 6d. net. Vol. II., Constitutional, Social, and Economic History, IQS. 6d. net. Vol. III., Diplomacy, Ecclesiastical Affairs, and Ireland, los. 6d. net.

HENRY VIII. By A. F. POLLARD, M. A., Littd. Crown 8vo. 4. 6d. net.

CUSTOMARY ACRES AND THEIR HISTORICAL IMPORTANCE; being a Series of Unfinished Essays. By the late FREDERICK SEEBOHM, Hon. LL. D. (Edin.), Litt. D. (Camb.), D. Litt. (Oxford). 8vo. i2s. 6d. net.

THE CONFEDERATION OF EUROPE. A Study of the European Alliance, 1813-1823, as an Experiment in the International Organisation of Peace. Six Lectures delivered in the University Schools, Oxford, at the invitation of the Delegates of the Common University Fund, Trinity Term, 1913. By WALTER ALISON PHILLIPS, M. A. 8vo. 75. 6d. net.

THE AGRARIAN PROBLEM IN THE SIXTEENTH CENTURY.
By R. H. TAWNEY. With Reproductions of Plans (1590 to 1620). 8vo. 9. net.

THE VILLAGE LABOURER, 1760 to 1832. A Study in the Government of England before the Reform Bill. By J. L. HAMMOND and BARBARA HAMMOND. Second Impression. 8vo. gs. net.

HISTORY AND HISTORIANS IN THE NINETEENTH CENTURY. By G. P. GOOCH, M. A. Second Edition. 8vo. TOS. 6d. net.

LONGMANS, GREEN, CO., 39 Paternoster Row, London;
New York, Bombay, Calcutta, and Madras.

RECENT HISTORICAL WORKSâ (continued).

THE FATE OF EMPIRES: Being an Inquiry into the Stability of Civilisation. By ARTHUR JOHN HUBBARD, M. D. (Dunelm). 8vo. 6s. 6d. net.

STOLEN WATERS: A page from, the Conquest of Ulster. By T. M.
HEALV, K. C., M. P., Bencher of King's Inns, Dublin, and of Gray's Inn, London. 8vo. lew. 6d. net.

This narrative is based on unpublished MS. State Papers, and historical trials or inquisitions. It brings to light the hitherto unknown frauds practised on the Crown and the City of London in the times of James I, Charles I, Cromwell, and Charles II. The narrative is woven round the controversy as to the title to two great fisheries in Northern Ireland â The River Bann and Lough Neagh.

THE FIRST TWELVE CENTURIES OF BRITISH STORY: A Sketch of the Social and Political Conditions of the British Islands from the year 56 B. C. to 1154 A. D. With 20 Sketch Maps and 3 Photographic Reproductions of Medieval Maps. By J. W. JEUDWINE, LL. B. (Camb.), of Lincoln's Inn, Barrister-at-Law. 8vo. I2J. 6d. net.

ESSENTIALS IN EARLY EUROPEAN HISTORY. By SAMUEL BURNETT HOWE, A. M., Head of the Department of History in the Plainfield High School, Plainfield, New Jersey. With Coloured Frontispiece, 168 other Illustrations, 31 Maps and Plans (10 Coloured), and 8 Charts and Genealogical Tables. Crown 8vo. js. 6d. net.

A HISTORY OF EUROPE. By ARTHUR J. GRANT, M. A., King's
College, Cambridge, Professor of History at the University of Leeds. With Maps and Coloured Chart. Large crown 8vo. js. 6d. net.

INDIAN HISTORICAL STUDIES. By H. G. RAWLINSON, M. A., Professor of English Literature, The Deccan College, Poona. With Illustrations and Map. Crown 8vo. 4. 6d. net. CONTENTS.â Gautama Buddhaâ Asokaâ Indo-Greek Dynasties of the Panjabâ
Chinese Pilgrims in Indiaâ Ibn Batutaâ Akbarâ Sivaji the Maratha- Robert Knpxâ

Ranjit Singh and the Sikh Nationâ Foreign Influences in the Civilisation of Ancient India.

ORGANISED DEMOCRACY: An Introduction to the Study of American Politics. By FREDERICK A. CLEVELAND, Ph. D., LL. D. Crown 8vo. IQJ. 6d. net.

A HISTORY OF WALES FROM THE EARLIEST TIMES TO THE EDWARDIAN CONQUEST. By JOHN EDWARD LLOYD, M. A. With Map. 2 vols. 8vo. 2is. net.

THE RISE OF SOUTH AFRICA: A History of the Origin of South African Colonisation and of its Development towards the East from the Earliest Times to 1857. By GEORGE EDWARD CORY, M. A., King's College, Cambridge, Professor in the Rhodes University College, Grahamstown, South Africa. In 4 vols. 8vo. VOL. I. FROM THE EARLIEST TIMES TO THE YEAR 1820. With Map, Plans, and Illustrations. 15. VOL. II. From 1820 to 1834. With 38 Illustrations and 2 Maps. 8vo. ibs.

THE FIRST DECADE OF THE AUSTRALIAN COMMONWEALTH: A Chronicle of Contemporary Politics, 1901-1910. By HENRY GYLES TURNER. 8vo. 9.

THE MAKING OF THE AUSTRALIAN COMMONWEALTH (1899-1900). A Stage in the growth of the Empire. By the Hon. B. R. WISE, formerly Attorney-General of New South Wales. 8vo. js. 6d. net.

THE MAID OF FRANCE: Being the Story of the Life and Death of Jeanne d'Arc. By ANDREW LANG. With 3 Maps and 3 Portraits. 8vo. i2s. 6d. net. Cheap Edition. With 3 Maps. Crown 8vo. 6s. net.

NAPOLEON I. A Biography. By AUGUST FOURNIER, Professor of History in the University of Vienna. Translated by A. E. ADAMS. With 2 Photogravure Portraits and 7 Maps. 2 vols. 8vo. 2U. net.

LONGMANS, GREEN, CO., 39 Paternoster Row, London;
New York, Bombay, Calcutta, and Madras.
S7S8
Stanhope, Ghita
The life of Charles
PLEASE DO NOT REMOVE CARDS OR SLIPS FROM THIS POCKET
UNIVERSITY OF TORONTO LIBRARY

Lightning Source UK Ltd.
Milton Keynes UK
UKOW052110020512

191896UK00003B/82/P